Custodians

❧ *of* ❧

Wonder

Custodians

 *of*

Wonder

ANCIENT CUSTOMS,
PROFOUND TRADITIONS,
and the LAST PEOPLE
KEEPING THEM ALIVE

ELIOT STEIN

ST. MARTIN'S PRESS
NEW YORK

For Julyssa and Oliver

Contents

Custodians

❧ *of* ❧

Wonder

Introduction

Minutes after I met Anna, she was gripping my wrist with one hand and patting my cheek with the other. I was 22 years old and had been wandering aimlessly through rows of squat pastel houses on the Italian island of Burano when I saw her outside her home. She was 90 years old, five feet tall, with her silver hair coiled into a bun. As she stared back at me from behind a thick cataract glaze, she asked if I could help her see something once more.

Anna led me through a striped curtain dangling from her doorway toward the back of her living room, where a mosaic of white designs hung framed on the wall. It took a moment for me to understand what I was looking at: each pattern was filled with thousands of microscopic stitches threaded with such detail and delicacy that they resembled embroidered spiderwebs. As I moved to inspect each piece, Anna moved with me, asking me to tell her what I saw. I said I was drawn to a fisherman seemingly stitched from sea foam. Anna told me he had been her husband. In another, I described the series of bridges arching over the Venetian canals, the gondolier portrayed in intricately tight points straining to moor.

I had never seen anything quite like these swooping, sinuous creations, and, as Anna explained, that's because she was one of the last living inheritors of an impossibly difficult style of needle-made lace known only to women on this small island—an artform she described as "embroidering the air." For more than 300 years, this tightly guarded technique produced one of the most prized products in the Western world. Burano-made lace was the boast of royalty, the height of fashion, and the target of international smuggling. But more than anything, it was the pride of Burano—the life's work of an astonishing thread of anonymous women who gave something beautiful to the world and, in the process, shaped an island. Machines eventually started replacing hands, and as fewer and fewer women continued the trade, that thread unraveled until all that was left were people like Anna, pleading with those who outlive her to find the eyes to see and the memory to recall how Burano came to be.

This chance encounter inspired the first travel story I ever wrote, but it also awakened a sympathy and reverence for these final custodians that still guides me 17 years later. So often, we hear stories about the first person to do something: the innovators, the pioneers, the ones who move us forward. But rarely is there a whisper for the last person to carry on a tradition, or a pause to look back and consider how these rites have shaped us and the places we come from. Instead, these gorgeous, irrational, gentle things humans do that make the world so inexorably fascinating often die a silent death, and it's only after they vanish that we realize what has been lost. I can't help but feel we owe these aging craftsmen, fading customs, and quiet gestures more. As one person in these pages told me after I met an elderly artisan who had saved an ancient craft from the brink of extinction: "This man deserves to be honored, but if you're going to do it, it should be while he's alive."

I'm currently a journalist at the BBC, and I've spent much of the past seven years profiling remarkable people around the globe who are each preserving a distinct cultural wonder that would otherwise be lost. It is perhaps an unusual way to make sense of the world, but I've found it to be as generous and humbling a teacher as I could ever ask for. These sentinels have entrusted me with more than their stories. They have shown me their process, revealed their most intimate joys and sorrows, and explained what inspires them to carry on. Along the way, they have reminded me that travel remains an exercise in curiosity, and that the world is always so much richer than our assumptions of it.

This book explores 10 of the world's rarest and most dazzling cultural marvels on the edge of disappearance as told through the last people alive preserving them. You'll travel to five continents and meet more than a dozen artisans, keepers, and protectors maintaining these traditions against all odds. In Italy, you'll find a lone woman living in a far-flung town clinging to the slopes of a mountain who makes the rarest pasta on Earth. In the Peruvian highlands, you'll get to know the last Inca bridge master, who balances precariously over a steep gorge every year to weave the last remaining Inca suspension bridge out of grass. And in southern India, you'll discover an extended family of alchemists who have guarded the formula for a rare and mysterious metal mirror that is believed to reveal your truest self. In an age when everything has seemingly been explored and explained, and where cynicism so often overshadows curiosity and wonder, these cultural custodians remind us how much there still is to discover, and invite us to fall back in love with the world.

Chances are you have never heard of a single person in these pages or the practices they're maintaining. These are unsung, unheralded, and relatively unknown people living simple lives. Yet, the extraordinary things that they do reveal a profound and little-known truth about a place's unique identity. This book isn't just about a rare pasta you may never taste, a bridge you may never cross, or a mysterious mirror you may never see. It's about why these unlikely things you likely never knew existed matter, why these individuals continue to carry on, and what it means when the unique traditions and customs that make us who we are fade away. Above all, it's a celebration of human ingenuity, imagination, and perseverance, and a love letter to the people, places, and practices that make the world such a wondrous place.

If the coronavirus pandemic revealed anything, it's how connected we all are; how the actions of one person echo across a community; and how the elderly, the working class, and those without safety nets are the most vulnerable in a crisis. Unsurprisingly, these truths apply to most subjects and stories in this book. When people were forced to quarantine in their homes, Scandinavia's last night watchman had no one to guard. When cigar factories closed across Cuba, the island's few remaining *lectores* lost their audiences. And when movie theaters shuttered in Taiwan, Asia's last billboard poster painters risked losing their jobs. Each of these once-upon-a-time rites was already on a perilous path toward extinction before the pandemic, and the last several years have only heightened the urgency of telling these stories now.

Similarly, while the pandemic heightened our collective sense of global interconnectedness, it also awakened us to the irreversible effects of globalization. When localism gives way to internationalism, we often lose the distinct vestiges that make our world so wonderfully diverse—and this global homogenization is happening before our eyes. Nine languages disappear every year. By 2080, that annual rate is expected to jump to 16, and if we don't do anything to halt this linguistic loss, more than half of the world's languages will be extinct in the next 100 years.[1] By 2030, 8.5 percent of the global manufacturing workforce could be replaced by robots.[2] Nearly 3,000 villages in Spain are at risk of becoming ghost towns;[3] 2,500 in Italy are perilously depopulated;[4] and 896 towns and villages across Japan are estimated to disappear by 2040 as better-paying jobs lure young people to cities—a phenomenon the country's former minister for internal affairs Hiroya Masuda described as "local extinction."[5]

None of this bodes well for those who travel to be stirred by the unfamiliar and enthralled by the boundless depths of how the natural world affects human expression. Nor does it for the endangered artisans and final custodians preserving a knowledge that would otherwise fade away. In many ways, these guardians are the closest thing we have to humanity's wise men and women. And while culture is an ever-evolving force, it isn't far-fetched to say that what's at risk of being lost with their disappearance is nothing less than the world's local, whimsical soul.

Finally, there's one more reason I feel compelled to share these stories now. Having profiled so many people around the world whose only wish is that the tradition they've devoted their lives to be passed on to their son or daughter, I was inspired to embark on this project after finding out that I would soon become a father for the first time. I'm unable to teach my son how to transform blades of grass into coils as strong as steel, or to fold and stretch 256 perfectly even strands of needle-thin pasta dough with the tips of my fingers. Yet, my hope is that I can leave something that inspires him to tilt toward the sun, to dare to listen, and to develop a sense of wonder and curiosity about the incredible world we all share.

As the distances and differences between us continue to diminish, I can't help but feel that we can learn something by looking toward these customs and custodians. Together, they remind us that culture is born slowly through a million tiny, personal moments; when one seemingly insignificant wonder fades, an irretrievable part of our humanity vanishes with it.

1

The Living Libraries of West Africa

Very old men, called griots, still to be found in the older back-country villages, men who were in effect living, walking archives of oral history . . . Throughout the whole of Black Africa such oral chronicles had been handed down since the time of the ancient forefathers . . . and there were certain legendary griots who could narrate facets of African history literally for as long as three days without ever repeating themselves.
—ALEX HALEY, *ROOTS*

Balla Kouyaté's first impression of the United States was utter confusion. His older sister, Kaniba, had become a well-known singer in West Africa and was invited to New York to perform. No one in the family had ever been to the US or spoke any English, so Kaniba asked her 27-year-old brother if he could accompany her, and in the summer of 2000, the siblings boarded a series of flights from their home in Bamako, Mali, to New York City. By the time they finally landed at JFK Airport 20 hours later, all Balla wanted was a cigarette. After waiting for his bag, Balla stepped outside, pulled a Dunhill smoke from his suit pocket, and had just reached for a lighter when a stranger approached him. Balla couldn't make out what the man was saying but eventually understood he was asking Balla for a cigarette—*his* cigarette. Balla stared back at the man incredulously. All he had ever heard about the US was that once you arrive, you become rich. In fact, when Balla received his three-month visa, he gave away everything he owned—his TV, his motorcycle, his bed, everything except the clothes in his suitcase and his *balafon*—thinking he'd never need them again. So, why was this stranger seemingly begging him for a cigarette? Balla gave the man his whole pack and then told his sister they had to hurry back inside the terminal to ask for help in French. Surely, they were just changing flights here, he thought. This couldn't possibly be the United States.

Balla and Kaniba stayed with three other Malian musicians in a housing project in the Bronx, sleeping on the couch in the cramped apartment. The only English word Balla knew was "hi," and in his first week in the Bronx, he said it to everyone he passed on the sidewalks. Back home in Bamako, it was customary to greet people whether you knew them or not, but that rule apparently didn't apply in this strange, new place. "They looked at me like I was crazy, or that I wanted something from them. It was culture shock on a lot of levels," Balla said, in his soothing Mandinka accent.

When Kaniba's gigs were done, she decided it was time to go. Things in the US seemed hard, and she missed home. Balla wanted to return, too, but one of the musicians he was living with convinced him to stay. He told Balla that there were hardly any other Malian balafon players in the US, and certainly none like him. Balla realized that if he was ever going to break out on his own, this was his one chance, but he had to find a way to support himself.

One of Balla's roommates got him a job at a car wash in Lower Manhattan. On his first day, Balla noticed there was another man from Mali working there, and when Balla went up to introduce himself, the man nearly dropped his water bucket in disbelief. "What on Earth are you doing here?" he asked. Balla explained that he was trying to make it as a musician in the US. A few weeks later, after word had gotten out that Balla was living in New York, he was asked to perform at a local West African wedding. The only problem was he didn't know how to tell his new boss that he'd need the day off, so he asked his Malian coworker to translate. The man explained to their young, white supervisor that Balla needed to perform at a ceremony.

"Sir, he plays the balafon," the Malian man said.

"He plays the *what?*" the supervisor responded. "Listen, I don't care. You tell him if he takes the day off, he's fired." And that's exactly what happened.

Soon after, a West African singer tipped Balla off that she knew a convenience store owner looking to hire someone—only, the store was up in Albany, New York. That autumn, Balla scraped his money together, bought a one-way Greyhound ticket, and got a job unloading inventory and stocking shelves. He had never experienced cold like that, and at night, he slept on a bare mattress in the hallway of an apartment above the shop wearing three pairs of pants, cradling his balafon under a blanket. Whenever Balla would call his parents back in Mali, he made sure never to tell them how cold or lonely he was. But more than 20 years later, he still remembers the words his father would tell him at the end of each long-distance call: "Balla, remember you are a Kouyaté. You are a *djeli*. Whatever you do, you cannot let this tradition die."

Nearly 800 years ago, Sundiata Keita founded one of the largest and greatest kingdoms in African history: the Mali Empire. When he did, he appointed a man named Balla Fasséké (Balla's direct ancestor, for whom he's named) as the guardian of a sacred instrument called a balafon. The precursor of the xylophone and marimba, a balafon is made by carefully cutting 21 wooden slats into different lengths, fixing them atop hollow calabashes, and striking them with mallets wound with the gum and sap of a rubber tree. Fasséké's job wasn't just to play the balafon but to be the keeper of the empire's history and pass it on to the public as he played.

Ever since, in an astounding tradition that continues to this day, male members of the last 27 generations of the Kouyaté family have learned to master the balafon and serve as living history books, preserving the ancient stories, culture, and traditions of the Mande people who live in Mali, Guinea, and eight surrounding West African nations. This tradition, as anyone who read Alex Haley's book *Roots* may remember,[1] is called a "griot" in English. But in the Mandinka language of West Africa, it is known as a djeli. The word "djeli" means blood, for it is said that just as people can't live without blood, a Mande community can't live without a djeli. To be a djeli is a birthright, and over the centuries, these ancient balafon-playing bards have served as equal parts historians, praise singers, and ambassadors of the kings and communities they serve. They memorize and recite national epics, recall family genealogies with encyclopedic fluency, announce births and deaths, oversee important family events, and facilitate marriages among bashful couples.

Remarkably, the original balafon that Keita (more commonly called Sundiata) first bestowed to Fasséké some 800 years ago still exists. Known as the Sosso-Bala, it is kept in a round mud hut in a remote 150-person village called Niagassola, Guinea, that has no running water or electricity. All modern balafons descend from this instrument, and it cannot leave the village unless it is carried on the head of its official guardian, known as the *balatigui*. In fact, it is only brought out of the mud hut once a year for a single ceremonial playing during Eid, and only the balatigui is allowed to play it. For the last 24 years, Balla's father, El Hadji Sekou Kouyaté, had served as the Sosso-Bala's loyal guardian. But shortly after I met Balla, his 90-year-old father passed, and that honor fell to Balla's oldest living uncle. Balla knows that one day, it may fall to him too.

In 2001, the Sosso-Bala was proclaimed by UNESCO as an Intangible Cultural Heritage of Humanity. Of the 678 global traditions, practices, and human expressions on the list—which include things like Argentine tango, Chinese calligraphy, and Indian yoga—the Sosso-Bala is the only one whose existence has remained within a single family.[2] When it was proclaimed, Balla was an undocumented immigrant hauling canned food off trucks in Albany by day and quietly practicing his balafon in the convenience store's upstairs apartment at night, gently tapping its wooden bars with the tips of his fingers to not wake up his roommates.

Balla still lives in the US, but his situation is quite different these days. The 49-year-old has been featured as a session player on more than 45 albums, including two Grammy Award–winning recordings by Yo-Yo Ma. His music has been archived in the Library of Congress; he's performed at the Kennedy Center, Carnegie Hall, and Lincoln Center; and he's led demonstrations at Harvard, MIT, and the New England Conservatory, where he currently teaches a class on musical improvisation. In 2019, he was named a National Heritage Fellow by the National Endowment for the Arts, the US government's highest honor in the folk and traditional arts. But while this award was received with a swell of enthusiasm back in Mali and Guinea, virtually no one in the US had ever written about him or his family's astonishing legacy.

And so it happened that in January 2022, after a weeklong search to connect the dots from a 13th-century emperor to Niagassola, Guinea, to an address in Medford, Massachusetts, I sent a hopeful email to a man I'd never met, asking if he'd be willing to meet me, to tell me his family's story, and to let me follow him back to the place where it all started. Within 30 minutes of hitting SEND, I received a call from a number I didn't recognize. It was Balla, and the first thing he told me was, "I've been waiting for an email like this for more than 20 years."

I had no way of knowing at the time, but Balla's life had recently been overshadowed by grief. Three months earlier, his wife, Kris, had succumbed to cancer, leaving Balla all alone to care for the couple's 15-year-old son and 14-year-old daughter. As Balla told me, Kris was more than just his partner; she was his anchor and biggest supporter. She was also instrumental in his success. Kris was the one who filled out each of Balla's grant applications, who found him teaching positions, and who arranged access to a studio at Harvard, where she worked as a media technician, so he could record his debut album in 2007. In 2017, Balla, Kris, and the kids took their only-ever family trip to Bamako and Niagassola to meet Balla's extended family and see where he grew up. It was on this trip that Kris saw how much Balla loved playing music with his siblings and suggested he record a family album. When I met Balla at his Medford condo, he was putting the finishing touches on this project that had been five years in the making and that he had dedicated to his late wife. It features not only his brothers and cousins as bandmates but also his two American kids on backing vocals in Mandinka.

Ten days later, I joined Balla and his children on a journey back to Mali and Guinea that he had been planning since Kris's passing. As he explained, it was a chance to come home, to heal, and to remind the kids of their roots. Along the way, I set out to understand how this 800-year-old tradition has survived, to meet the current balatigui, and to seek his permission to become one of the first foreign journalists in history to set eyes on the Sosso-Bala.

———————

In 1216, two hunters approached the throne of Naré Maghann Konaté in the West African savanna. With them was a humpbacked woman named Sogolon Kondé, and when the Mandinka king laid eyes on her, he gasped in disbelief. Her presence had already been envisioned by Konaté's djeli, Balla Fasséké, who had told Konaté that were he to take an unattractive woman as his wife, she would bear the mightiest king the land had ever seen. Konaté already had a wife and son, but recalling Fasséké's prophecy, he took Sogolon as his second wife, and the following year, she gave birth to a boy. They called him Sundiata, yet he would also go on to be known by another name: Mari Djata, meaning "The Lion King." It is said that Sundiata's true story is what inspired the animated Disney film.[3]

This famous tale comes from the *Epic of Sundiata*,[4] which has been passed down by an unbroken line of djelis since the 13th century. Prince Sundiata was born in the shattered remnants of West Africa's first major civilization, the Empire of Ghana, which straddled the borders of modern-day Mauritania and Mali. By the time the humpbacked woman appeared at the Mandinka court, the empire was little more than a collection of small, warring fiefdoms. Despite Fasséké's grand prophecy, Prince Sundiata was born feeble and unable to walk throughout his childhood, which led him to be ridiculed by his stepmother and half brother. Konaté died when Sundiata was only seven years old, and though it was the king's wish that Sundiata succeed him, his half brother swooped in and assumed the throne. Fearing for their safety, Sundiata's mother fled with the young prince to a neighboring territory to seek asylum, and through the help of an iron rod, Sundiata soon took his first heroic steps.

As Sundiata grew, he not only became a great hunter like his father, but he became so strong that it was said he could uproot a baobab tree. He would soon need this strength, because while Sundiata and his mother were in exile, the leader of the nearby Sosso people, the evil "Sorcerer King" Soumaoro Kanté, had seized the former Ghanaian capital and began attacking the Mandinka people. Soumaoro was so cruel that djelis tell of him keeping the heads of nine defeated kings and wearing shoes made of their skin. Sundiata's half brother was terrified of Soumaoro, and instead of facing him, he fled in fear, leading the Mandinka to summon their exiled prince to help liberate them from Soumaoro's reign. Sundiata vowed to defend his homeland, and as he left his exiled post to unite a coalition of Mande clans to fight Soumaoro's forces, Fasséké had a second vision.

One night, Fasséké dreamed that a genie had given Soumaoro a magical malleted instrument, and that in order to help the Mandinka people defeat the evil king, Fasséké must obtain it. So, the next day, he set out to find Soumaoro. When he approached the Sosso ruler's chamber, Soumaoro wasn't there, but he saw the percussive instrument and started to gently strike it. Soumaoro was so taken by the harmonious melodies coming from his balafon that when he found Fasséké playing it, he asked him if he'd be his djeli. Recalling his vision, Fasséké agreed, but he told the evil king that he was loyal to the Mandinka people, saying *"Ku Yann Tea"*— meaning, "there is an unspoken, secret connection between us." From that moment, the devoted Mandinka djeli became known as Balla Fasséké Kouyaté, and this surname has passed to all his descendants ever since.[5]

Sundiata's united Mande forces defeated Soumaoro's Sosso army at the Battle of Kirina in 1235, and at just 18 years of age, Sundiata became the first ruler of the Mali Empire. When he did, he took Soumaoro's mythical "Sosso-Bala" balafon as a war trophy and appointed Fasséké Kouyaté as his trusted djeli, just as his father had. Sundiata asked Fasséké Kouyaté to guard the sacred instrument and requested that he and all those who came after him serve as the keepers of the empire's culture and memory.

Eight centuries later, there remains an unspoken connection between the Kouyatés and the Keitas they have served. I got my first glimpse of this when Balla and I met in Manhattan at the Mali Mission to the United Nations so his children and I could apply for our visas before the trip. When the registrar identified herself as Miriam Keita, Balla launched into a breathtakingly long monologue in Mandinka, recalling the *Epic of Sundiata*, recounting how the registrar's forefathers had hailed from northern Mali and migrated south, and reciting her family's entire 800-year history.

When Balla finished, as a group of Malian onlookers crowded around him, the registrar turned to me and said, "You are so lucky to know this man. In our culture, we say when a djeli dies, an entire library of knowledge dies with him."

Today, nearly everything we know about Africa's real Lion King and the early Mali Empire comes from this continuous chain of djeli oral historians, and Sundiata remains a near-mythical figure among many West Africans. In addition to uniting the Mande peoples (of which the Mandinka—or Malinke, as it's sometimes written—are the largest subgroup), Sundiata is also said to have issued one of the world's first human rights charters, an oral constitution known as the Kouroukan Fouga, or Manden Charter. Among other things, it advocates for peace within a diverse nation, food security, education, and freedom of expression.[6] Sundiata governed his new empire more as a multiethnic federation than an authoritarian regime, with each of the 12 tribes he united having equal representation in his court. This governmental model proved so successful that it not only ushered in one of the longest prolonged periods of peace among the once-warring clans of the West African interior, but it also allowed Mali to soon surpass Ghana and become one of the largest and richest civilizations in African history.

"In terms of sheer size, influence, and wealth, Mali was West Africa's greatest empire," said Kevin MacDonald, who has worked in Mali for more than 30 years as an archaeologist and is the director of University College London's Institute of Archaeology. "What makes it unique from prior empires is its system of governance. Instead of controlling different ethnic groups through alliance and threat, by the time we get to the mature Mali Empire, you're looking at a sophisticated territorial empire that had regional governors known as '*masa*.' There was more coordination from the center, and regions and statelets were better integrated into the empire."

According to MacDonald, at its height starting around 1300, the Mali Empire stretched for some 2,000 kilometers west to east, from the Senegalese coast across modern-day Gambia, Guinea-Bissau, Guinea, southern Mauritania, the Ivory Coast, northern Ghana, Mali, northern Burkina Faso, western Niger, and northwest Nigeria—a distance roughly the size of Western Europe. Like Ghana before it, the empire grew rich by taxing the many Imazighen (sometimes offensively called "Berber") traders from North Africa who traveled south through its territory along the trans-Saharan trade route to exchange salt for gold. But unlike Ghana, whose borders sat between the salt deposits to the north and the gold mines to the south, the Mali Empire grew to strategically control both the salt and the gold. Throughout the Middle Ages, Mali was far and away the world's largest gold producer.[7] Thanks to an insatiable appetite for the mineral from North African and Mediterranean societies to craft jewelry, decorate mosques and churches, and mint coins to pay armies, droves of camel-bound Imazighen traders braved the monthslong journey across the Sahara's scorching sand dunes to obtain it. By the 1320s, Mali had become one of the wealthiest kingdoms in history.[8]

Yet, for all its dazzling prosperity, one of the most striking aspects of the Mali Empire is how little the outside world knew about it at the height of its power, and how little scholars still know about it today. Aside from the enormous distance that separated Mali from its main trading partners in North Africa, the empire was also thought to have been notoriously secretive. It used its highly organized military to guard its caravan routes and ensure that once traders entered its borders, they didn't venture too far from the state-sanctioned trading hubs to sightsee.[9] It is precisely because of the empire's shrouded history and the fact that so few foreigners were able to travel through it that the oral histories passed down by the djelis within it are so valuable.

In the absence of indigenous written histories, what little else we know about the empire aside from these djeli-narrated tales comes from a few other sources. One is the Tunisian intellectual Ibn Khaldūn, who never visited Mali but spoke to many who did to write his historical book on North and West Africa, *Kitāb al-ʿIbar*. Two others are the West African chronicles of *Taʾrīkh al-fattāsh* and *Taʾrīkh al-Sūdān*, which were written hundreds of years after the empire's fall. As a result, if you were to stop anyone on the streets today outside of West Africa and ask them if they've ever heard of the Mali Empire, they may only be able to vaguely recall two things: the city of Timbuktu and the emperor Mansa Musa—the richest person who ever lived and the guy who, literally, put the Mali Empire on the world map.

Musa was Mali's 10th emperor, and during his 25-year reign from 1312 to 1337, the empire reached the height of its power. He developed Mali's trade routes; increased its territory; and annexed 24 cities, including Timbuktu. As the empire expanded, so did Musa's wealth. According to the British Museum, during Musa's rule, nearly half of the gold in the Old World came from the Mali Empire—and Musa owned all of it. His wealth has been characterized as "indescribable" by the BBC, with some estimates placing his net worth between $400 and $500 billion[10]—roughly twice the amount of Elon Musk, the richest person in the world today.[11] Yet, Musa didn't just want Mali to be rich; he wanted it to be recognized and respected throughout the Muslim world.

Though Islam had reached sub-Saharan Africa as early as the eighth century via the camel-bound Arab traders from North Africa, it wasn't until roughly 1300 that Mali's kings became Muslim.[12] As a result, even though the empire controlled the lucrative trans-Saharan trade routes, it was still viewed as something of a far-flung, "backward" power by its North African trading partners. It also remained relatively unknown by the outside world. Musa, a devout Muslim, wanted to change that, so he embarked on the greatest hajj history had ever seen—a part pilgrimage, part publicity stunt to Mecca designed to flaunt his empire's wealth and dazzle the Islamic world.

In 1324, Musa and an entourage of 60,000 officials, soldiers, slaves, and djelis set off on a 6,500-kilometer journey across the Sahara. Arab writers describe his caravan as being draped in Persian silks, the travelers clutching golden staffs, with 100 camels each hauling 300 pounds of pure gold. It was a gilded, glittering city moving through the desert—a procession so brilliant that chroniclers said it "almost put Africa's sun to shame."[13] Others claim the emperor handed out fistfuls of gold dust to beggars along the way. But the most well-documented part of Musa's journey took place when his caravan passed through Cairo, where he and his royal entourage spent three months bestowing lavish gifts to sultans, emirs, and diplomats. Musa apparently gave away and spent so much gold during his time in Cairo that he single-handedly caused the value of the currency to crash, wrecking the economy across the Middle East for 12 years.[14]

By all accounts, Musa's calculated expedition to attract the world's attention did just that. According to 14th-century Syrian historian Shibab al-Umari, who visited Cairo a dozen years after Musa left, residents were still raving about the ruler's generosity.[15] Tales of his extravagant cross-continental journey continued long after his death, eventually reaching Europe. In 1375, the Mali Empire appeared on a map for the first time, with Musa depicted in the Catalan Atlas wearing a golden crown, grasping a golden scepter, and holding a giant golden nugget. Musa's world tour also brought other benefits back to the empire. The king returned with a host of religious scholars and architects who would later transform Timbuktu into a famed intellectual and religious center.[16] But while Musa's hajj led him to become a larger-than-life figure across the Arab world, he has a far different legacy back in West Africa today—and this is because the djelis who accompanied him never let their descendants forget how he gave away the empire's wealth.

"There is a reason there is an *Epic of Sundiata* but no epic of Musa," Daouda Keita, the director of the National Museum of Mali, told me in his Bamako office. "His tales reached many people, but he spilt our riches and he turned his back away from local animistic traditions to embrace a more mainstream idea of Islam."

One of the people Musa's exploits reached was the explorer and Islamic scholar Ibn Battuta. In 1325, the 21-year-old set off on his own pilgrimage from his home in Tangier, Morocco, to Mecca. Along the way, he stopped in Cairo, where he heard that just two years earlier, a king had come bearing more gold than the residents had ever seen. Battuta completed his hajj and continued roaming the globe. During the next 29 years, he covered an estimated 120,000 kilometers (nearly five times as far as Marco Polo wandered), visiting nearly every corner of the Muslim world from Andalusia to Indonesia and becoming the greatest traveler of the Middle Ages.[17] Along the way, he was attacked by bandits, nearly drowned in a shipwreck, and hid in a swamp for seven days after rebels ordered his execution. Yet, Battuta never forgot the tales he had heard about the African king, and though it would take him 25 years to reach this distant land, it would prove to be one of the explorer's greatest adventures. In 1351, Battuta set out from

Fez, Morocco, on a 2,400-kilometer journey across the Sahara to a land few foreign travelers had ever seen: the Mali Empire. Today, his book *The Travels of Ibn Battuta* remains the only surviving eyewitness account of the kingdom.[18]

After crossing the Atlas Mountains, Battuta reached a small oasis town where he spent four months buying camels and waiting to tag along with the great North African trade caravans heading south across the Sahara. The group traveled in the early morning and late afternoon to avoid the scorching sun, and in April 1352, after crossing an 800-kilometer stretch of desert with only one oasis and navigating a windswept expanse of the Sahara that was "haunted by demons," the caravan finally entered the elusive Mali Empire. During the next eight months, Battuta would venture extensively across Mali's sub-Saharan trade routes, visiting the capital and Timbuktu and meeting with governors, judges, and the king himself. In many ways, Battuta's account of the empire is colored by his outright contempt for Black Africans; his demands that a man of his stature receive a monetary welcome versus the pounded millet, honey, and milk dinner he was initially offered; and his general disapproval of how many of Mali's residents still clung to traditional religious beliefs rather than being fully absorbed by Islam—a fact that continues across much of the former empire's territory today. It probably also didn't help that after being served a meal of "gruel," Battuta fell ill for two full months while his travel companion died.

Yet, for all his grumblings about the food and Malian women not veiling themselves in the presence of men, there was a lot Battuta admired about the empire. He waxed about the "fine Egyptian fabrics" people wore; the "surpassing beauty" of the ladies; and the egalitarian attitudes toward gender dynamics, with women being free to have "'friends' and 'companions' amongst men outside their own families." He was also struck by the empire's immense safety, noting, "neither traveler there nor dweller has anything to fear from thief or usurper."

One of Battuta's most vivid encounters came when he attended a festival held by the empire's ruler, Mansa Sulayman (the younger brother of Mansa Musa, who had died 15 years earlier).[19] Though Battuta had nothing good to say about the "miserly king," he was thoroughly taken by his djeli, whom he identified as a Kouyaté. He describes the djeli as playing an instrument "with sticks to produce a wonderful sound," adding: "he beats on an instrument which is made of reeds with tiny calabashes below it, [a 'balophon'], praising the sultan, recalling in his song the expeditions and deeds. The wives and the concubines sing with him . . . about 30 of his pages . . . each has a drum tied to him and he beats it. Then . . . [come acrobats and jugglers of swords]."[20]

What makes Battuta's account of Mali so fascinating is that it provides a singular look at a great African power just before the trans-Atlantic slave trade. Sulayman died six years after Battuta's visit, and when he did, a string of ineffective leaders plunged Mali into civil war, bankrupted the state, and overextended the empire. By about 1450, MacDonald notes that Mali became increasingly susceptible to raids and revolts from its rural territories, and around this time, the newly forming Songhai Empire that would eventually absorb most of Mali began carving up its northern and eastern territories. To adapt, the empire looked west, focusing its attention on the Atlantic Ocean and the Portuguese ships that increasingly started snooping around its coasts.

Thanks to Musa's exploits, tales of Mali's wealth had reached European rulers, and by the mid-1400s, the Portuguese were eager to bypass the crowded trans-Saharan trade routes and gain direct access to what would later be called Africa's "Gold Coast." With the rival Songhai Empire increasingly controlling West Africa's north-south trade routes, partnering with these strange, white visitors offered a unique economic opportunity for Malian leaders. However, it would have devastating consequences. In 1456, Portuguese explorers reached the mouth of the Gambia River and made an agreement with a Malian governor to exchange silk, arms, and horses for gold, ivory, and people—thus, launching the large-scale African slave trade.[21] By the turn of the 16th century, as Portuguese and Spanish explorations of the New World flooded Europe with the plundered gold of South and Central American empires, the value of Mali's most prized mineral plummeted. Soon, European ships weren't coming to Mali for gold, but for slaves to work their colonial plantations.

In many ways, the Mali Empire ran on slavery. Slaves from Mali's conquered territories worked the salt and gold mines, served as soldiers in its army, produced the food surpluses that bolstered the economy, and were sent north through the Sahara to Arab rulers along with its vast minerals.[22] But as scholars have noted, Mali's system of slavery was more likely akin to the sort of serfdom that also existed in various forms throughout medieval Europe.[23] Today, the Mali Empire's role in the trans-Atlantic slave trade remains a highly controversial topic, but what's certain is the magnitude, cruelty, and long-lasting effects of European chattel slavery that endured for the next 350 years was far more horrific than anything that existed in West Africa. Yet, there's an even deeper controversy surrounding Mali's legacy of slavery—one that, until recent decades, had been guarded in secrecy by centuries of Mandinka djelis.

According to Wâ Kamissoko, Mali's chief djeli in the 1970s, one of Sundiata's greatest achievements was his abolition of the slave trade within the empire. However, Kamissoko claimed that, 20 years after the Lion King's death, slavery resumed within Mali. This betrayal of Sundiata's command apparently caused such national shame that a consensus of djelis felt compelled to erase Sundiata's abolition from the annals of the empire's history. Kamissoko said that for centuries, the balatigui and other high-ranking djelis were taught the true history but had to swear to never reveal it publicly. It was only just before his death in 1976 that Kamissoko decided to break this vow of silence and divulge this kingdom's hidden history in the 1973 book *Soundjata la Gloire du Mali*.

As the trans-Atlantic slave trade intensified, it drained manpower across West Africa, making the region more vulnerable to invasions from Moroccan forces, who effectively ended what was left of the Songhai and Mali empires in the late 1500s and the early 1600s. At the same time, the end of the trans-Atlantic slave trade in the 1800s also had devastating effects for West Africa, as it crippled the region's economies that had come to rely on it and left them open to conquest and colonization. By the turn of the 20th century, the French controlled most of the Mali Empire's former territory. The colonies of French West Africa gained independence by 1960, but France's exploitation of natural resources and its imperialist monetary policies still cripple the region. Really, the only good thing to come from French rule is that anywhere you go in Mali and Guinea today, you're never too far from a fresh baguette.

Yet, through centuries of wars and occupiers, the Mali Empire's two main linguistic legacies have remained: its language (Mandinka) and its oral historians (djelis). Though according to Dr. Nubia Kai, the author of the book *Kuma Malinke Historiography: Sundiata Keita to Almamy Samori Toure*, djelis have always had a much broader role than simply storytellers. "In the traditional precolonial era, griots were the principal political advisors to kings, chiefs, and other high government officials. They were the mediators in international, national, and local disputes. They served as ambassadors and diplomats to neighboring countries. They were the chief judicial advisors and advisors of national defense. They were also the officiators of rites of passage ceremonies, puberty rites, marriage, naming ceremonies, funerals, national inaugurations, harvest festivals, religious festivals, sporting events, and other national holidays. They negotiated marriage and dowry arrangements between the families of the bride and groom. They were foremost historians, archivists, genealogists, social and cultural anthropologists, educators, musicians, and dramatic performers."[24]

Today, the roles of djelis have remained relatively unchanged. There may no longer be Malian kings, but Mande politicians and presidents rely on their djelis to act as advisors and peacemakers. "Our role is to help people make decisions—both among each other and if they're having a conflict within themselves," said Balla's cousin Alieu Diabate, who served as the djeli to former Malian president Ibrahim Boubacar Keita, and whose Bamako living room is filled with images of him shaking hands with West African leaders alongside a framed certificate confirming his knighthood from the National Order of Mali.

Many Mande families still have a djeli who knows their ancestry and who participates in their most intimate affairs. As Ibrahima Diabate, a djeli from the town of Kela, 100 kilometers south of Bamako, told me: "A djeli [family] stays with a person for life. When a baby is born, the djeli is there. In our culture, the imam whispers the name the family has chosen into a newborn baby's ear, so that he is the first to know who he is, but it is the djeli who announces that name to everyone. When that person wants to marry, it is the djeli who goes to the other family to introduce himself, give kola nuts, and explain this person's intention and history. At the wedding, the djeli is there. If there are problems in a marriage, the djeli is there to help resolve them. And when that person dies, the djeli buries them and recounts the life they led. We make that person eternal."

As Balla explained, there are several types of djelis. One is the "grand" advisors and guardians—such as the Kouyatés—who have historically served royalty. Then there are the more "local" djelis, who maintain the histories of the specific towns and villages from which they hail, such as Ibrahima. Once upon a time, the only djelis were the Kouyatés, but over the centuries, this social caste of musicians has expanded to include other families, such as the Diabates and Sissokos. And while the balafon may be the most famous djeli instrument, it's far from the only one. Google "griot music," and in addition to balafon performances, you'll find renditions of ancient epics, folk songs, and modern Afropop performed by men on the *djembe* (a goblet-shaped drum), the *ngoni* (a lute-like instrument widely believed to have inspired the banjo), and the kora (a sort of 21-stringed harp that produces one of the world's most enchanting sounds). Women, like Balla's sister Kaniba, can also be djelis and usually specialize in singing historical narratives. These days, djelis are essentially the pop stars and divas of Malian music, and if you wander into any café or club in Bamako playing music videos, you'll notice many of the artists have the last name Kouyaté.

While MacDonald noted that Western scholars have traditionally been suspicious about the reliability of the oral histories djelis have performed, their contributions to uncovering the mysteries of the Mali Empire have been immense. Between 2005 and 2013, MacDonald and Malian historian Seydou Camara interviewed more than 70 village elders and djelis in Mali's south-central Ségou region. Their work took them to Sorotomo, a vast ruin long rumored to have been a political and military force thanks to the long memory of djelis. The site had never been excavated, and upon digging, the team uncovered one of the largest ancient centers ever discovered in West Africa: a thriving 72-hectare city dating from the 13th to the 15th centuries that dwarfs the empire's capital of Niani and has led experts to wonder whether Sorotomo and the surrounding Ségou region was actually the epicenter of the kingdom.[25]

"In a sense, oral history and archaeology are very good partners because archaeology can provide frameworks of settlement geography and dating, and oral history provides a possible narrative," MacDonald said. "Griots are negotiators and praise singers who don't just perform to the royal courts, but also for the people in smaller communities. They have shaped the minds of a civilization."

Indeed, it was a Kouyaté who wrote Mali's national anthem. The call sign of Radio Mali is a refrain from the *Epic of Sundiata* that Fasséké Kouyaté first performed. And stories recounted by generations of Kouyatés have inspired Malian films and soap operas. This is the legacy that Balla was born into. As Keita at the National Museum of Mali told me: "We are a society of oral tradition. Only the djeli knows that history, and the Kouyatés are the original djeli. They preserve the collective memory of our people. If we lose them, we lose the history of our culture."

In an eerie coincidence, like Sundiata, Balla was unable to walk for the first seven years of his life due to an unknown condition. The youngest of 11 children, he grew up between his father's ancestral home in Niagassola and the closest city, Bamako. Neither mud-brick home had electricity or running water, and like many families in Mali and Guinea today, the Kouyatés cooked outside over a wood fire and used shea butter candles to light their compound at night. When Balla was six, his father placed two mallets in his hands and told him he was ready. "Back then, there was no doctor or hospital to diagnose my condition," Balla said, sitting in the living room of his Medford condo, his trademark fedora cocked to the side. "But the good thing about the balafon is you play it sitting down, so I was okay."

Balla eventually learned to walk, and when he wasn't climbing mango trees or chasing geckos, he was happiest kneeling beside his father and cousins practicing the balafon. As soon as he learned the basic accompaniments, he started memorizing the *Epic of Sundiata*, whose many episodes and countless variations can take djelis several days to narrate. Balla's father performed across West Africa as a djeli, and he taught each of his sons the basics of the balafon, but Balla took to it in a way that none of his eight older brothers had. "I remember watching my father and cousins and telling myself I'd never give up until I could do what they did. Any cassette I could get my hands on, any music with the balafon, I would spend days listening to it, only coming out when it was time to eat." Balla explained that, to be a djeli, it isn't enough to memorize the epics and play an instrument; you have to learn to make the instrument your family has historically played too. "Whenever my dad would come back from traveling, he'd want to repair his balafon or make a new one, so that's how I learned to cut, shape, and tune it. The frame is made from bamboo. The keys are typically rosewood that you get from the forest and dry in the sun. With the Sosso-Bala, the keys are tied with antelope skin, but growing up [with the balafons we regularly played], we typically used strips of goat skin. You can't do that here in the US, so I use nylon string," Balla said, laughing as he showed me the many balafons he crams into his condo's closets.

Balla's father hoped that at least one of his sons would follow in his footsteps, but as each gravitated toward singing and other instruments, Balla's love for the balafon only grew. "I wanted to be just like my dad. He never went to school. He couldn't read or write. But he was generous, and people loved him so much that they'd carry his balafon for him until his next performance. I didn't want this tradition to disappear in my family," he said. When Balla was 12, he dropped out of school and started performing for farmers outside Niagassola with his mother. He was so small his mother placed him on top of a large rock, and while she sang and played the *karinyan* (a sort of two-handed cowbell), Balla performed historical epics for hours on end, as teams of 25 men plowed the fields to the rhythms of the family's synchronized beat. "The farm owner paid us a sack of rice or corn or peanuts each day," he said. "And if we did that for two or three months, we'd get a whole year of food for our family, so we started doing it all around Guinea and Mali."

At 13, Balla headed to the Mali-Guinea border to take a job so rooted in Mandinka culture that it predates even the balafon: "I worked in the mines, digging for gold with a pick," he said. "I hated it. Every week,

there would be a plane from France that would come and take it all away."
During the planting and harvest seasons, he'd return to the fields to play
for the farmers with his mother. As word of his balafon ability spread, he
started getting asked to perform at baby showers, coming-of-age ceremonies, and weddings from Bamako to Niagassola. Thanks to his sister's rising stardom, Balla was able to quit the mines as an 18-year-old and began
accompanying Kaniba on tour to Burkina Faso, the Ivory Coast, Senegal,
and the Republic of the Congo. Soon, musicians across West Africa began asking him to record with them, and by the time he was 26, Balla
was one of the most in-demand session players in West Africa. But Balla
didn't just want to back up other artists; he wanted to do his own thing.
So, in 1999, a year after his father became appointed as the guardian of the
Sosso-Bala, Balla did something previously unheard of with the ancient
instrument: he started playing two at the same time. "With one balafon,
you have seven notes. With two, I tune them so that I can make 12 and a
half notes, and lots of quarter notes. With this [full chromatic scale], I can
play any music in the world—traditional djeli music, but also music that a
balafon is not supposed to play."

I had never heard a balafon before, let alone two, so before our trip I
went to Queens to see Balla perform. The instrument sounds like a much
richer marimba, with the hollowed-out calabashes below each slat acting
as a resonator, amplifying each woody note. For the first hour, Balla played
traditional djeli music. As a Malian woman belted out joyous epics in a
piercing vibrato, Balla looped a syncopated, head-nodding rhythm behind
her. Later, when an American blues band asked Balla to join them onstage,
he used his double-balafon setup to seemingly tap into a deeper range of
human emotion, darting off on rolling, improvised solos and wringing a
sense of pining and pain from his family's ancient tool of praise.

Naturally, this decision to break from tradition was met with controversy, especially within Balla's family. "My father thought I was out of my
mind. In our culture, no one had ever played two balafons. He thought it
was out of line. But when I explained it to him, he started to accept it. I
said: 'Dad, I don't just want to keep this tradition alive, I want to bring it
to more of the world.'" And so, a year later, Balla followed his sister and
boarded a plane for the US.

One day when Balla was working at the convenience store in Albany, he got a phone call from a kora player he grew up with. The musician was now living in Somerville, Massachusetts, and playing Sundays at a local Middle Eastern bar. He invited his childhood friend to come play with him, so Balla bought a Greyhound ticket to Boston. At the end of the show, an American woman with an easy smile approached the balafon player. She was born and raised in Massachusetts, but she spoke perfect French from her time studying in Paris. She had even spent time in Mali studying African dance. "That's how I met my wife," Balla said, gazing at several pictures of Kris in his living room, some with her curly brown hair falling over her shoulders, and later ones where she's wearing a chemo cap. Balla made $30 that night, which wasn't even enough to cover his return bus fare, but he told the kora player he'd be back the following Sunday. He wanted to see her. "Originally, my attention wasn't to have a girlfriend or get married, but to have a friend." He smiled. "I didn't get to meet many people here who knew my culture."

Balla and the kora player soon hooked up with another musician from The Gambia and started playing more regular gigs. Balla left Albany, moved into a studio in Harlem, and started going to jazz clubs. "I said I played the balafon and they'd say, 'What's that?' so I'd say, 'It's a xylophone with a *b*,' and we'd start jamming. I loved it!" Balla recalled. He also started performing at West African naming ceremonies and weddings from New York to New England, which gave him an excuse to see Kris in person versus just talking to her on the phone. As the years passed, Balla realized that his feelings for his American friend had deepened, and in 2005, the two married and relocated to the Boston area. "When you talk about *djelia*, it's a man and a woman together. The man usually plays and tells a story, and the female will sing. It's kind of like a back-and-forth," Balla said. "She was my *djeli moussa*, which means my female djeli, my equal."

Two years later, Balla's bandmate was nominated for a Grammy for an album Balla played on, which encouraged Balla to finally record his own album, *Sababu*. Its success and his subsequent tour led to collaborations with artists like Yo-Yo Ma (who asked him to join his Silkroad Ensemble), banjo virtuoso Béla Fleck (whose family remains close with Balla), and guitarist Ben Harper (who cried the first time he heard Balla play, saying it tapped into something deep within his African roots). Though Kris would never get to hear Balla's second album, which she inspired, Balla is sure she would have liked it as much as she loved getting to see where he came from during the family's lone trip to West Africa. "I'm telling you, it's nothing like this," Balla told me, looking out the window at Medford's Victorian homes on a 37-degree-Fahrenheit December day. "You'll see."

I awoke at 7:00 A.M. to the sharp, shrill sound of a sheep being slaughtered at a few meters away from where I lay on the floor. Four hours earlier, after we landed at the Bamako airport and were welcomed by signs reading WELCOME TO MALI: LAND OF GOLD, a mob of family and friends swarmed Balla and his two children before whisking us in a five-car caravan through the darkness to Balla's new home. It was so new, in fact, that Balla had never stepped foot in it. Over the last several years, he had slowly put money aside to build a compound where his 90-year-old mother and two sisters could live, and where he and his family could stay when they came to visit. As we unlocked the black gate leading into the sleek, white-and-red stucco house, I noticed one of Balla's cousins dragging a lone sheep by a rope into the compound's courtyard. After a sleepless 30-hour triangle from New York to Istanbul to Mali, I briefly wondered what was happening but soon plopped down on a mattress on the other side of the wall from where the animal was tethered.

A few hours after I became an ear-witness to a sheep decapitation, Balla knocked on my door and told me he wanted to show me something. We walked into the courtyard where a pool of blood and the sheep's head lay on the ground baking in the 90-degree-Fahrenheit heat. Balla explained that in his culture, it's good luck to sacrifice an animal when moving into a new home. "There'll be a big party later," he said, as women in bright-patterned *boubou* dresses balancing giant bowls of rice and freshly carved mutton on their heads began to descend on the compound. "But first, I want to show you the conservatory, named after my direct ancestor Balla Fasséké."

I piled into the back of a car next to Balla's 16-year-old son, Sekou, and his 15-year-old daughter, Jossira—both of whom are named after Balla's parents. From the time Sekou could sit up, Balla propped him next to a tiny balafon and placed two mallets in his palms, gently guiding his tiny hands toward the right notes. When Jossira was a toddler, Kris began teaching her the basics of Malian dance, and the kids started accompanying their father on the road from New England to New York, crawling into his empty balafon case to fall asleep while he played gigs. As the kids got older, Balla began inviting them onstage at his shows, with Sekou playing the balafon rhythm that his sister would move to as their father tore through improvised solos. But aside from their family's musical legacy, a basic understanding of Mali's French colonial tongue, and their impeccable West African politeness and generosity, the kids reminded me of normal American teens. They both love trap music and TikTok; they play on their high school soccer teams and like video games; they work after-school jobs; and after just four hours of sleep and still severely jet-lagged, the last thing they both wanted was to be dragged out of bed by their dad.

"It's important you two see this place," Balla said, turning around from the front seat.

"The good thing about growing up on the road and falling asleep in balafon cases is we can sleep anywhere now," Jossira muttered to me, as she laid her head on Sekou's shoulder.

We bumped along a powdery road away from the compound, kicking up a cloud of the red-sand dust from which Bamako is built. Our car swerved to avoid free-range bulls and children passing tattered soccer balls amid the squat cinderblock houses. Bamako feels much more like an overgrown village than a capital city—a parched 2.7-million-person sandcastle made entirely from paprika. When it's not raining, it's hot, and when it's hot (as it is during the November-to-May dry season), life happens outside on the dirt streets that serve as kitchens, living rooms, landfills, playgrounds, and animal pastures. The smell of burning wood and charcoal grills smoking fish and simmering stews drifts into a dense smog of diesel as you approach the city's few paved thoroughfares, where a chaotic stream of scooters driven by men with women clutching their backs and babies strapped to the women's backs share the lane-less roads with children galloping atop white horses. Wooden stalls topped with thatched and tin roofs line the roads, selling everything from watermelons to purses to tires. A French-built bridge carried us away from the two soaring minarets of the Grand Mosque and over the Niger River—the lifeblood of the arid, landlocked country—where fishermen were hauling Nile perch into wooden canoes. We soon wound up a hill toward the Malian president's white palace and into the Balla Fasséké Kouyaté Arts Conservatory. The school's director, Dr. Bourbaïma Fofana, was waiting for us, and as our four-car caravan arrived at the palm-fringed campus, he beelined to Balla to greet him and his children before whisking us into a large, oak-paneled room. Fofana explained that the school's purpose is twofold: to enable Mali's most promising young balafon, kora, djembe, and ngoni players to hone their crafts, and also to honor the legacy of the world's first and most famous djeli.

"There are 54 countries in Africa, and in 16 of them, they practice the djeli tradition," he told me. "You can't go anywhere in Africa today where people have not heard of Sundiata, and when you mention him, you have to mention Balla Fasséké. We don't want to forget that history, but lately, that history has been disappearing. We have television, radio. People are getting their influences from other places, and we are losing this culture little by little. So, in 2004, the president started this conservatory and named it after him because he didn't want this tradition to die."

As I sat surrounded by Balla's extended family, I asked Fofana to tell me what makes the Kouyaté family so important to the Mande people today. After considering it for a moment, he said, "The role of the djeli is to create peace between human beings and hold our history. When we praise Kouyaté, it's different than any other djeli, because he is connected to Sundiata. It's like this: Muslims believe the Prophet Mohammed was a messenger from God. Christians believe Jesus was a messenger from God. We believe Kouyaté is the messenger of Sundiata, the ruler who ended the violence and united all of us. There would be no Mande society without Kouyaté."

By the time our caravan returned to Balla's house, the entire neighborhood had descended on the compound. I was greeted by a crowd of smiling school-aged children wearing donated t-shirts that had traveled as far as I had to Bamako: CITY OF BRIGHTON YOUTH SPORTS, BEIJING

CHINJING HIGH SCHOOL 2011, ROMA MINI BASKET CAMP 2004. I left my shoes by the pile at the door, and two of Balla's brothers, Fantamady and Dianguine, who play guitar and sing on Balla's latest album, led me up to the roof where giant bowls were waiting filled with Mali's take on jollof: *zaame*, a medley of rice, eggplant, garlic, and tomato topped with the sacrificed lamb. The boy wearing the Beijing shirt handed each of us a square bag of water. I watched the men bite it open, letting the trickle dribble over their palms to clean their hands before I followed suit. Fantamady offered me a spoon, but not wanting to stick out any more than I already did, I politely declined, squatting beside the four other men and rolling up my sleeves like everybody else. As in so much of the world, you eat with your hands in Mali. But unlike in India and Southeast Asia, where you guide the food into your mouth with the thumb, Malians pack each bite into a ball with the tips of their fingers, and genders scoop from different bowls. From the roast chicken and onion *diabadji* to the baobab-leaf-and-peanut-sauce-spiced *naboulou*, no two dishes I had during my trip were quite the same. The only constant was Balla's family always insisting I take the first bite, nudging the juiciest cuts of meat toward my side of the bowl until I'd inevitably slide it back toward my hosts—an unending show of generosity and hospitality in a country still struggling to move beyond subsistence.

When the last bowl of zaame had been devoured, three kufi-clad imams wearing knee-length tunics entered the compound and sat on a rug in the living room. After a 30-minute reading from the Quran to bless the Kouyaté family's new home and appease the Prophet, it was time to party. The imams cleared, and several of Balla's nephews appeared at the doorway carrying balafons above their heads. Outside, two cousins soon started slapping *n'taman* talking drums slung over their shoulders to a hypnotic beat. Across the street, a cluster of Balla's brothers and nephews brought out guitars and began to pluck the type of plaintive melodies and walking pentatonic scales that would feel at home on a Mississippi Delta porch.

I wandered from performance to performance at this impromptu Kouyaté music festival, until the percussive plinking of balafons led me back into Balla's living room, where two teenagers were thrumming an irresistibly danceable melody. As soon as I walked in, Balla's 90-year-old mother locked eyes with me. While a circle of women clapped in unison, she slowly raised herself from the couch, playfully pointed at me, and began bending her knees in her floral-patterned boubou as she placed her hand to her forehead to lead the family in the "Kouyaté dance"—a choreography that women in Balla's family have passed down for hundreds of years as men beat the balafon. She shook her head left and right, tugged at her dress, and rotated clockwise as the rhythm built. Soon, each of the 20-some women in the room, including her two-year-old great-great-granddaughter, was on their feet—five generations stepping, shimmying, and whirling with such joy that it felt like they were smiling with their entire bodies. For the Kouyatés, the night was a reunion; for me, it was a reminder of what led me to become fascinated by Mali so many years ago.

Mali is one of the world's great musical cradles, and its sounds have been beguiling foreigners ever since Battuta first saw a Kouyaté perform. Centuries later, enslaved Malians would bring their melisma singing style, call-and-response narration, and knowledge of making plucked and strummed stringed instruments like the kora and ngoni to the cotton fields of the American South, leading many musicologists to declare Mali to be the origin of the blues.[26] In fact, when you listen to Malian superstars like the late Ali Farka Touré, whose pensive, spiritual guitar riffs born from a life working the land led him to be dubbed "the African John Lee Hooker," it's often difficult to distinguish between Malian folk and Mississippi blues. But as Touré famously said, "This music has been taken from here [Mali]. I play traditional music and I don't know what the blues is."[27] African Americans would mix and morph these West African sounds into jazz, rock and roll, soul, funk, and hip-hop. But since djelis were the only social caste permitted to play music in the Mali Empire—and in its former territories long after the empire's collapse—they are likely the ones who introduced many of these African traditions to the New World during the slave trade. This makes their legacy doubly important: not only have their long memories and handed-down epics formed the backbone of Mali's history, but their transplanted sounds helped form the backbone of much of Western music as well. As Balla told me, "Our role as djelis has always been about storytelling, about talking about what's going on in the communities. When you hear these rap lyrics or blues or country songs, it's like they're American djelis."

Today, echoes of this rich musical legacy still reverberate everywhere you look in Bamako. The following afternoon, Balla and I piled back into the car, passing clusters of children blaring Malian Afropop from tinny radios, threading vendors hawking fruit in a call-and-response cry from opposite sides of the street, and into Fantamady and Dianguine's dusty compound, where the steady drumbeat of women pounding millet under a mango tree reverberated from the cinderblock walls. The plan was to caravan as a large, extended family to Niagassola, the fabled home of the Sosso-Bala—but not on an empty stomach. To my surprise, the decapitated sheep's head that I had seen swarming with flies and slowly decomposing in the heat the previous afternoon was now the centerpiece of a viscous soup. The Kouyatés squatted around the skull, tore off pieces of a baguette, and looked at me, motioning that the sinuous, spidery veins spitting from the sheep's eye socket were the best part. I crouched down alongside the family and closed my eyes as I scraped the gooey cavity with the baguette's crumb. The meal would later make Sekou and Jossira violently ill. Somehow, I managed to stomach it.

We set out in four cars and began the 215-kilometer trip to the Kouyatés' ancestral home. I drove with Balla, his kids, and Balla's much younger cousin, Makane, who plays the balafon alongside Balla on his new album. We listened to a few of the album's tracks as we snaked southwest through Bamako's sprawling, traffic-choked tentacles. Dianguine's voice soared and swooped over Balla and Makane's layered balafon rhythm, and Fantamady's guitar riffs rose up and peeled away in a sunny, toe-tapping melody. The scenery softened with the soundtrack, and soon, Bamako's mountains of metal scrap were replaced by the sandstone ridges and sharp pinnacles of the Mandinka Mountains. According to the *Epic of Sundiata*, it was here, amid the wind-whipped buttes and barren spaghetti-western landscape, where the Lion King united his 12-nation alliance against the evil Sorcerer King. The villages went by in an ochre blur, punctuated only by the towering baobab trees, white minarets, and pointed tufts of the circular mud huts that pierced the horizon.

As he drove, Makane told me that he'd visited the Kouyatés in Boston several years earlier, and the conversation quickly turned to the one member of the family not with us. Makane said he never forgot how Kris treated him like her son, mothering him to eat more vegetables during his stay and tucking him in each night in New England with an extra blanket. Sekou told me how his mom always used to leave an orange at the bottom of his and Jossira's stocking each Christmas—a tradition the two of them continued just six days earlier on their second Christmas without her. Soon, the kids were recalling their parents' drastically different parenting styles. "When we were really young, Dad used to hire these West African nannies to watch us," Jossira said, already giggling. Balla leaned forward, chiming in. "I wanted to expose you two to the culture, but your mom never liked any of them."

"Dad! Do you remember what that one did?" Jossira asked. "Which one?" Balla replied. "The one who pierced my ear when I was a baby without telling you or Mom because she decided I was ready!" Jossira exclaimed.

"Oh, yea! Your mom called me yelling that I needed to get rid of her," Balla said, as the kids burst into laughter. When things finally quieted, Balla looked out the window and said softly, "We always had different ways of doing things, but we worked," seemingly to himself, or perhaps to Kris.

We crossed into Guinea in total darkness, and 15 kilometers later, after stopping to buy several live chickens that we'd bring to Niagassola to kill and cook, we turned off the paved road and began a 77-kilometer, four-hour roller coaster through a desolate, crater-pocked moonscape so bone-jarringly bumpy that it made my teeth ache. Every few minutes, Makane had to swerve into the scorched bush because the off-road jolting was smoother than the pummeling we would have endured had we drilled into the waist-high termite nests studding the dirt path. The only thing keeping me going was the knowledge that, somewhere up ahead in the darkness, Balla's 90-year-old mother was in a car braving this road too. Balla explained that since this route is the only way in and out of Niagassola, it serves as something of a protector of the Sosso-Bala, insulating the ancient instrument from the outside world. But as the beams of our headlights darted from side to side in the lonely landscape, he added, "Still, my one goal in life is to get this road paved."

Just when I felt the nausea well up in my throat, our caravan suddenly stopped. Dianguine approached my door with an ear-to-ear grin and cheered, "*Bonne année! Bonne année!*" I looked down at my phone. It was midnight, and the start of a new year. We each staggered out of the car, any discomfort suddenly swept aside by delirious joy, and we embraced one another in the moonlight. A few moments later, we heard a rustling in the darkness, and the faint silhouettes of nearby villagers who'd heard us approach emerged from the bush. Soon, we were dancing, hugging, and taking photos together—a constellation of strangers celebrating another year around the sun under a sea of stars.

We pulled into the cement compound that Balla had built for the family at 2:00 A.M.—10 hours after we left Bamako. I carried my suitcase into the dimly lit home with one hand and a clucking upside-down chicken by the legs with the other. Dianguine pointed me toward one of the four bedrooms, and after Sekou recommended I bathe myself in bug spray before falling asleep, I lay down on a thin floor-bound mattress, letting the sounds of Balla's three snoring cousins wash over me, knowing that tomorrow was going to be a big day.

Dawn broke and I padded out of the compound's cool, concrete floor and into the fire-red sand to take in the home of the Sosso-Bala. At first glance, Niagassola is an unlikely final resting place for a sacred instrument revered by 11 million Mandinka people across West Africa. It's also an unlikely pilgrimage destination. During the annual *Tabaski* (Eid) holiday marking the end of Ramadan, thousands of people from across Guinea and Mali brave the dirt road and descend on the hamlet to see the Sosso-Bala and listen to it being played alongside a chorus of modern balafons. Throughout the other 364 days, Niagassola is decidedly quieter.

The 150-person village is a cluster of circular mud-brick huts topped with conical thatched roofs. I watched as scarf-wrapped women and their barefoot, knee-high children pushed wheelbarrows filled with plastic jerrycans to the village's three water pumps. Free-range bulls, sheep, goats, turkeys, and chickens shaded themselves under a cluster of towering banyan trees and nibbled on burnt, crackly shoots that were more kindling than grass. The billowing crimson dust gave the place an ethereal fairy-tale feel, like being inside a snow globe of ground sumac. Three men with weatherworn faces carrying old-timey musket rifles sat crouched outside the lone saloon-like café, looking straight out of a wanted ad from the 1900s. One of them, Neramani, told me they had one of the most respected—and only—jobs in the village: they were hunters, tasked with protecting and feeding Niagassola. On a normal day, they might bring back a few rabbits, monkeys, or a warthog. On a good day, they'd shoot an antelope or a lion.

Aside from the mosque, the Kouyaté compound, and the gated-and-locked building where the Sosso-Bala is held, the only other concrete building in the village is the school (which doubles as the post office). I got the sense class wasn't in session during my morning ramble. At one point, I turned around and found no less than 20 small children trailing me, all of whom burst into laughter as soon as this strange, alien-looking visitor smiled at them. I then took a few more steps, turned, and shot them a silly face, which made them laugh even harder. We continued this mimed game of cat and mouse for a few minutes until all the kids finally ran up to me, many hesitantly reaching for my bare arms with innocent curiosity as they exclaimed *"Toubabou!"* (white skin). The children soon became my village guides, leading me by the hand and offering a tour of their world: the palm grove where they play hide-and-seek, the dusty pitch where they kick cloth-rag soccer balls around loitering cattle, and the sandy warrens where they race old moped tires by pushing them with sticks.

By the time I returned to the compound, Balla's family was seated under the tin awning, drinking sweet, Tuareg-style tea heated over glowing embers. Balla handed me a glass and said, "When you're finished, come into the house. We're going to have a family meeting, and it's important you're there." After a few nervous sips, I headed inside the living room, where Balla, Sekou, and seven elder male Kouyatés were already seated in a circle. I couldn't tell if this was some sort of Mandinka initiation or intervention.

Balla explained that tradition dictates any outsider who wishes to see the Sosso-Bala needs to first state why they have come and their intention to the Kouyaté elders. The elders would then relay that message to the current balatigui, Siriman Dokala Kouyaté, who would approve or deny the request. I took a deep breath, faced Balla's oldest siblings, Mambi and Mamandi, and said that I had come to learn about this tradition and to write about it, and that just like Balla, I am hoping to awaken people to something profound and beautiful they may otherwise never know about. I explained that while we come from different backgrounds and speak different languages, I couldn't help but feel that each of us inherently understands one another. The Kouyatés have historically served as peacemakers, storytellers, and historians; I am a Quaker pacifist, a writer, and a firm believer that every community's present is a reflection of its past. I said your lives as djelis are marked by public recitations, and mine by quiet contemplation, but our hearts beat to the same rhythm. Just as Balla Fasséké felt an unspoken connection with the Mandinka people, I felt a certain kinship with this tradition, and I would love to see where it all started.

With that, Mambi and Mamandi disappeared outside into the blinding light. A few moments later, they shuffled back into the dimly lit room and addressed the Kouyaté clan. A sign of uncertainty flashed across the faces of those who had come from Bamako, including Fantamady and Dianguine, who started motioning toward me, somewhat protectively. The Mandinka conversation soon grew more and more animated.

"What's going on?" I asked Balla.

"Siriman has allowed you to see the Sosso-Bala," he said. "But there's a problem. Apparently, anyone outside the family who comes to see the Sosso-Bala outside Tabaski needs to offer the village a cow. This is true whether you're a neighboring farmer or the president of Guinea." Balla was extremely apologetic, and a touch embarrassed. He said that because the elder Kouyatés living in Niagassola oversee the traditional process, he and his brothers from Bamako weren't aware of it. Plus, so few outsiders ever make it through the rugged, 77-kilometer death trap to see the Sosso-Bala outside Tabaski that it hadn't occurred to him to ask. "To be honest, the only time anyone can remember a foreign journalist coming to see the Sosso-Bala was a Frenchman 40 years ago," Balla said. I guess he came with a cow.

After learning how much a cow costs in rural Guinea, I sheepishly told Balla that this was far more money than I had on me. "Dad, can he just Venmo someone the cost of a cow?" Sekou said, lifting his face up from a white bucket where he'd been heaving up the sheep's head soup. "Sekou, look around," Balla said. "Does it look like there's Venmo here?" There was no electricity in Niagassola and I had no cell signal, but Sekou's thought gave me an idea, so I asked Balla if I could wire him the cost of a cow once we returned to Bamako. Balla relayed this message to Mambi and Mamandi, who promptly disappeared outside again. After a long deliberation, they returned and muttered something to Balla in Mandinka that caused all of the brothers to stand up and exhale in relief. "Siriman will allow it." Balla smiled. "But he said this has never happened in the history of the Sosso-Bala." Now, there was only one more thing left to do before I could see the mythical instrument: meet its keeper.

Siriman Dokala Kouyaté is 70 years old and easily the largest of the roughly 40 Kouyatés I met in West Africa. A girthy hulk of a man with leathery jet-black skin and graying hair showing under his brimless kufi cap, Siriman, like Sundiata before him, looks like he could easily uproot a baobab tree. He greeted me in a royal purple robe, and as I faced him under the Kouyatés' outdoor awning, I thought back to something Dianguine had told me in Bamako: "To be the balatigui is to be like a king."

The balatigui spoke in a deep, resonant timbre, as if talking through a balafon's hollowed-out calabash. I asked him how this 800-year-old war trophy ended up in Niagassola. Siriman spread his two palms apart, as if making an invisible timeline, and recounted the instrument's journey. "After Sundiata's death, we think it has only traveled to six places: Kéniéba, Narena, Kita, and Karan, in Mali. Then to Kéniékourou, in Guinea, and in 1930, it arrived in Niagassola. Back then, this was all one land. Even today, the border [between Guinea and Mali] is somewhat artificial, so whenever anything happens with the Sosso-Bala, both governments have to be informed." In the rare instances the instrument has historically traveled, Siriman explained that it must be carried on the balatigui's head. I asked, rather delicately, how gentlemen of a certain age carry what must be a very heavy weight atop their heads for days on end in the scorching savanna heat. "There is a long procession," Siriman said, laughing. "When the balatigui tires, he hands it to the next person, and the next, and the next, but it always starts and stops with him."

Siriman asserted that he is the first-ever "intellectual" to guard the Sosso-Bala. He splits his time between Niagassola and Conakry, Guinea's capital, where he is a judge appointed to Guinea's Supreme Court. "Of all my professional responsibilities, guarding the Sosso-Bala is my greatest one," he said. "It is more than 800 years old, and I am responsible for its health and safety. When I am not here, I have to delegate the eldest Kouyatés to guard it, the hunters, the entire village. It is all Mande people who bear this gift." I asked him if his experience as a djeli helps him resolve conflicts as a judge, and he leaned forward and recounted the following: "One time, I was overseeing this case between two families who had been fighting over land for generations. No judge before me had been able to resolve it, so during a pause in the court proceedings, I changed out of my magistrate clothing and into my traditional clothing. I pulled them aside and I said to them, 'I am the direct descendant of Balla Fasséké. If you two claim to be descendants of Sundiata, you will end this conflict right here.' They both wept like babies and that was the end of it."

By this point, the entire Kouyaté family had gathered to watch our interview. I wasn't sure how appropriate my final question was in front of Balla's older brothers, but I asked it anyway: "If one day Balla were to become the balatigui, do you think he would uphold this tradition well?" The judge considered this for a moment and then issued his verdict: "You know, there are many people ahead of Balla, but you never know. Like Balla, I have many older brothers, and I never thought in a million years I would be the balatigui."

By all accounts, Siriman shouldn't have become the balatigui, but as Balla explained to me back in Medford, his predecessor had forsaken an ancient belief. "When my dad passed, his brother, Mamoudouba, was supposed to become the balatigui. But when the balatigui dies, traditionally, the wife and family don't go out for 40 days and the Sosso-Bala doesn't leave the hut. My uncle [Mamoudouba] didn't believe that concept and didn't follow it, and guess what? He didn't have a chance to become the balatigui because he suddenly died. He wasn't sick or anything; he just went to bed and died because he didn't do the things the right way."

This wasn't the only mystery surrounding the Sosso-Bala throne. Whenever I would ask the Kouyatés about the line of succession to become the balatigui, I was met with an air of ambiguity bordering on secrecy. Officially, the role is passed along a line of brothers from oldest to youngest before it moves to the eldest male in the next generation. Siriman is the younger brother of Balla's father, and if things move in perfect succession, the role would pass from Siriman to his only younger brother (Balla's youngest uncle) before then moving to Balla's oldest brother. By that logic, there are nine people between Balla and the balatigui. However, Balla's three oldest brothers are each roughly 20 years older than him, so it's unlikely this perfect succession will happen. I also sensed there was more to becoming the balatigui than just age. On several occasions, Balla hinted that, just as a doctor should have a mastery of medicine or a lawyer a mastery of law, a balatigui should have a mastery of the balafon—and despite the family legacy, that's not exactly true today. "The balafon is my family's instrument. We all learned it growing up. But I have brothers who play other instruments now and can't play a single song on the balafon," Balla told me. "I also have an older brother who has nothing to do with music and works as a mechanic." When I asked Balla what would happen if the would-be balatigui didn't know how to play the balafon, he said that the family may not allow it. Therefore, while a long branch of the family tree may stand between Balla and becoming the official guardian of Mande memory, in many ways, he is its logical, likely future heir.

With Siriman's blessing, the Kouyatés and I rose up from our chairs and we walked to a cream-colored building guarded by several sheep and two bulls sunning lazily outside. As Siriman's brawny younger cousin unlocked a barred, prison cell–looking security door, Balla explained that the family used the money from the UNESCO inscription to surround the small, circular mud hut holding the Sosso-Bala with a more secure structure. We shuffled inside the new stronghold to the outside of the old hut, where a small, one-meter-tall gnome-sized wooden door was fastened shut by an oversized steel padlock. The brawny cousin unbolted it and slowly creaked the door open as a stream of daylight poured into the ancient hut's pitch-black interior. One by one, 20 Kouyatés and I slipped off our shoes, lowered ourselves through the elfish doorway, and stepped onto the windowless shelter's dirt floor. The hut measures about four meters across, with a thick, fork-shaped branch standing in the center to support its thatched roof. A hush of silence fell over the family as we lined the hut's circumference. Everyone's attention was drawn to a white sheet draped over a bulging 1.5-meter object propped upright against the hut's wall. Directly above the sheet, seven framed photographs hung on the mud wall. Six of them showed the Sosso-Bala's most recent balatiguis with small, handwritten notes indicating the years each served. The seventh was of an elderly woman, her head cocked back, frozen mid-serenade, who sang alongside the Sosso-Bala for 40 years and whom everyone in Niagassola called "Mother." To the side of the white cloth sat a wooden casket-like case that's used to transport the Sosso-Bala on its rare excursions, as well as a pointed iron spear that is said to have been seized, along with the balafon, from Soumaoro.

Mamandi clutched the spear and eyed me through the dim light. "Are you ready to see the Sosso-Bala?" he asked. I nodded. He and Mambi then carefully removed the white cloth, revealing a bulbous cluster of dark-brown calabash gourds fastened by strips of antelope skin to wooden slats that had aged to the point that they were nearly ebony. The keys and calabashes were supported by a sturdy, rectangular frame wrapped so heavily in antelope hide it looked like a mummy. I wasn't allowed to touch the instrument, but when I bent down to get a closer look, I noticed each of the slats was the exact same shade, so I asked if any had ever been replaced. "They are all original," Mamandi said, in a deep voice. "The only things that have been replaced are several calabashes, and the antelope skin." Balla also explained another Sosso-Bala anomaly. "This instrument has 20 keys, but because all other balafons come from this instrument, no other balafon can have 20 keys. Some have 19, mine generally have 21 or 22, but never 20." I asked how, exactly, you tune an 800-year-old instrument. "You don't," Balla said with a laugh. "Everyone is afraid to tune something this old, so instead of tuning the Sosso-Bala, for Tabaski, all the other balafons have to be tuned to the Sosso-Bala." By this point, everyone was dripping sweat, so I asked the family if they did anything to protect the instrument from the hut's suffocating heat and humidity.

Several Kouyatés tried to politely hide their laughter, which told me all I needed to know, and as Mambi and Mamandi started fanning themselves, it became clear it was time to go.

I stepped out of the dark hut and followed the family back into the blinding light toward the Kouyaté compound. As the rest of the Kouyatés dispersed, I took a seat under the tin-roof awning beside Balla, Sekou, and Jossira and silently weighed what I'd just seen, pondering the impossibility of it all. I wasn't questioning whether the Sosso-Bala was born from a genie and bestowed to a "Sorcerer King," how it managed to survive eight centuries, or why it hadn't melted into a puddle after 90-some years locked inside a muggy mud hut. Instead, I was finally grasping the duality Balla has had to navigate since leaving West Africa, and what it would mean for him and his family if he were to ever return as the balatigui.

To leave home is ultimately to end one story and start another, and while we may journey back to where we came from, it's never quite the same because we're no longer the same. Anyone who has ever dared or been forced to immigrate is the sum of two disparate chapters: who they once were and who they're becoming. As outsiders, we're blind to the lives they've left behind. In Nicaragua, my mother-in-law was the first woman in her family to ever work in an office; in Washington, DC, she used to avert her eyes so that the women whose offices she cleaned each night wouldn't see her cry. In West Africa, Balla was the descendant of royalty, the torchbearer of an empire's collective memory; in Manhattan, he was an anonymous car washer with a boss who couldn't be bothered to remember his name. But as with my mother-in-law's family, somewhere along the way, the Kouyatés came to rely on who Balla was becoming in his new home to provide for them back in his old home. The new house he built in Bamako for his mother and sisters, the family compound he financed in Niagassola, and the financial support he regularly sends to a network of relatives in Guinea and Mali are only possible because Balla chose to sever ties with tradition. Were he to one day become the balatigui and return to Niagassola, the career he's built for himself in his new home and the support he's able to send loved ones in his old one would both come grinding to a halt—a fact he's keenly aware of.

With his extended family out of earshot, I asked Balla whether he wrestles with this, and what he wishes for the two most important people left in his life. "There are a lot of people here who rely on me to make things happen, and when I come back, even for a short visit like this, I go through a lot, financially. But I'd rather do that for my kids to know where they came from, and to know how important their family is to this society," Balla said. "The truth is, this tradition is disappearing. The internet, journalists, they've all replaced the djeli job these days. So, the way things are going, if we don't care for our traditions and teach our kids, this will disappear. If that happens, Mande people, my family, would lose our identity. In 100 years, I won't be here, probably my kids won't be here. But what is going to happen to my grandchildren if I don't preserve this tradition? I've always said to my kids, you don't have to be balafon players if you don't want to. You can be anything, even the next Obamas—so long as you bring the balafon to the White House."

The sun dipped below the horizon until the sky and sand were the same shade of red. I asked Balla if, one day, he were to be named the balatigui, whether he'd give up his life in Medford and everything he'd worked toward to return to Niagassola. "Only God knows if it'll be me one day," he said. "All I know is that anything can happen in the future, good or bad." He's right. You never know when your life can be upended by a three-month visa, a woman speaking a familiar language in a faraway bar, or the discovery of an abnormal mass during a routine mammogram. "But if it ever happens, I would give it all up to come back here, yes. It's not even a question. This is something much bigger than me."

2

Scandinavia's Last Night Watchman

People always leave traces. No person is without a shadow.
—HENNING MANKELL, *THE TROUBLED MAN*

On a wet November night, a cold wind howled across the Baltic Sea and through the narrow cobblestone streets of Ystad, on Sweden's southern tip. Huddled under an umbrella, I followed rambling rows of half-timbered cottages toward a 13th-century church whose dark spire towered over the medieval market town like a witch's hat, and gently knocked on the wooden door below. A man cloaked in a long blue tunic slowly creaked it open, his face hidden in the shadow of his wide-brimmed felt hat. "I'm Roland," he said, stepping out of the doorway to peer up at the hands on the clock tower. "We should go."

In a flash, the stout 74-year-old slammed the door shut and began to climb the 14 stories leading from the base of the tower to his office above the belfry. I followed the figure up a dimly lit spiral staircase caked with cobwebs whose 110 worn wooden steps groaned under each stride. After unlocking a steel fireproof door at the top of the staircase, Roland briefly paused to let me catch my breath before swiftly scaling a ladder two more stories, squeezing past three hulking bells, and climbing one final ladder. He then ducked under a thick wooden beam and hoisted himself through a small hatch into the pitch-black tower keeper's room. Inside, he flipped on the room's two lights, cranked a loud metal lever round and round to lower the hatch to the floor, and flashed a smile.

"You don't want to be caught in the bell room when the clock strikes nine," he said. Moments later, the wooden floorboards began to vibrate as the grinding of metal gears swung the 3.3-ton bells into orbit just below our feet, creating a clanging cacophony that shook the bowels of the sanctuary. I held onto a joist to steady myself while Roland gripped a four-foot-long copper horn and quietly gazed out of a window in the bell tower's north wall at the town below, scanning the horizon for fires and any signs of potential danger. When the peal of bells softened to a hum, he heaved the horn through an open windowpane and blew a haunting, bellowed cry across the rooftops, reassuring the town's 29,000 residents that all was well. Like clockwork, he would repeat these calls every 15 minutes from the tower's four windows in a north-east-south-and-west order between 9:00 P.M. and 1:00 A.M., just as he has done for the past 57 years.

Today, Roland Borg is one of the world's last night watchmen, and probably the closest thing to a medieval guardian we have in the modern world. Nearly every night for the last 500 years, as darkness has descended on this coastal community, a lonely sentinel has clambered up the tower of Ystad's Saint Mary's church to watch over the town below—and for the last 103 years, that person has been a Borg. Roland's grandfather, Fritz, assumed the role in 1921, and the 18-kilogram wool coat that he wore to brave the frigid Swedish winters still hangs in a corner of the keep's rafters. Twenty years later, Fritz's son, Helmer, succeeded him and cast the seven-kilogram heraldic trumpet that Roland sounds through the night.

Roland's role as Scandinavia's only remaining night watchman is truly singular. Night after night, he moves alone through the tower, hidden away like an invisible ghost, seemingly seeing everything, but seen by none. Wrapped in his ankle-length cloak and cutting through the flickering light to man his post, he's a portrait from a different time; his short frame, copper wand, and rounded glasses call to mind something between a wizened wizard and a white-haired Harry Potter. There's no bathroom, kitchen, bed, or Wi-Fi in Roland's humble wood-paneled perch. There isn't even central heat, and the only respite from the long, cold Swedish nights is a tiny, insulated hovel built into the corner of the keep that's big enough for a plug-in radiator, an IKEA chair, a TV, an old touch-tone phone to call the fire department in case of emergency, and a collection of Elvis posters and hand-drawn art from Roland's grandchildren that he's tacked to the walls.

For the last 49 years, no one has been officially allowed to go up in the tower with Roland. "Back when my dad was working, visitors could come up here every night between nine and 11," he said, winding up an alarm clock held together with tape that he uses to time his calls instead of a watch. Ironically, in 1975, the fire brigade deemed Ystad's oldest fire lookout a fire hazard and effectively sealed it off from the outside world to anyone other than the man on duty. But when Roland learned that I hoped to speak with him, he urged town officials to make a rare exception and grant me access to the tower so I could watch the watchman work. "Roland is quite unused to people wondering what he is doing. The night watchman has formed his own bubble, his own universe up there," one government employee told me before I arrived. "He's really looking forward to meeting you," another wrote. "This is important for him."

I got the sense that Roland could feel his time in the tower was coming to an end, and that this might be the last chance to talk about his life's work. So, over the course of seven days in Ystad and four bitterly cold nights squeezed into the tower's hovel with Roland, I learned the unlikely story of how this idyllic medieval town became the fictional murder capital of Sweden, how a partially blind watchman helped defend it against one of the country's most infamous criminals, and how this cold-blooded fugitive has promised to return to Ystad to exact his revenge. But above all, in an age of smoke detectors, street lighting, and video surveillance, I pondered who the last night watchman needs to watch when technology sees everything.

Night watchmen have existed in some form since the dawn of time, harking back to the days when people first learned to become afraid of the dark. Studies have shown that our earliest ancestors likely slept outdoors in large groups, taking turns staying awake so that one person was always keeping an eye out for potential dangers lurking in the darkness.[1] In fact, it has long been claimed that the world's oldest profession isn't women of the night but these men of the night.

The first recorded night watchman was the Prophet Ezekiel, who, according to a story in the Old Testament (Ezekiel 33:1–9), was appointed by God to warn the people of Israel when he saw would-be invaders.[2] It was a deadly serious job, and God warned that if anyone were to die because Ezekiel spotted danger and didn't blow his trumpet, He'd "hold the watchman accountable for their blood." In Ancient Rome, Emperor Augustus created the Vigiles (the watchmen) after a blaze ripped through the city in AD 6. Commonly considered the world's first public fire brigade, they served as the official night watch of the empire, patrolling the streets and keeping an eye out for thieves and robbers when they weren't extinguishing blazes with their water-filled buckets.[3] Yet, the image of a night watchman that most people recognize traces back to the Middle Ages, when agricultural advances led Europeans to start migrating from scattered countryside communities and feudal manors to fortified towns to sell and trade their surplus crops.[4] The coming of darkness to these crowded, unlit streets often brought a heightened threat of danger. In addition to providing cover for pickpockets, burglars, and foreign foes, night was also when towns were most vulnerable to a far greater everyday threat than plagues or enemy attack: fires.

In a world filled with thermostats and electricity, it can be easy to forget how cold and dark life was before them, and how much people relied on flames to survive. "If you wanted to stay warm, you needed to start a fire. If you wanted to cook something, you needed to make a fire. And if you wanted to see something at night, you needed to light a candle," said Ingela Bergils, an antiquarian at Ystad's 13th-century Greyfriars Abbey. "But because it was sometimes difficult to make a fire, you often had to borrow a flame from your neighbor and carry it through the cobbled streets, which made it easy to fall—especially at night."

Since many medieval towns were densely packed with wooden buildings and topped with thatched roofs, a live fire could quickly engulf the whole community if it wasn't immediately spotted. So as early as the ninth century, cities and towns across Europe began employing nightly guardians to help defend themselves against the night's many dangers. From patrolling dark streets and announcing the time to watching for incoming enemies, storms, and smoke from church parapets, these eagle-eyed constables were equal parts gumshoes, timekeepers, medieval meteorologists, and firefighters, rousing residents in the event of an emergency with a series of coded calls that only local citizens knew.

In Ystad, that code changed as the hands moved around the clock tower. "If there was a fire or crime in the daytime, the watchman would go downstairs to the bells, hit them with a hammer, and hang a red flag out of the tower in the right direction so people knew where to go," Roland said, rubbing his hand across an indented cleft of the largest bell's lip down in the belfry. "At night, instead of a flag, they lit a red lamp." This practice continued until 1884, when Ystad's first telephone was installed up in the tower to connect the watchman with the fire department and police.

"At one time there were probably tens of thousands of night watchmen all across Europe," said Carole Rawcliffe, Professor Emeritus of Medieval History at the University of East Anglia and the coeditor of the book *Policing the Urban Environment in Premodern Europe*. "They were a rudimentary police force before there was such a thing, and while there were basic similarities in what they were doing, there was an awful lot of local variance from one place to the next."

In Vienna, Salzburg, and towns across Germany, watchmen wandered the streets wielding long ax-blade halberds to convey a sense of law and order. In Danish territories from Reykjavík to Ribe, they preferred spiked "morning star" maces. Watchmen in Prague often worked in tandem and communicated to one another across the city by blowing into bull horns.[5] Guards in Bruges called to one another with wooden shawms (the precursor of the oboe). As these signal-callers learned to flute more notes than just a single, sustained signal, noble families started hiring them to perform at banquets and weddings, making night watchmen Europe's first professional wind musicians.[6] Across Madrid, 16th-century *serenos* assumed an even more familiar role. So named because they'd announce the time followed by the all-is-quiet "Sereno!" call, these dusk-to-dawn patrolmen worked for tips by opening doors, running late-night errands for families, and even arranging secret trysts between lovers—flashing a covert all-clear sign to cheating partners as they snuck in and out.[7]

One of the earliest and most extensive national networks of watchmen was in England. As early as 1252, the Assize of Arms required local shire-reeves (the origin of "sheriff") to appoint nightly wardens to "keep the Watch all night from sun setting unto sun rising."[8] For hundreds of years, these men were responsible for everything from ringing the curfew bell and guarding city gates to imposing a sense of morality. In London, watchmen frequently detained those found drunk and urinating in public overnight, and ensured prostitutes didn't stray outside their designated quarters. They carried a stick to push unlocked doors closed and used wooden rattles to alert sleeping citizens to threats.[9] England extended this practice to its colonies in the New World, too, and the US's earliest public police forces were lantern-clutching watchmen who started patrolling the streets of Boston, New York, and Plymouth in the 1630s–1670s—a tradition that lingered on in these places for the next 200 years.[10]

In addition to keeping an eye peeled for dangers hiding in plain sight, watchmen were also tasked with defending their towns against invisible threats, like disease. "In Europe, if you had an infection in your home during plague times, you were often ordered to stay home," Rawcliffe said. "You needed someone to ensure these rules were kept, so that was the night watchman. It was a medieval form of lockdown." But while the night watchman had one of the most important jobs in society, it wasn't one of the most coveted. Many places like Ystad initially sought volunteers for the position, enlisting all able-bodied men to assume the role on a yearlong rotating basis alongside their regular day job as a civic duty. Predictably, few people were keen to sign up for a dangerous gig with bad hours and no pay, so wealthy families across the continent started paying deputies to serve in their places. By the 16th through the 18th centuries, many towns across Europe had established a system of salaried, professional night watchmen who were often funded through payments each household was obliged to make to their local church. But as Europe's population doubled between 1500 and 1750, and a cultural shift ushered in by the Baroque era spurred a boom in late-night theaters, operas, and entertainment, the role of the watchman began to be viewed as outdated. And though the responsibilities of the night watch were great, the reputations of those who carried them out weren't.[11]

In parts of Germany, the only jobs considered lower than the *Türmerin* (tower guard) were the gravedigger and the executioner. The watchman's children were even forbidden from joining other guilds.[12] In England, patrolmen were notorious for being drunk, lazy, and corrupt. In Shakespeare's *Much Ado About Nothing*, Constable Dogberry tells his comically bumbling band of watchmen that sleeping on duty is perfectly fine, and that if they see a thief, they could try to apprehend him, but it'd be easier not to bother. "Charlies" (so-called after Charles II established a force of paid watchmen in 1663) were often old codgers with rattles who took bribes, colluded with criminals, and played cards at the pub. In Georgian times, it became common practice for bored teens to tip over the wooden watch boxes where passed-out Charlies had fallen asleep on the job.[13]

When the Great Fire of London torched one-third of the city and left 100,000 homeless in 1666, it laid the foundation for modern fire brigades to form across Europe in the decades ahead.[14] That same year, Louis XIV created Europe's first centralized, uniformed police force in Paris, and by the late 1800s, most major European cities had established both a professional firefighting and police unit. With the watchman's two main roles outsourced, this already-antiquated profession was effectively snuffed out.[15]

Today, Europe has lots of watchmen reenactors but very few actual watchmen. In many well-trodden towns that once employed them, costume-clad guides now lead tourists through the streets at twilight, recycling rehearsed lines as they "make their rounds." Since many cities now rely on things like facial-recognition software, artificial intelligence, and thermal-imaging cameras, it's a wonder this seemingly obsolete vocation hasn't vanished entirely. But against all odds, a handful of places do still cling to elements of this medieval practice.

In Lausanne, Switzerland, someone has served as the city's official timekeeper for more than 600 years, cupping their hands from atop the Notre Dame Cathedral to call out the hour between 10:00 P.M. and 2:00 A.M. in a tradition dating back to 1405.[16] Since at least 1392, a rotating group of musicians in Kraków, Poland, have played a five-note bugle call from atop the St. Mary's church tower every hour on the hour.[17] In Nördlingen, Germany, Horst Lenner watches the town from the Daniel church tower, alongside his cat, Wendelstein, and a few barn owls. Above a circular freight elevator once powered by prisoners who ran in it like it was a giant hamster wheel, Lenner funnels his hands to his mouth and calls out, "*So, G'sell, so!*" ("Everything's fine, mates! Everything's fine!") every 30 minutes between 10:00 P.M. and midnight.[18] In the German town of Annaberg-Buchholz, Matthias Melzer and his wife, Marit, live in a small apartment nestled in the St. Anne's steeple and frequently dry their wet laundry from the church's Gothic spires.[19] In Münster, Germany, Martje Saljé became the city's first watchwoman in more than 600 years after assuming the role at St. Lambert's Church in 2014.[20] And in a brilliant rite in Ripon, England, a tricorn-hat tooter has "set the watch" with a ceremonial horn blast each night at 9:00 P.M., without interruption, since 886. According to David Winpenny, the vice president of the Ripon Civic Society and the author of numerous books on the town's history, when the night watch ended in Ripon in 1604, the wakeman who oversaw the watchmen became the town's first mayor. He didn't trust the horn blower to fulfill his duty, so he imposed an additional one that has remained to this day.

"After setting the watch each night in the Market Square, he is to find the mayor, wherever he may be—the pub, the church, his home—doff his three-cornered hat, and say, 'Mr. Mayor, the watch is set.'"

"How does he know where the mayor is?" I asked.

"Oh, these days it's easy," Winpenny replied. "He just texts him."

But while each of these places steadfastly maintains their own medieval timekeeping traditions, nowhere does it exist quite like in Ystad. For starters, the town is the only place on the planet that still employs a full-time tower guard 365 days a year whose job description is to help defend it against fire. In Lausanne, Krakow, Nördlingen, and Annaberg-Buchholz, the towers have evolved into popular tourist attractions. In Ystad, a lovely tradition holds that if you wave up at the watchman, he will always wave back, but the fact that the tower and its keep are off-limits to the outside world adds to its frozen-in-time mystique. The watchman is also an inescapable presence in Ystad. Unlike in bigger cities, Ystad's compact core means you can look up from anywhere in town and see the copper horn appear through a tiny windowpane in the spire each night, and the fact that this deep, foghorn-like peal is trumpeted rather than voiced makes it impossible to ignore. "We live with the watchman's call the way we live with the wind and sea," said Peter Schönstrom, whose Anno 1793 Sekelgården Hotel is built into a medieval tannery near the tower, and comes with soundproof windows. But most importantly, of the world's few remaining night watchmen, no one has been carrying on the tradition anywhere near as long as the Borg family.

"It's amazing. There is no other place in Europe where such a tradition is occurring in one family as in Ystad," said Johannes Thier, the head of the European Guild of Night Watchmen and Tower Guards, an association of guides and reenactors representing 10 countries and 67 cities that once employed such guardians. "In other cities, it is more ceremonial, but in Ystad, it's a job."

Roland's grandfather, Fritz, already had a job in 1921 when he began the night watch. A no-nonsense Ystad prison guard who knew how to follow orders and didn't ask too many questions, he was the ideal candidate, and didn't even have to apply. "It was so simple that my grandfather was asked if he wanted the job. Unlike other places, it was a well-respected profession here and it came with a uniform, so he said, 'Yea, why not,'" Roland recalled, his breath forming a cloud as the yellow thermometer nailed to the keep's central joist showed 4 degrees Celsius.

There was no separate room when Fritz started, no plug-in radiator to escape the cold—no electricity, for that matter. Watchmen were on duty from 10:00 P.M. until 4:00 A.M., and in the late 1920s, the town installed an early, uninsulated version of the corner room where Roland keeps warm. It had a short straw mattress that Fritz had to bend his knees to fit on, and he was expressly forbidden from lighting any candles or smoking, for fear it would ignite the straw bed. Fritz remained at his post for 20 years, ringing the church bells by hand; looking for smoke in the darkness; and blowing his horn once at a quarter past the hour, twice at half past, three times at a quarter to, and four times on the hour, as has always been the custom here. "After two decades, my grandfather told my father, 'Okay, it's time for you to take over now,' so he did," Roland said.

Roland's father, Helmer, was a busy man. By day, he worked as a sheet metal laborer, waking up at 6:00 A.M. to spend all day plating metal roofs. He'd then come home to eat dinner and head to the tower to work from 10:00 P.M. until 4:00 A.M. Some of Roland's earliest memories are of

Helmer staggering home before dawn, going into the kitchen, and leaning against a wall to sleep for an hour until it was time to start his day again. "Still, he always shaved and combed his hair before coming to the tower," Roland recalled, glancing across the keep to a black-and-white painting showing Helmer blowing the horn he cast through the tower window. "He was a very, very proud man—proud of the job and proud of the town."

Helmer had eight children, and while the first seven didn't seem too keen on the family trade, the youngest did. Helmer built his family a house within earshot of the night watchman's horn, and Roland remembers staying awake as a three-year-old to hear his father's deep, droning calls. "Because I showed an interest in it from a very early age, my father decided I would be the watchman after him," Roland said. By the time Roland was five, he was romping up the spiral staircase to accompany Helmer in the keep. During a royal visit to Ystad in 1956, King Gustaf VI Adolf couldn't believe that a night watchman still existed somewhere within his country, so he insisted on trudging up the tower to see him for himself. When the king came through the hatch, Roland said he shook Helmer's hand and told him how wonderful it was to meet him, but Helmer couldn't hear a word. "He had gone deaf from ringing the bells," Roland said. "After my grandfather, they installed a rope to ring them, and it was so heavy it would lift my father off the ground, like the Hunchback of Notre Dame!"

Roland started working alongside his father in the tower in 1967, learning everything from how to distinguish a distant flame from a glowing light to how to sound the same tone with each call by breathing in deeply from your stomach and expelling it in one long, continuous motion. That year, a violent storm tore through Ystad, ripping the metal plating off the spire and causing the tower to sway two feet in both directions. When it passed, 64-year-old Helmer replated the tower roof himself, and carried on mentoring Roland for another four years. Then in 1971, after 30 years on duty, Helmer told his son that something was wrong. At first, he struggled to climb the stairs. Soon, he didn't even have the energy to blow the horn. Helmer wasn't the type of man who went to the doctor, but he wasn't stupid. As Roland looked out the southern window toward the harbor, he recalled his father pulling him aside shortly after falling ill, placing his hand on Roland's, and saying, "You're ready. Take this job, and you'll never regret it."

Roland's family drove Helmer to a doctor, who told them a highly aggressive cancer had spread throughout his body. Three weeks later, he passed, and Roland became the latest in a long line of Ystad watchmen to steadfastly maintain this tradition. There was only one problem: all alone up in the tower, Roland soon realized he was afraid of the dark.

———

Like the origins of the night watch itself, no one is exactly sure when and how this job started in Ystad. As Bergils handed me a stack of old, archived documents in the Greyfriars Abbey one morning, she explained why. "I think the night watchman came to Scandinavia around 1300, and by the 1500s, we have more and more images of them in Danish towns," she said, noting that Ystad and all of Sweden's southern Skåne County was part of Denmark until 1658. "When it came to Ystad is another story. We know the town formed around 1200 and the church is the oldest building in the town, but all of the town's archives were destroyed in 1569." She paused. "That's when the Swedes set fire to everything. There were a lot of fires back then, you know."

In 1748, King Frederick I of Sweden issued a document formalizing the roles and responsibilities of the country's night watchmen, a copy of which Roland still keeps in the tower as a reminder of bygone times. It stipulates that "the watchman must keep sober and awake and carefully look for threatening fire." If he comes to work late, falls asleep, or smokes while on duty, the penalty would range from "being dismissed" to "18 pairs of rods," or "in grave cases, being executed." By 1913, floggings and hangings were considered outdated in Ystad, and the town's mayor felt the role of the watchman was too. When he proposed abolishing the position, Ystad's fire chief protested, declaring, "All means to prevent fire should be retained!" and the Town Council voted overwhelmingly to retain the institution. "People here love their traditions, their old ways," Roland told me one night, waving back at a couple down in Stortorget, Ystad's central square that surrounds the church. "Every time it's suggested we should finish with this tradition, the people here protest."

Walking around town, it doesn't take long to understand why this once-upon-a-time job has lingered on in a place like Ystad. With its winding stone streets, wood-framed cottages splashed in cheery Easter egg colors, and Hansa Gothic red-brick architecture, the town is a picture-perfect image of medieval idyll. It has more half-timbered homes than anywhere else in Scandinavia (roughly 300), and many of them date back to the 15th century. It's also home to Sweden's best-preserved medieval monastery (the Greyfriars Abbey), the country's oldest hotel (Continental du Sud), and one of its oldest theaters (Ystad Teater). The afternoon I arrived, a swarm of rosy-cheeked children were helping their parents line Ystad's main street, Stora Östergatan, with Christmas trees, and as they burst into carols, I couldn't help but feel like I'd just walked into an advent calendar.

The town radiates out from Stortorget square, a quaint-as-can-be marketplace wrapped by gable-roofed buildings, where vendors sell everything from fresh-picked raspberries to locally caught herring, just as they have since Ystad was settled in the early 1200s as a fishing settlement. Echoing Ystad's multinational past, many homes proudly fly the Skåne flag—which combines the red of the Danish banner with a yellow Swedish cross—and several transplants told me that locals here still speak Swedish with a Danish accent. Even in the moody, autumnal weather, there's a measured calm in the air. Bikes bounce along cobbled, pedestrian-only streets; cafés swell each afternoon as friends pour in for their daily *fika* coffee break; and roses climb up the Lilliputian-like cottages squeezed together in the town's historical center.

It didn't exactly feel like the kind of place I'd normally associate with murder and mayhem, but thanks to Henning Mankell's bestselling series of Nordic Noir novels about Ystad police detective Kurt Wallander, this tranquil seaside town has become the undisputed homicide capital of Scandinavia. Through 11 books, a Swedish TV series, and a hit BBC spin-off starring Sir Kenneth Branagh, millions of people around the world have followed Wallander—a divorced, out-of-shape, whiskey-loving antihero—as he stalks the shadows of killers and villains along Ystad's narrow alleyways. In Mankell's Ystad, the town's brightly colored veneer masks an evil lurking within, and this contrast extends to the cinematic, big-sky landscapes, rolling rapeseed fields, and steep seaside cliffs that surround it, where dead bodies routinely turn up.

"Ystad is primarily known for two things: the watchman and Wallander," said Jack Lofving, a business developer at Ystad Studios, located in a former military barracks a mile east of the Saint Mary's tower. Since 1994, 54 Wallander films have been shot here. Not only has the franchise made Ystad Studios the largest film studio in Scandinavia, it's also meant most everyone in Ystad has unwittingly been an extra at some point, as fictional villains have exploded cars and dragged blood-soaked bodies through the streets. Over the years, Wallander has fought a criminal mastermind hell-bent on bringing down the world economy in Stortorget square, confronted a suicide bomber below the tower, and cornered a hostage-taker who blows himself up just outside the Saint Mary's church. In each instance, directors had to time their filming around Roland's quarterly calls.

"They asked me if I'd stop blowing, just for a little bit, but I said I can't," Roland told me, unwrapping homemade cakes and pouring caramel-colored Julmust soda as he and I sat by the radiator on our second night in the tower. "When I blow the horn, everything is calm. When I stop blowing, there's a problem. The people of Ystad need their watchman."

Ystad may be synonymous with Wallander for thriller fans, but for locals, the watchman is the figurative—and in some cases, literal—symbol of the town. "The church is in the center of town, and the night watchman is at the top of the church. He's always been at the heart of Ystad," said Johan Lenngerd, who manages the local Hotell Tornväktaren (The Tower Guard Hotel). Over pastries at Café Lurblåsaren (The Horn Blower Café), Anna Röing, who owns an antique shop in a half-timbered building from the 1500s, put it bluntly: "Ystad without the night watchman wouldn't be Ystad. It'd just be another old town."

Röing also helped me solve a mystery I'd been wondering about. As I wandered through Ystad each day, I'd often peer through the cottages' closed windows to admire their suspended fireplaces, functional minimalism, and sleek Scandi interiors taken straight from a design catalog. Then at night, as the temperatures fell below freezing and the wind screamed through the town, I'd notice that nearly every home had cracked their windows open. Was this some bizarre Swedish sleeping custom I didn't know about? "No, that's something unique to here," Röing said, smiling. "Many people in Ystad open their windows to hear the horn better. They can't sleep when they don't hear it. It gives us a special feeling, a comfort. We get used to it as children, we love it."

In my seven days in Ystad, most everyone I spoke to who grew up here echoed the same sentiment, including 77-year-old Lena Palmgren. "Sometimes the new people come to town and live near the tower, and they think, 'Ugh, every quarter hour? I won't be able to sleep!' But I live near the church, and I can't sleep if he's *not* blowing. It's so special that we have a watchman who looks after us. When I was young, I felt safe going in town and knowing that he was up in the tower," Palmgren recalled, explaining how she used to climb up the tower and visit Roland's father, back when it was permitted. "I've been enchanted with the night watchman since I was a little girl. When we were in school, we had a competition to make something, and I drew the night watchman and won a prize. That inspired this," she said, handing me a clay figurine of a watchman sounding a copper horn. For the last 61 years, Palmgren's been firing, hand-painting, and selling the little sentinels in her 1600s wood-framed shop, Krukmakaren Ystad (The Ystad Potter), off Stortorget square, making sure to paint their eyes "kind, like Roland's." As Palmgren wrapped a pint-sized horn-blower for me, she said, "All traditions are nice, especially the old ones. Ystad would be empty without the night watchman."

But what is it about the night watchman and Roland, specifically, that breathes so much life into this place? To find out, I tracked down Fredrik Sjöstrand, a reporter at the local *Ystads Allehanda* newspaper who has interviewed Roland nearly 50 times in the last 24 years. When we met outside his office, I looked up and noticed that the paper's logo is, unsurprisingly, the night watchman. "There's no getting around the fact that people in Ystad are very proud when it comes to their traditions and history," he said. "Here's a guy who personifies that. He puts on his suit and hat and he's the symbol of the city. He doesn't say much, but he exudes the role. He loves what he does, and it turns out, he's quite good at his job."

There was a learning curve, though, and after Helmer died and left

Roland to spend his nights up in the tower all alone, it took him a full year to get over his fear of the dark. "When I was with my dad, we were two, but when I was by myself, I heard everything creaking and thought, 'Oh, what was that?'" Roland told me the following night, as rain splattered against the copper roof Helmer had rebuilt. "There wasn't so much light before. Until last year, it was just one flickering light and it was very dim, sort of like a horror film."

Roland wasn't the first night watchman to get scared up in the Saint Mary's spire. When digging through the town's archives, Bergils found records of tower keepers throughout the centuries encountering "Johanna," the headless daughter of a priest from the 1600s who was said to drift through the walls in the rain. One young watchman was so spooked by the apparition that he asked a senior watchman to escort him down the stairs and never returned. Helmer, too, had warned Roland that many guards often sensed that someone was following them as they descended the spiral staircase after their shifts. "I did everything I could that first year to confront my fears and get over it, and the best thing was to read horror stories. I could open up a horror thriller up here and then I was living in that world," Roland said, his green eyes widening.

A few moments later, eerily on cue, the two lights in the tower keep suddenly shut off and everything turned black. I heard Roland feel his way through the darkness across the keep to the light by the hatch, and with the flip of a switch, he reappeared. "That happens," he said, unfazed. "When someone turns the lights off downstairs in the church, they go off up here too. Anyway, where was I . . . ?"

Between his father passing and confronting his fears in the tower, 1971 was a dark year for Roland, but in the midst of it, an unexpected light appeared. One night when the deputy watchman was on duty, a friend dragged Roland to a local dance. A woman across the room caught his eye, and he built up the courage to talk to her. "She was attractive, she was stylish, she was honest, and I danced like a camel," Roland said, rather matter-of-factly. He learned that her name was Yvonne, and they made plans to meet again. Yvonne didn't balk at Roland's irregular hours—she sang in a choir, loved knitting, and had enough hobbies that she was always busy. They married that summer, and 52 years later, Roland said his first instinct was right: "She is the most beautiful, honest person in the world."

She also saved Roland's life. In addition to inheriting Helmer's job, Roland also inherited his father's tireless work ethic, and for 43 years he worked as a forklift operator during the day before coming to the tower at night. "There was very little time between these two jobs, and I was working very intensively, sleeping just two hours every night," Roland said. One morning in 2000 after a double shift, Roland woke up next to Yvonne trying desperately to grasp onto anything he could. She asked him what was wrong, but he was unresponsive. Yvonne knew right away he was having a stroke, so she called an ambulance. At the hospital, doctors told Roland that if he'd waited any longer to seek help, the stroke would have affected his brain or killed him. Instead, the damage was limited to his eyes. "I have no peripheral vision in my right eye," Roland said, which begs the question: how does the night watchman watch if he can't fully see?

Roland was ordered to rest up and not return to the tower for a month, an experience he described as "terrible." But in that time, he learned to adapt to his new vision. "After so many years, I'd learned how to look. I can see perfectly straight ahead, like a falcon. So the only thing I do differently now is to move my head a little bit more," Roland explained, demonstrating how he pans his head left to right at each window before sounding the all's-well horn over Ystad. "It didn't affect my job."

It did affect how Roland gets to his job, though. Since the stroke, Roland hasn't been able to legally drive, so for the last 23 years he has walked from his home in the tiny town of Gärsnäs to the train station, boarded a 30-minute train to Ystad, and then walked up the hill to the Saint Mary's tower. After lowering the hatch and bellowing his first call across the rooftops, the first thing he does each night is to pull out his old cell phone from his cloak pocket, flip it open, and tell Yvonne that he's arrived safely. Yvonne has always told Roland, "I don't mind you working at night, so long as you make it home," and after another train ride back, he eventually does—long after midnight.

Roland's commute isn't the only thing that's changed since he started working in the keep. The belfry's three iron ore bells became automated in 1980, and before that, it was Roland's job to ring them. "But unlike my father, I wore protective earmuffs," he said, as we watched a nature documentary in his insulated man cave between his calls. TV is another luxury Helmer didn't enjoy. When Roland scraped together enough money to haul a black-and-white television up here in 1971, he remembers there was only one channel and it turned off at 10:30 P.M. These days, he gets six channels, and thanks to a closet full of DVDs he's collected over the years (including every Wallander film), he never gets bored. An old boom box dangles from an extension cord above the hatch, and Roland listens to CDs and the radio every night. He loves classical music, especially Beethoven and Wagner, and says he sometimes stares down at the town below, imagining its sounds, lights, and people are all players in a vast, orchestrated concert. "But there's one person in particular I listen to," Roland said, leading me toward the keep's eastern wall, where he's created a floor-to-ceiling collage of more than 30 Elvis posters. "He became so big, but Elvis the person was a simple, ordinary man. I have always liked that," he said. Roland then angled his horn through the open windowpane and started softly humming "Are You Lonesome Tonight?" before calling out to an Ystad warm in their beds.

Remarkably, in 57 years, Roland said he's only ever forgotten to sound the horn once, and it was back in the 1970s. "The owner of the Continental du Sud was extremely proud of the night watchman tradition and took all his guests to the balcony at one o'clock in the morning," Roland recalled. "He told them 'Look up at the tower now. You're about to hear it!' but they didn't hear anything. After some time, he rang me on the telephone here and said, 'What the hell are you doing?' And I said, 'I'm sorry, but I must admit I've actually fallen asleep.' It's the only time it's ever happened, and I promised myself that I'd never again fall asleep up here."

Naturally, Roland has formed his own rituals in the last half century. Every Christmas Eve, as he hears friends and families singing in their warmly lit homes, Roland watches *Lady and the Tramp* alone up in the tower. On New Year's Eve, he brings the boom box over to the eastern window and blasts Elvis as revelers in the square below count down to midnight. In the summer, Roland spends most of his vigil looking out from the glass. His favorite view is from the southern window, where the moon glimmers over the Baltic and boats bob in the quay. Because it remains light this far north in June and July until 10:30 P.M., Roland says the sun-scorched keep can feel like an oven, with temperatures reaching 40 degrees Celsius. "Sometimes I just have my shorts on." He chuckled. In the winter, when the uninsulated part of the keep is bone-chillingly cold, Roland generally stays near the radiator in his enclosed hovel, wrapping himself in his grandfather's woolly coat whenever it's time to go out and blow. "It used to get down to minus 20 degrees [Celsius] at night," he said, as Otis Redding crooned from the boom box. "But these days, it doesn't get so bad because of climate change."

When you consider that Roland has manned his post long enough to feel the planet physically change, it's hard to fathom how else the world around Roland has changed since he's been squirreled away in the tower, measuring time in 15-minute increments. Two years after he started alongside his father, a man walked on the moon. He remembers being in the tower in 1980 when he heard that "the Western film star" Ronald Reagan was going to be the US's next president; when they interrupted the nightly news in 1986 to announce that Sweden's prime minister, Olof Palme, had been gunned down; and when his black-and-white TV showed young people in 1989 taking sledgehammers to the Berlin Wall. In 2000, he peered out from the tower's windowpanes as fireworks exploded around him, a medieval timekeeper ushering in the advent of a new millennium.

Ystad has changed too. Compared to when Roland started, there's more of it to watch. The town has expanded outward from the port as suburbs have swallowed up farms. When Fritz began working, a man was in charge of lighting Ystad's gas streetlights with a burning stick each evening. Now, solar lights automatically kick in at dusk, illuminating once-dark alleys. By the 1970s, residents could dial 112 to quickly report a fire, theft, or emergency. By the 1980s, smoke detectors became common in Ystad homes. These days, families and businesses rely on security alarms, CCTV, and the police and fire department to protect them, and while Roland's job description may call for him to guard the town, he understands that his real role is much more about safeguarding the town's cultural heritage.

"With modern technology, they can discover fires long before I can, but if I see anything strange or out of the ordinary, I call the police or the fire brigade," Roland told me. "This is my job, my duty, and I do it for my father and my grandfather. I'm carrying on their life's work."

Over the years, Roland estimates he's rang the authorities roughly 20 times after seeing something alarming from the tower. There was the blaze he spotted down at the harbor when old cranes were lifting bales of hay, the band of thieves he saw breaking into a radio shop late at night in Stortorget square, and a recent SOS flare out at sea, among others. A month before I'd arrived, Roland heard an explosion just west of the tower. The 112 dispatcher asked him where the blast had come from, and based on a lifetime of looking and listening from his keep, Roland not only identified the street where he thought the explosion occurred, but the exact house. The dispatcher called Roland back an hour later to say he was right, and that the fire department had been sent into the same building where they located a detonated bomb inside.

Yet, in between blazes, burglars, and bombs, Roland's role can seem quite paradoxical. When nothing out of the ordinary happens—often for years on end—his job is to lean out the window every 15 minutes; float a long, hanging note in the air; and reassure people, "You're okay." As Sjöstrand told me: "He's like the opposite of a SWAT team member."

"The reality is, this is Sweden today, and you'd think we don't need this job," said Tina Westergren, an Ystad municipality employee responsible for hiring the night watchman. "You'd think we live in a modern society, and we haven't needed it for centuries, right?" But as Nordic Noir readers know, even in a seemingly idyllic place like Ystad, chilling things can happen.

In a real-life story ripped straight from the pages of Wallander, in 2000, a man named Ulf Borgström began systematically setting fires across southern Sweden. A lifelong outsider who had been bullied as a child and frequently incarcerated for theft as a juvenile, Borgström targeted structures of cultural or historical significance as a way to seek vengeance on a society he felt had wronged him. During the next 10 years, Borgström is believed to have torched more than 200 buildings and terrorized communities throughout Skåne. As each building burned to the ground, authorities were certain that Borgström was responsible, but he consistently managed to elude police by not leaving the faintest trace of evidence behind, daring authorities to try and catch him in the act. As he continued to ravage the region, Sweden's *Expressen* newspaper labeled him the nation's "most wanted criminal."[21] After setting fire to a string of 18th-century churches and homes throughout Skåne, Borgström set his sights on Ystad. He moved into a caravan on the outskirts of town and used it as a base to scorch everything from a nearby 14th-century farmhouse to a historical paper mill. "People here were scared because no one knew what he was capable of," Lofving recalled. "It was only a matter of time."

Then one night while on duty in 2003, Roland looked out from the tower windows and saw something no Ystad watchman had ever seen before: four fires were burning across the town at the same time—one in every direction. "I rang the fire brigade and yelled, 'It's burning everywhere in Ystad!'" Roland said. His quick action not only helped save people inside two restaurants, a youth center, and an apartment building, it also coined the nickname of Sweden's most infamous arsonist.

"The media started calling him 'The Dawn Pyromaniac' because when he started, he'd set his fires at night, but Roland and others would identify it, so he started waiting until dawn when [Roland] was off duty," Lofving said, noting that a Wallander story was later based on The Dawn Pyromaniac. "The police never, ever caught him red-handed. By the time they arrived, he was always long gone. This was a long, complex case. Over the years it made national and international news, and it changed Swedish crime."

It also changed how many people in Ystad viewed the symbolic role of the night watchman. The Ystad Fire Department, which had long deemed Roland's tower keep a fire hazard, started asking Roland if they could use it as a lookout post each day. So, after finishing his shift at night, Roland would leave a key to the tower for firefighters in a tiny crack outside the door. As more and more buildings burned across Skåne and police were left without footprints or fingerprints and with little more than crumpled newspapers and half-burned candles as evidence, national media began interviewing Roland about when and where he thought The

Dawn Pyromaniac would strike next. "When the fires started, it was so interesting because the people should have been looking at the police and saying, 'Protect us,' but we were looking to Roland," Lofving said. "This was always our history going back centuries, but now, it was in the present day, and he was doing his job and we felt safe because of it."

As with Wallander, who pours himself into his cases at the expense of his health, searching for The Dawn Pyromaniac took a toll on Roland too. Even though Borgström now operated after the watchman clocked out, Roland started becoming much more attentive to small details up in the tower—lights in homes that weren't normally on, shadows that weren't there the night before—anything that could help the police. He started sleeping less and followed news reports about Borgström religiously. "It was the hardest part of my career," Roland admitted. "He was every-where."

This pattern went on for years, seemingly with no pattern to Borg-ström's arson at all. He'd torch a home in the city of Vimmerby, and then a historical old barn 250 kilometers away near Kristianstad the next month. He'd burn down new villas in Ystad, and then half-timbered houses in Hammenhög. He'd set a knife factory in Mora ablaze, but also burn down an ice cream factory the same night. Borgström was charged and stood trial several times, but there was never enough evidence to convict him. Just when Roland was ready to give up and leave things to the police, he lumbered down the tower's spiral staircase one night in 2009 after his shift to find something that caused the hair on the back of his neck to stand up. Jammed against the door was a stack of crumpled newspapers and shreds of ripped rags doused with kerosene. It seemed Borgström had set his sights on Saint Mary's—or its tower keeper. "He'd already set fire to other churches, so I suspected this one was next," Roland said.

Catching The Dawn Pyromaniac in the act soon became a national se-curity issue, and in 2010, the Swedish police deployed a new tactic. For the first time in the nation's history, Sweden used an estimated seven to eight million krona from taxpayer funds to monitor and follow Borgström 24–7. They called it *Operation Punktmarkering* (Operation Man-Marking). Two undercover civilians and two uniformed surveillance officers were ordered to stay within 1.5 meters of him at all times. They'd wait outside the tent where Borgström was now sleeping in the middle of Ystad, shadow him as he hung out in Ystad parks, and accompany him as he dined at Ystad restaurants. Remarkably, he still managed to elude them. "It was surreal. They were on him like glue wherever he went. You'd see police officers trailing him everywhere and you'd think, 'Oh, there he is,'" said Carl Johan Engvall, a reporter at the *Ystads Allehanda* who covered the case. "I remember one time they lost him and he went on a train, changed trains, and managed to burn down an old windmill."

Borgström was finally convicted of aggravated arson in December 2010 after his man-markers witnessed him leaving an Ystad apartment building minutes before it went up in flames. He was sentenced to eight years in prison and has since been in and out of custody more than five times. In 2018, he was released and promptly set fire to a social services office in Köping. A month before I arrived, he'd cut off his foot shackle, burned down another building, and was apprehended again. Through it all, he's consistently promised to come back to Ystad and burn it to the ground. "Revenge is what I live for," he told Swedish journalists from behind bars. "It will burn in Ystad."[22]

"There's no doubt in anyone's mind he's coming back, and he's going to create mayhem," Lofving told me. "We hope Roland is here when he does."

Yet, after 57 years of guarding Ystad, Roland's future in the tower—as well as this 500-year-old tradition itself—is increasingly in doubt. When Roland started, the night watchman's shift was from 9:00 P.M. until 3:00 A.M. In 2005, the municipality cut it back to 1:00 A.M., and in 2021, they reduced it again to midnight. In December 2019, the town realized the tower's working conditions weren't up to code and ordered Roland to stay home for six full months as they replaced the keep's light, several warped and wobbly steps, and the windowsills worn into U-shaped scallops by hundreds of years of horn calls. According to Bergils, it was the longest time in Ystad's history a watchman hadn't been on duty. Even still, Roland showed up on Christmas Eve and New Year's Eve to watch *Lady and the Tramp*, listen to Elvis, and work for free.

"I don't think we will ever have another tower watchman who is as dedicated to the role as Mr. Borg, but he won't be here forever, unfortunately," said Anders Andersson, who manages the Saint Mary's church. "We've had a lot of discussions about how to maintain this duty after him. Is it possible to recruit anyone else? He's different. He has a big heart for this work, a big heart for this tradition."

"Look, it's hard work going up to that freezing tower, sitting there alone," Sjöstrand said. "It's not very glitzy. It's also not that very well paid. The hours are horrible. But for Roland, it's where he gets his energy. So, yes, today it's hard to see who would replace him." But if you ask Roland, there is one obvious choice.

One night while he was on duty in 1985, Roland watched a report about a civil war in a country he'd never heard of, far, far away. The government of Guatemala was massacring tens of thousands of ethnic Mayans, and leaving countless babies orphaned in the process. Unable to sit by, Roland told Yvonne about the genocide. The couple had long wanted children, but they hadn't had any luck. So, in the midst of a humanitarian disaster, Roland and Yvonne arranged for a nun to airlift an orphaned brother and sister from the Guatemalan Highlands to Sweden in order to adopt them—one of whom required an immediate operation to repair an inguinal hernia. "The nun didn't tell us about his condition until we met him. She was afraid we wouldn't want him," Roland said, wiping away tears. "But of course we would have. How could we have not?" Today, Robert and Carolina Borg are 39 and 37 years old, and Roland and Yvonne have seven grandchildren.

Unlike Fritz and Helmer, Roland promised that he'd never ask his son, Robert, to take over the family trade—he just hoped he might naturally gravitate toward it. For a while, he did. Between 2000 and 2006, Robert apprenticed alongside his father up in the tower, just as Roland had done with his father. "He's got it in him. He's got the feeling for it and he's a quick learner," Roland beamed. "This job has been in my family for more than 100 years and it's my dream that he takes over, though I'm never going to force him."

Like Fritz, Helmer, and Roland before him, Robert now has a family of his own to support. Roland makes 137 SEK ($12.55) an hour as Sweden's last night watchman, which is well below the national average of 193 SEK ($17.70). And like every Ystad watchman who has come before him,

Roland is considered an hourly employee, meaning he has no vacation and few benefits. So, in a bitter twist of irony, when Robert started having children and needed a full-time salary to support them, he left his job as a medieval watchman and became a modern-day watchman. "He works as a security guard in Landskrona," Roland said, flatly. "I still have a glimmer of hope that he wants to follow in my footsteps, but you never know what the future is going to bring."

In the meantime, there are three deputies who step in when Roland is away. One is Lars Persson, a business developer who collects watchman figurines from around the world. Another is Eva Milberg, a former IBM employee from Stockholm who became Ystad's first-ever night watchwoman when Roland recommended her for the position in 2020. ("It's not a man's job," Roland told me. "She gets the job done just as well as I do.") And the third is Ludvig Olsson, a 42-year-old member of the Ystad Fire Department who plays his 200-year-old clog fiddle (a wooden clog whittled into a fiddle, sometimes called the "national" instrument of Skåne) up in the tower. While each adamantly told me they felt this tradition should continue after Roland, they also worry it may vanish with him.

"This is Roland's life, and when he can no longer be in the tower, it will fade," Persson told me. "If it does, then it would only be a talking piece: 'Once upon a time, we had a man who stayed up in a tower . . .' Our history would be forgotten."

No one in Roland's family has ever had to apply to become a night watchman: Fritz was handed a uniform, Fritz told Helmer to take over, and Helmer's dying wish was that Roland succeed him. In order to become a deputy 24 years ago, Persson said he was asked three questions in the Greyfriars Abbey. "They said, 'Do you smoke? Do you drink? Are you scared of ghosts?' I said no to each, so I was hired. They don't let *anybody* up to be a watchman," he said, without the slightest bit of humor.

But how do you become a watchman today? If the big question is who is going to replace Roland, how does that process happen? Is there an application process? Does the municipality just post it on LinkedIn?

"I've been wondering that as well, and I'm a little concerned because it should be my job to hire it," Westergren told me in her office. "The truth is, it's not under control. No one has thought it through. Roland is quite old now and no one has had a real serious thought on it. I worry it will just become another story among all the other lost occupations. Once things are lost, you can't recover them."

I was having a hard time wrapping my head around the idea that the world's last true night watchman likely isn't going to be replaced by technology but rather killed off by bureaucracy and bad planning. When Wallander needs space to gather his thoughts, he often goes to Ales Stenar, a megalithic monument east of Ystad. So on my last full day in town, I borrowed a bike from Westergren and pedaled 19 windy kilometers through patchwork farmland and bluffs pounded by the cold, crashing Baltic Sea to the site.

Sometimes called "Sweden's Stonehenge," Ales Stenar is one of Europe's great unsolved mysteries. The monument is perched high above a bluff on the southern coast where Sweden slopes down into the sea and abruptly ends. Ancient Skånians somehow managed to drag 59 mammoth stone boulders each weighing nearly two tons up this hill to form a 67-meter oval shaped like a Viking ship. Experts think this enigmatic formation appeared about 1,400 years ago, but no one knows exactly how or why. Since the stones are positioned so that the sun sets exactly at the ship's "stem" each summer and rises at its "stern" each winter, some historians believe the boat is an ancient astronomical clock—which suggests that people around here have had a fascination with timekeeping long before the night watchman.

As I looked out across the sea, I thought about a story I had written a few years earlier about an island's last lighthouse keeper. Like Roland, he worked alone in a tower that had been continuously manned for hundreds of years, but after 88 keepers before him, he had been told that he'd soon be replaced by an automated control panel that didn't require sleep or a salary. In a way, the lighthouse keeper's job was much more straightforward than Roland's. Night after night, he peered across the ocean, looking for a lone glimmer in an endless sea of black. Meanwhile, the watchman's task is somewhat the opposite: to scan a nightscape increasingly engulfed in artificial light and find the rare light that doesn't belong. Still, every captain and fisherman I spoke with told me that what they'd miss most when the lighthouse became automated wasn't a practical function, but a physical presence—a feeling of comfort knowing that someone is up there watching over you. It's the same in Ystad. There haven't been invading ships in the harbor or armored enemies at the gate in centuries. There's no curfew to enforce. People wear watches and carry cell phones to tell the time. But as Palmgren told me in her pottery studio, "When I hear Roland blow the horn, I feel home."

There have been talks about sticking infrared cameras atop Saint Mary's spire and automating the horn calls, like a church bell. But I have never been anywhere in the world where people keep their windows open in freezing temperatures to hear an automated church bell. "The horn call is a piece of our heritage, our history. It means something," Andersson told me.

Maybe I was wrong. Maybe the most important part of the night watchman's job isn't to float a warm note through the air to reassure people "You're safe," but rather to remind people that things weren't always so safe. That, long before we were warm and cozy in our beds, there were real dangers lurking in the darkness, and that each of our lives today is the result of millions of invisible choices, sacrifices, and miracles from the past we'll never know about. For anyone who believes that gratitude and wonder is a practice, I can't think of anything more stirring than this nightly call to contemplation.

I began pedaling back to Ystad for my final night in the tower with Roland, but the wind whipped so viciously across the salt-sprayed coast that it blew me off my bike and tossed me into a roadside potato patch. By the time I made it back to Stortorget square, it was dusk, and there was a noticeable tension in the air. Several of the square's usually cheery vendors wore concerned expressions and residents clustered together looking down silently at their cell phones. I asked a barista at a nearby café if everything was all right.

In the six hours I had been away, The Dawn Pyromaniac had been released from a high-security prison in Kumla after completing his sentence.[23] That night, I asked Roland what he made of this as we watched the nightly news in his radiated room. "He's always said when he's released, he's going to come back and burn the whole of Ystad down, but I don't believe that myself. It's only threats. Still, I keep an eye on him from here," Roland said, glancing over toward the tower's windows.

Only time will tell if Borgström comes back to terrorize Ystad again, or if Roland, Robert, or anyone will be here in the tower if he does. I asked Roland what he'd do if he woke up one day, his nights were suddenly free, and he had all the vacation time in the world. He wasn't sure. Maybe he'd go to Graceland, he said, or see more of Sweden. He'd never been on an airplane before, because he's afraid of heights. But up here, 14 stories above Ystad, it was different. "When I started, my father told me, 'You'll never regret this job,' and I've never regretted one single day," Roland said, reaching for the horn before his last quarterly call of the night. "Just like him, I'll keep doing it until I can no longer go up the stairs."

I clutched the vertical handrail and carefully descended the creaky, cobwebbed staircase with Roland to say goodbye. At the base of the tower, the medieval watchman stuffed his cloak into a bag, zipped up a black Gore-Tex jacket, and disappeared into the night. Soon Roland would be just another guy, riding the express train home.

3

The Last Inca Bridge Master

I believe since the history of man, there has been no other account of such grandeur as is to be seen on this road, which passes over deep valleys and lofty mountains, by snowy heights, over falls of water, through the living rock, and along the edges of tortuous torrents.
—PEDRO CIEZA DE LEÓN, 1548

A blast from a conch shell cut through the canyon. Two men in white wool jackets and brightly colored *chullo* caps placed a glistening llama fetus atop the glowing embers of a fire still feeding on a bloody sheep's heart. As they lifted their hands to the heavens in hopes the gods may accept the offering, Victoriano Arizapana slung a golden coil of rope over each shoulder and walked toward the edge of a cliff. A hush fell over the sea of sombrero-clad men who parted as the 60-year-old slowly approached the abyss. With a deep breath, Arizapana carefully lowered himself onto four tightly braided cables spanning the 30-meter crevasse, each the circumference of a man's thigh, and straddled them with his bare feet dangling over the sides. He then poured a few drops of clear *cañazo* cane liquor on each cable, whispered the names of the four mountain spirits who would decide his fate, and pushed himself off the end of the stone abutment into the gaping chasm.

Balancing precariously 22 meters over the rushing Apurimac River, Arizapana worked slowly. With each advancing scoot, he reached high above his head to grab the smaller ropes from the top of the handrails, tying them tightly to the outside cables to join them with the base as balusters. He then leaned forward so that his torso was parallel to the four braided cables he teetered on like a seesaw to pass the smaller ropes underneath, uniting the four bottom beams into a single, wobbling plank. Sparrow hawks swooped under Arizapana's feet, darting back into their nests pocked into the sides of the rock face. It was 11 degrees Celsius, and the last gasps of day painted the sky pink and dappled the Spanish moss drooping from the canyon's basalt wall. As the wind whipped up, the suspended structure began to sway back and forth like a giant hammock. Arizapana suddenly stopped working and gripped both handrails to balance himself, causing the small ropes to fall from his hands and plunge into the foaming river below. In Quechua, Apurimac means "the God who talks," and like all *apus* (mountain spirits), it's a living being that needs to be fed in order to keep the flame of life burning. Arizapana wouldn't be the first man to be swallowed up by the river, and he knew that one wrong move now could be the difference between life and death.

As the cables continued to tremble above the gorge, Arizapana remembered the words his father once told him: "Trust yourself, have faith in the apus, and don't look down." He reached over his head for a new rope, bent himself so far forward that his face touched the careening cables, and continued diligently fulfilling a duty that men in his family have maintained for more than 500 years: weaving the Q'eswachaka, the last suspended rope bridge from the Inca Empire.

Located on the western edge of South America, tucked between Earth's largest rainforest (the Amazon), its driest desert (the Atacama), and the tallest mountain range in the Western Hemisphere (the Andes), the Inca were one of the world's most unique empires. They developed in near isolation, expanding their territory from Cusco, Peru, in the 1430s and ruling for just 100 years until the Spanish conquest of 1532. But through an ingenious system of engineering and strict organization, they managed to create the largest empire ever seen in the Americas—a sprawling two-million-square-kilometer civilization that extended across parts of modern-day Colombia, Ecuador, Peru, Bolivia, Chile, and Argentina—encompassing as many as 12 million people and 100 languages. It was roughly 10 times the size of the Aztec Empire and had twice its population. Remarkably, the Inca managed to forge this vast society without the wheel, the arch, money, iron or steel tools, draft animals capable of plowing fields, or even a written language.[1]

Instead, one of the keys to the Inca's rapid expansion was an extraordinary network of roads used for communication, trade, and military campaigns known as the Qhapaq Ñan (The Royal Road). Considered one of the greatest engineering feats in the ancient world and rapturously proclaimed "the most stupendous and useful works ever executed by man" by 19th-century geographer and explorer Alexander von Humboldt, the Qhapaq Ñan extended for nearly 40,000 kilometers—roughly the circumference of the globe.[2] It stretched from Quito, Ecuador, past Santiago, Chile, on two main north-south arteries, along with more than 20 smaller routes running east to west like a giant ladder. Second in length only to the Roman Road system, the Qhapaq Ñan was in many ways even more impressive, as it traversed some of the planet's most extreme geographical terrains. This prehistoric highway linked the snowcapped peaks of the Andes at more than 6,000 meters with the continent's steamy rainforests, barren deserts, and yawning canyons. To do this, the Inca bore massive tunnels through mountains, lined valleys with immaculate stone paths, and carved spiral staircases up cliff faces. Where the earth abruptly ended, they used a brilliant system of suspension bridges to leap canyons and stitch their road network together. But the Inca didn't build their bridges out of metal or wood. They wove them from grass.[3]

At the empire's height, it's estimated that some 200 suspension bridges spanned the cliffs along the Qhapaq Ñan, each one strong enough to support the weight of a marching army.[4] Today, nearly 500 years after the collapse of the Inca Empire, only one bridge remains, and it dangles over the Apurimac River near the 500-person village of Huinchiri in Peru's southern highlands. In the past, each Inca bridge was overseen by a bridge master (*chakacamayoc*) who was responsible for guarding and repairing it. These days, the last Inca bridge is overseen by the last living Inca bridge master: Arizapana, the latest in an unbroken line of chakacamayocs that he says stretches back to the Inca, like braided rope.

Arizapana uses the same method to build and repair the Q'eswachaka as his forefathers did half a millennium ago, which means the bridge only lasts one year and needs to be constantly rebuilt in order to prevent it from collapsing. Weaving enough grass to make a 30-meter suspension bridge requires a lot of manpower. So, every year in the second week of

June, 1,100 people from four surrounding communities living at more than 3,600 meters elevation come together to cut, braid, and transform blades of straw-like *q'oya ichu* into golden coils as strong as steel. For three straight days, Arizapana oversees every aspect of the bridge's construction, from measuring the length of its cables and crossbeams to the thickness of its handrails. After the cables have been heaved to the edge of the rocky canyon and painstakingly pulled into place by teams working on opposite sides of the river, the villagers cut down the old, sagging bridge, letting the all-natural structure plummet into the Apurimac and slowly decompose. Then, when the time is right, Arizapana murmurs a blessing to Pachamama (Mother Earth) and upholds this sacred expression of the Inca's bond with nature by taking a leap of faith that his ancestors, the community, and the gods have commanded of him.

In 1911, an American lecturer-explorer from Yale University named Hiram Bingham III was chasing a rumor that had been circulating for years: somewhere, high up in the Peruvian Andes, lay a lost city hidden in the clouds. After compiling clues about the alleged location of the city in the Inca's ancient capital, Cusco, Bingham set off toward the Urubamba Valley. Four days later, he was entombed more than a mile deep in a canyon surrounded by towering crags. As the cliffs closed in and dusk fell, he hacked his way through the thicket before spotting a grass-thatched hut. The owner identified himself as Melchor Arteaga, and when Bingham inquired if there were any ruins nearby, the man pointed to the top of the mountain. The next morning dawned in a shivering drizzle and Bingham asked Arteaga if he could take him to the place where he'd pointed. Arteaga demurred, saying it was too cold and wet, so Bingham agreed to pay him several days' wages of one *sol* (roughly $0.25), and off they went.[5]

At the bank of a gushing river, the men slowly crept across a flimsy plank made from four slender branches lashed together with vines. "It was obvious that no one could have lived for an instant in the rapids, but would immediately have been dashed to pieces against granite boulders," Bingham wrote.[6] On the other side, the men scrambled up a near-vertical bluff. "A good part of the distance we went on all fours, sometimes hanging on by the tips of our fingers," Bingham continued.[7] As they climbed higher, the rush of the river softened under the thick canopy below. After a grueling two-hour ascent, the cliffs sloped into hills, and the men collapsed into a grassy clearing. Several mountaintop farmers soon welcomed Bingham with gourds full of water. Arteaga couldn't continue any farther, but one of the farmers volunteered a new guide to lead Bingham on the final stretch to the lost city: his barefoot son, who was no more than 11 years old.

The small boy bounded down the hill in tattered pants and a striped poncho, ducking under tangled branches and thorns that stopped the lanky American in his tracks. Bingham didn't expect to find anything particularly interesting, but as he followed the boy's shadow through the riot of vines and rounded a promontory, he gazed up and saw it: Machu Picchu, a towering Inca citadel of temples, fountains, and palaces fashioned by men without mortar. The site had been forgotten by the outside world for nearly four centuries and never revealed to the Spanish. Bingham had stumbled upon one of the most extraordinary architectural ruins on Earth.

"It fairly took my breath away," he wrote. "What could this place be?"[8] Decades after his death, it would be declared one of the New Seven Wonders of the World.[9] Bingham's self-proclaimed "discovery" of Machu Picchu effectively introduced the Inca Empire to much of the modern world. His story was immortalized in swashbuckling first-person accounts with hundreds of captivating photographs in *National Geographic*[10] and *Harper's*[11] magazines in 1913, and later, in a bestselling book, *Lost City of the Incas*. But what's been lost in this intrepid tale is what led Bingham to explore Peru in the first place.

Years earlier, Bingham had come across a book published in 1877 by the American archaeologist and painter E. George Squier called *Peru: Incidents of Travel and Exploration in the Land of the Incas*. "In that volume is a marvelous picture of the Apurimac Valley," Bingham later wrote. "In the foreground is a delicate suspension bridge which commences at a tunnel in the face of a precipitous cliff and hangs in midair at great height above the swirling waters . . . in the distance, towering above a mass of stupendous mountains, is a magnificent snowcapped peak." The bridge Bingham was referring to was located 58 kilometers upriver from the Q'eswachaka, and Squier's spellbinding painting of men and horses crossing these cliffs at dizzying heights on a 45-meter drooping, grass-woven walkway also inspired Thornton Wilder's Pulitzer Prize–winning novel, *The Bridge of San Luis Rey*. "The desire to see the Apurimac and experience the thrill of crossing that bridge decided me in favor of an overland journey to Lima," Bingham wrote. "As a result, I went to Cusco."[12]

Bingham and Squier were far from the first foreigners to marvel at the Inca's suspension bridges. When the Spanish arrived in Peru in 1532, they must have been astonished at what they saw. They had never seen anything like the woven bridges of the Andes. The Inca suspension bridges cleared spans of more than 45 meters, which was longer than any European masonry bridge at the time. The longest Roman bridge in Spain had a maximum span between supports of 29 meters.[13] Chroniclers wrote that Spanish soldiers were so terrified of these braided fiber cables strung across the gorges of the Inca's realm that they called them "the work of the devil" and would stand in awe before crawling on their hands and knees the entire way across.[14]

"To someone unaccustomed to it, the crossing appears dangerous because the bridge sags with its long span . . . so that one is continually going down until the middle is reached and from there one climbs until the far bank; and when the bridge is being crossed it trembles very much," wrote conquistador Pedro Sánchez de la Hoz in 1543.[15] But despite their frail appearance, these dangling walkways were incredibly sturdy, each "so strong that horses can gallop over it as though they were crossing the bridge of Alcántara, or of Cordoba," Pedro Cieza de Léon, another chronicler, wrote in 1553. They were, in his estimation, as solid "as the streets of Sevilla."[16] According to modern tests conducted by MIT professor and structural engineer Dr. John Ochsendorf, the Q'eswachaka's four base cables can support 9,388 kilograms—or roughly 110 men spaced evenly apart.[17] And unlike the arched stone bridges of Europe, the Inca's grass-woven creations could quickly be cut as a defensive measure to avoid advancing armies, and then rebuilt. In some cases, the very sight of these engineering wonders was enough to force foreign clans to surrender. "Many tribes are reduced voluntarily to submission by the fame of the bridge," wrote Garcilaso de la Vega in 1609, the son of an Inca empress and Spanish conquistador and one of the few chroniclers of Inca descent. "The marvelous new work that seemed only possible for men come down from heaven."[18]

The Inca wove their world from fiber, so when it came to solving the problem of how to carry people over cliffs, it was the natural solution. They lined their homes with thick rugs and blankets from llama and alpaca fur. They used cotton and wool to fashion the most prized clothing and textiles the Americas had ever seen, with up to 120 wefts per centimeter. They built boats out of reeds that were nearly as long as Columbus's ships. They stitched cotton and alpaca wool between layers of leather to make armored helmets and body suits that were lighter and nearly as strong, pound for pound, as Spanish steel. These quilted garments were so effective at stopping fired arrows that conquistadors adopted them during the conquest and reported leaving battles with so many projectiles lodged into them that they looked like porcupines. One of the empire's deadliest weapons was the *warak'a,* a fiber-bound sling that launched rocks with such force they could crack open a human skull and split a Spanish sword in two.[19]

The Inca even communicated in fiber, relying on a sophisticated system of colored-and-spun knotted cords called *quipus* to store information.[20] These intricate necklace-looking webs could hold hundreds of strings and record decimals up to 10,000. In the absence of a written language, the Inca used quipus for everything from documenting family genealogy and sending military orders to measuring state taxes and taking the census. However, as the Spanish established control over the Inca, the ability to read quipu faded away, and the 600 or so that remain are indecipherable to the modern world. As a result, much of what we know about the Inca Empire today comes from these Spanish chroniclers, and it paints a fascinating (if incomplete and biased) picture of this vast federation.

Ancient Peru was one of the world's six cradles of civilization where ancient societies abandoned their nomadic hunter-gatherer lifestyles and settled down in one place. Between 8000 and 3000 BC, people here domesticated llamas and alpacas, along with an immense variety of crops, such as potatoes, quinoa, corn, and squash. The Inca Empire—or

Tawantinsuyu (The Four Regions Together, as it was known)—was the final great civilization to emerge here, though for some 200 years after its founding in the early 13th century, it was little more than a chiefdom.[21] That all changed in 1438, when the ninth Inca ruler, Pachacuti, took the throne.

During Pachacuti's 33-year reign, this "Inca Alexander the Great" embarked on a staggering series of engineering and military campaigns. He rebuilt Cusco into an imperial city paved with perfectly cut stone; ordered many of the empire's crowning monuments, such as Machu Picchu; and expanded the Inca's territory from Chile to Ecuador, transforming the once-humble hamlet into the largest empire on Earth at the time. To do this, Pachacuti created the Qhapaq Ñan, a vast highway system that originated in Cusco's central square and spread in opposite cardinal directions to connect Tawantinsuyu's four *suyus*, or regions.[22]

Pachacuti dispatched groups of spies along his Royal Road to assess the military strength and wealth of nearby regions. He would then try to persuade the chiefs of these lands to join the empire by promising that they would grow more powerful if they became Inca, and negotiating with a not-so-subtle threat that came marching down his highway. "The typical Inca strategy for getting communities to join them was to roll up to the edge of a place of, say, 5,000 people, with an army of 50,000 people and say, 'We invite you to become part of the Inca Empire. If you do, we will build you buildings, we will feed you, we will protect you. And if you don't, we will escort you to the edge of the empire. One way or another, this land is ours. Would you like to join?'" said Dr. Edwin Barnhart, an archaeologist specializing in ancient civilizations of the Americas. "It was a very successful strategy, and it wouldn't have been possible without the Qhapaq Ñan." Any communities who resisted were crushed by Pachacuti's ever-growing army, but those that accepted were peacefully folded into the Inca's multicultural empire.[23]

As the Inca army marched along its immaculately maintained Royal Road, they slept in barrack-like shelters called *tambos* that were placed a day's walk from one another (roughly 20 kilometers) and were fed from stone storehouses called *qullqas*. In addition to housing long-lasting staples such as corn, beans, and freeze-dried potatoes, each of the Inca's estimated

10,000 qullqas also had clothing, blankets, tools, and weapons. All of this inventory was recorded with quipus and communicated across the empire through a sprawling communication system of relay runners dispatched along the Qhapaq Ñan.[24]

Known as *chasquis*, these runners were the fastest, fittest men from nearby towns. From their designated stations, these white-robed couriers would tear 10 to 15 kilometers through the mountains on the Royal Road, carrying memorized messages and clutching quipus that were so important that if they were misinterpreted, they could plunge the empire into chaos.[25] From his imperial seat in Cusco, Pachacuti and his successors used quipus and chasquis to quickly mobilize and direct the Inca army. Yet, unlike many Christian empires, the Inca didn't forcefully supplant local beliefs and customs as they expanded their territory. Instead, they absorbed new cultures and skills while incorporating the trademark elements of Inca infrastructure into each new conquered land: the runners, the storehouses, and their paved-and-swept Royal Road. "The Inca came in and said, 'You don't have to change your religion or your way of life. You're just under new management, so whatever you guys do best— whether it's pottery, weaving, or metallurgy—you're going to keep doing that and we're going to get that moving through the empire on our road system.'" Barnhart said.

This new "management" system was one of the most fascinating aspects of Inca society, and without it, many of their crowning achievements never would have been possible. In a land without draft animals, all plowing, farming, and building had to be done by hand.[26] Ancient Andean societies quickly realized that groups could do this more effectively than individuals, and the only way to survive in such an extreme environment was to band together. As a result, a system of reciprocity and societal cooperation emerged in remote highland communities. The Inca codified this practice into law, and in doing so, created what some have called the first socialist civilization.[27]

The Inca ran the world's largest empire without money. The production, storage, and distribution of goods was wholly controlled by the central government. The concept of private property didn't exist, and all assets and resources were shared. No one had anything to sell, cash to spend, or a reason to buy anything. When an Inca couple got married, the state provided them with a house, land, and tools from the nearby storehouse, as well as two llamas and enough seeds to grow their own food. A portion of each family's food was to be offered to the gods. Anything else they didn't eat would be turned over to the storehouse as a form of tax. The most common form of tax was something called *mit'a*, or communal labor.[28]

If the Qhapaq Ñan was the highway of the Inca Empire, mit'a was the engine, and the two worked hand in hand. Through mit'a, the Inca government could quickly call on citizens to become soldiers and laborers, summon massive forces of 140,000 men on a day's notice, and move them across the Royal Road to tackle the most pressing civic projects in the empire—be it conquering new lands or building new roads. All men, aged 15 to 50, were required to perform this imperial tribute for roughly three months a year. Mit'a is the secret to how the Inca were able to construct towering citadels in the clouds and weave 200 suspension bridges from grass in their short 100-year reign.[29]

Ironically, the same highway system that built the Inca Empire also helped lead to its collapse, as Spanish forces (and more devastatingly, the deadly smallpox they introduced) traveled along the Qhapaq Ñan to defeat the already-decimated Inca military. Yet, centuries of colonial rule failed to rid much of the empire's former territory of Inca culture. Today, eight million people across the Andes still speak the Inca's official language, Quechua. Vast portions of the Royal Road remain in use from Argentina to Colombia. The Inca rainbow flag flies proudly above a statue of Pachacuti in Cusco's central Plaza de Armas, where the Qhapaq Ñan originated. And in the remote grasslands near the Q'eswachaka bridge, the ancient Inca tradition of mit'a has been kept alive by the empire's direct descendants as *minka*.[30]

The construction of the Q'eswachaka requires more than 25 kilometers of woven rope, and hundreds of rural families still use the bridge to cross the Apurimac. Just as every household in the empire was expected to contribute their labor to civic projects for the greater good, each household in the four communities surrounding the bridge is responsible for contributing 40 double-arms' lengths (roughly 70 meters) of braided q'oya grass. Yet, unlike in Inca times, this is no longer a compulsory tax. In fact, no one even orders the Q'eswachaka to be rebuilt each year. According to Guido Jara Ugarte, an anthropologist at Peru's Universidad Nacional de San Antonio Abad del Cusco, "the bridge's renovation is a living expression of a time and culture that is still deep within these communities." Residents here proudly identify as Inca, so while they may have been under new "management" for the last 500 years, they've simply continued doing what they do best: weaving fiber.

"The beautiful thing about the Q'eswachaka is that you have this physical artifact from the Inca period, but you also have a perfectly preserved process of Inca organization and construction that has survived too. It all creates a powerful symbolism," Jara Ugarte said. "The Andean worldview is full of complementary duality: chaos and order, water and earth, and life and death. The Q'eswachaka represents this duality by connecting both sides, physically and spiritually."

And so it has gone for centuries. In a world of contrary forces, men gather on opposite sides of a river and pull against one another, transforming tension into order, bridging water and earth, and celebrating the renewal of life year after year with each new bridge. In doing so, they remind us what made "The Four Regions Together" so special. Each blade of grass in the Q'eswachaka represents an inhabitant of the Inca's remote realm: fragile by themselves, but invincible when they join forces.

———————

From its source in the snowy glaciers of Mismi Mountain, the Apurimac tumbles over cliffs and shoots through narrow slot canyons during its 700-kilometer journey to the Amazon River. As it carves a rift through the high-altitude puna grasslands of Cusco's southern region, it divides the district of Quehue in two parts. On one side is the administrative capital, Ccollana Quehue. On the other side are the villages of Choccayhua, Chaupibanda, and Huinchiri. Traditionally, the only way to travel from these villages over the river was to cross the Q'eswachaka, and the area's inaccessibility has helped preserve many of its pre-Columbian customs. Some 200 years after the Spanish conquest, traditional *kurakas* (Inca magistrates) still ruled the land. As a result, the rhythms of rural life remain startlingly similar to those during Inca times. More than 90 percent of people here speak Quechua as a first language.[31] The region's few scattered residents still wear traditional handwoven *pollera* skirts, *lliclla* capes, and chullo hats, whose vivid colors contrast with the arid, dusty scrubland that unfurls toward the horizon. Most villagers survive as subsistence farmers, growing the same hardy staples on the slopes of the mountains as their ancestors did. And a short walk from where the Q'eswachaka spans the Apurimac River, the last Inca bridge master lives alone in a small adobe home on the side of a mountain.

At 5'10", Arizapana towers over most other Inca descendants in the region. He is soft-spoken with short jet-black hair, leathery-brown skin weathered by a life outdoors, and high cheekbones that angle in toward his narrow chin. When I arrived in Huinchiri after a dizzying four-hour drive south from Cusco, the three-day bridge-building festival was four days away, and each person—including the bridge master himself—was busy preparing their share of braided grass. Sitting outside his whitewashed home in a sloping field of golden q'oya that faced a flaming sunset, Arizapana demonstrated how to transform cut grass into coiled rope.

He starts by using a curved scythe to hack off fistfuls of q'oya at the base and lays them on the hillside to dry in the sun. It takes Arizapana a full day to harvest enough q'oya to braid 70 meters of rope and several days for the cut q'oya to dry. He then splashes the dried q'oya with water, places a bundle of it atop a flat rock, and bangs it gently with a circular stone to make each shoot more pliable without splitting the q'oya itself. Once the straw-like shoots are as supple as possible, he takes the moistened q'oya and rubs it between his hands, twisting it into a braided twine and adding more q'oya shoots to extend the braid whenever he feels that it's becoming too thin. While he does this, he keeps one foot on the rope he's already braided, so that the cord remains taut as he lengthens it. Arizapana said that it often takes some households a full day with the whole family working to weave their 70 meters of grass, but he's been doing this so long that he can finish his share in less than three hours working alone.

As the bridge master twisted the q'oya between his palms, he looked over his shoulder to a one-room clay hut, a short walk away, where he was born and explained that he has lived on this same small plot of land his entire life. Growing up, he used to idolize his father, Leonardo, the bridge master before him. "I remember watching him weave the Q'eswachaka when I was seven or eight years old, and I wanted to be just like him," Arizapana said, wearing a yellow-and-red chullo and white wool jacket. Leonardo insisted that Victoriano get an education, so every morning, he would wake up at 6:00 A.M. and walk two hours to the top of the mountain to attend the closest school. "I went to elementary school for four years, but I used to escape and come back here to be close to my dad. I was always attached to him."

Victoriano had two sisters and no brothers, and Leonardo used to tell his only son about "the pride of the family bloodline"—an ancient thread that had remained entwined in his mother's side of the family since the Inca Empire. When Victoriano was 12, his father let him help build part of the bridge for the first time by asking him to balance atop the four base cables and weave a few of the balusters that connect the two handrails to the walkway. "I was very nervous and scared about the height, and I made some mistakes, so my father had to correct me," he said. "By the time I was 15, I was more confident, and when I was 16, I started to construct sections so my father could take a break when his hands were full of scars."

Traditionally, the current bridge master decides who will become his successor, and after Victoriano proved himself as a teenager, his father leaned in close one day and told him, "You will keep my hands after I die, and like me, you will be a respected man by everyone in the community." Leonardo passed when Victoriano was 35, and though Victoriano had blossomed into a confident apprentice under his father's watchful eye, becoming the lone chakacamayoc proved far more challenging than he'd expected.

"I was afraid to fall, to do things the wrong way without the support of my father," Arizapana remembered. "For the first three years after I became the chakacamayoc, I had recurring dreams that I'd fall from the bridge and get shot up into the heavens. I used to make terrible sounds during these nightmares that would wake my wife up. It took me years to become comfortable in this job." The nightmares eventually subsided, but several years later a real-life tragedy befell the bridge master. One night during a village-wide party, Arizapana's wife reached for a glass of what she thought was cane liquor. She took a sip, collapsed in Arizapana's arms, and died as dozens of people looked on in horror. The community's Andean healer later told Arizapana that, amid the revelry, he suspected his wife had accidentally drunk from a bottle of nearby pesticide, but the fact that Arizapana was helpless to protect her still haunts him. "It was the saddest moment of my life," he said, looking away. "I've never remarried, and I no longer go to parties."

Instead, Arizapana poured himself into his young children and the Q'eswachaka. "The bridge is part of my life," he said, raising his eyes and peering down the mountainside toward the river. "I look after it as my son." Victoriano now has two grown sons, Vidal and Yuri. For years, it has been his dream that his oldest son, Vidal, follow in his footsteps, but as the years have passed, that hope has slowly slipped away. "He knows how to make it, but he gets nervous and afraid," Victoriano said. "He used to help me during the renovation, just as I did with my father. Now, he has other interests."

A lack of jobs in the puna means that many younger Quechua-speaking residents are forced to adopt Spanish and migrate to nearby cities in order to support their families. As a result, the population of the rural Canas Province, where the Q'eswachaka is located, has been steadily declining for the last three decades.[32] For years, Vidal lived in Lima, plying his trade as a charango-strumming musician, before settling down with his wife and daughter in the nearby provincial capital of Livitaca. Of Victoriano's five children, only Yuri still lives in Huinchiri, and Victoriano has made no secret that his "dying wish" is for Yuri to "keep my hands, and continue this bloodline of Inca chakacamayocs," if Vidal refuses.

During Inca times, the chakacamayoc usually lived in a small hut at or near the bridge. In addition to maintaining the bridge, the bridge master was also responsible for protecting it. Tampering with any part of the Qhapaq Ñan was serious business, and the destruction of a suspension bridge could have halted all traffic and communication to a huge section of the empire. As the Spanish Jesuit missionary Padre Bernabé Cobo wrote in 1653, anyone who burned an Inca bridge was subject to the death penalty, "applied rigorously."[33]

These days, Arizapana is one of the only people in the puna with a year-round job. Twice a week, he goes to the Q'eswachaka to repair any loose planks and unraveled threads damaged by the elements, ensuring that villagers and their llamas can continue to cross the river safely. He earns 200 soles ($52) a month for this work, but when he's not at the bridge, he lives much like everyone else in this remote region.

During the seven days that I was in town, it dropped to minus 3 degrees Celsius each night, and I slept curled in a ball under an alpaca blanket. Like other residents here, Arizapana's four-room home doesn't have heat. It's topped with a lean metal roof, and a mixture of glass and cotton sheets covers the windows. He sleeps on a thin mattress, and a calendar, newspaper clippings, and photographs of his children are tacked to the clay walls. A small wood-burning adobe fireplace is built into the corner of his home and a wooden outhouse is located a short walk away in the pasture. He grows potatoes, lima beans, barley, oats, and quinoa. In the dry season, he mainly survives on potatoes that he cooks in an earthen Andean oven, dating back to the Inca Empire, called a *huatia*. In the wet season, he eats lima bean and quinoa soup and forages for bird eggs on the banks of the Apurimac. If he's lucky, he may catch a wild partridge up the mountain. Once a week, he piles into the back of a large truck with other Huinchiri residents to go to Ccollana Quehue to buy rice, oil, and sugar. Before 1987, there was no truck, so he'd cross the Q'eswachaka, walk three hours to buy supplies, and carry them three hours home.

Each of Victoriano's five children now have families and homes of their own, and ever since Leonardo died, Victoriano had looked after his elderly mother, Cecilia. When she finally passed four years ago, the world's last chakacamayoc buried her and then contemplated his own fate. "Who will come for me?" he said, looking at the empty rooms where his children used to sleep. "I feel lonely when I'm here by myself. Sometimes I distract myself by turning on the radio and listening to music, but when my children come, I feel happy. The bridge makes me less lonely. It brings me a lot of joy, especially when it's time to renovate it. I may live alone, but on these three days, I am the most important person."

While in Huinchiri, I stayed across the mountain with Arizapana's nephew, Gregorio Huayhua Callasi, and his wife, Josefina, who weaves the family's clothes from sheep and alpaca wool. Gregorio is one of the spiritual leaders in the community, and as he led me into a field to help him harvest his household's portion of q'oya the day before the festival started, he whispered the names of the four apus and dropped three coca leaves on the ground. He then placed a pinch of the leaves in his mouth and gave me some to chew. I asked him about these regular daily rituals I had observed from Arizapana and others. Gregorio explained that the Inca and their descendants believe that before any human intervention in the natural world—be it plowing a field, harvesting q'oya, or weaving a bridge—you need to recite the names of the local apus, ask for their protection, and then feed them an offering. "Of the four apus, the Q'eswachaka is the most important, because it bridges the land and can speak to all of the apus," he said. "If you don't ask for the apus' protection, very bad things can happen."

"What kind of things?" I asked, as I struggled to tear the sharp skeins of q'oya with the curved scythe and bloodied my hands.

"Starvation, disease, pain, and punishment," he said, rather nonchalantly. "If you want to know more, you should talk to Balthazar Puma. He remembers everything."

Balthazar Puma is a 104-year-old Andean shaman who lives at the very top of the mountain. He also happens to be Josefina's grandfather. When I asked her how to get to Puma's house, she gave me the following directions: "Go up the mountain, cross the stream at the waterfall, go left when you see cows, pass the fox dens, and follow the canyon to the very top." After a 90-minute scramble, I was at 4,050 meters elevation and gasping for air. When I finally arrived at the centenarian's mud-brick home, I found him sitting outside on a pile of rocks, holding a wooden walking stick and silently looking out over the valley below. He wore a brown chullo hat under a gray sombrero that was ringed with dried white flowers. As I introduced myself, he told me to speak up, because a witch had put a spell on him 40 years ago and he's been largely deaf ever since. Over the next several hours, through a chasqui-like relay system in which I'd ask questions to the shaman's great-granddaughter in Spanish, who would lean over and lift the flap of his chullo cap up to holler the question into his good ear in Quechua, Puma recounted several historical details about the Q'eswachaka that may soon fade from memory. He recalled his great-great-grandmother telling him that her ancestors cut the bridge to escape from the advancing Spanish army during the 1780 Rebellion of Túpac Amaru II—the largest Indigenous-led uprising in colonial Spanish-American history. He also remembered that there used to be other suspension bridges spanning the canyon nearby that would fall down in the wet season, but never the Q'eswachaka. "This bridge has a certain power," Puma said, looking at me with glassy brown eyes that had seen a distant world. "We revere it, and we're scared of what can happen if we don't honor it."

The shaman also explained what could happen if men don't invoke the apus when building the bridge. He recalled the time as a young man when he and the other healers didn't perform the offering properly, and three days later a car accident killed three people. Then there was the time 75 years ago when a doctor who didn't believe in the apus helped cut the old bridge, lost his balance, and drowned in the river. About 20 years ago, an employee at the Ministry of Culture told the Andean healers that the offerings were unnecessary. During the bridge's construction, he fell into the Apurimac and died in a Cusco hospital. One year, Puma remembered that they didn't rebuild the bridge at all, and "hail destroyed most of the crops, animals died, and there was great hunger."

Puma also said that a short walk up the river from the Q'eswachaka, there was an even earlier relic of Inca engineering that existed until relatively recently: an *oroya*. In what was perhaps the most terrifying way to cross a river in the Inca Empire, oroyas were tiny, wobbly baskets suspended from a single grass-braided cable that spanned a gorge. To get from one side to the other, you had to pull yourself, arm over arm, across the canyon with a rope. Puma said he and many others used the oroya to cross when the Q'eswachaka was busy, and that some people were so afraid they closed their eyes as they pulled themselves across. It was only when a woman fell out of the basket to her death in the 1960s that they finally replaced the oroya with a steel bridge.

And therein lies the great irony of the Q'eswachaka. Not only is there no longer an empire that orders it to be built, but residents and livestock no longer need to brave its trembling plank to cross the Apurimac. The steel bridge is located just 200 meters away from the Q'eswachaka and was refortified in 2013. It's now strong and wide enough to support a large truck. But for reasons that I'd soon learn are hard to explain, many residents in these four communities still prefer to use the sagging, grass-woven platform.

On the first morning of the bridge's three-day renewal, there was a flurry of activity on the normally silent puna. Trucks full of men clutching their 70 meters of braided q'oya bounced down the dusty mountain road toward Huinchiri from the three surrounding communities. Women in brightly colored *jobona* jackets with infants strapped to their backs appeared from across the wrinkled highlands, some walking since nightfall. After offering rice, garbanzo beans, and anise to the apus with Gregorio and Josefina while their four-month-old alpaca Quya ("Queen" in Quechua) nuzzled against my jacket, I trekked down the steep mountain path from their home to take in a rite more than 500 years in the making.

By noon, each of the surrounding communities had gathered along Huinchiri's lone dirt road above the Apurimac. Some families had yet to finish making their 40 double-arms' length of rope, so while women sat on the hillsides busily braiding the last of their q'oya between their palms, an appointed *teñiente* from each village measured the coiled rope from those who had, crossing their names off a list if their share was suitable, or ordering them to add to it if it wasn't. Families poured cups of yellow Inca Kola for their neighbors, and the wafting smell of grilled guinea pig fanned across both sides of the river. As I wandered across the modern steel bridge from where one community was huddled to another, I asked villagers why they continued to rebuild the Q'eswachaka since the modern bridge's construction.

Serapio Diaz from Chaupibanda told me that building and crossing the bridge "brings me closer to my Inca ancestors." Sixto Huanca from Huinchiri said, "I can feel the bridge when I cross it." And Walter Oroche from Ccollana Quehue explained, "The Q'eswachaka is part of the Qhapaq Ñan, and by walking on it, we feel a connection with our forefathers, the apus, the mountains, the river, and the valley. We receive their energy." This all points to a greater truth that Jara Ugarte told me: just as the Inca believed the natural world is filled with spirits that people must revere, they believed the Qhapaq Ñan had its own spirit that people absorbed as they traveled along it. "Where parts of the Qhapaq Ñan are still preserved, I have heard testimonies from the local people that, when they walk on it, they are able to maintain a certain type of energy. They never tire, while on other roads, they do," he said. "The Inca Road is a living road."

In a way, this living road perfectly captures the strikingly different worldviews of the two empires who fatefully clashed here. The Inca navigated their way through a carefully balanced dance of duality, gauging whether each man-made act would be environmentally sustainable or disruptive, absorbing new cultures, and relying on a system of tension-built suspension bridges made by men pulling equally on both sides to connect their universe. The Spanish worldview was essentially the opposite: places were to be conquered, people converted, and lands connected through a system of arched compression bridges. It was a philosophy of force. How anything from this past universe managed to survive that force is a wonder, let alone something as awe-inspiring as the Q'eswachaka.

By the early afternoon, every household in the puna had finally completed its required quota of rope. When the teñientes read each family's name from a list, they would place an end of their pre-inspected rope under one of three large stones, and then run the other end 70 meters away, laying it on the dirt road in a straight line. It takes roughly 40 strands of rope to form a cord, but as Arizapana explained, since each family's rope may be a different width based on the thickness of their q'oya, there is no uniform number. Instead, the bridge master walked up and down the dirt road, examining each stack of rope, and instructing the teñientes to add or remove rope so that each cord was roughly the same size.

When Arizapana signaled his approval, some 50 men in each community picked up the 70-meter-long bundle and worked together to slowly twist it into a coiled cord from one end to the other. They then determined where the middle of the cord was, divided into two teams, and pulled against one another in a giant game of tug-of-war to tighten it. This took more than an hour and required the strength and coordination of every able-bodied man in the village—or in my case, any able-bodied outsider willing to help. Once the men tightened one cord into place, they used the 40-odd bundles of rope under the other two stones to make two more cords. These three cords would form one cable. Villagers braided the cords together like hair by crossing one side into the middle, stepping on it to tighten it, crossing the opposite end into the middle, and repeating this over and over. As the men took turns twisting and tugging, Arizapana examined every meter with his hands, telling the workers whether the cables were too thin or thick. In all, the Q'eswachaka has six cables—four for the base and two for the handrails—and like the cords, each cable should be roughly the same width. Since nothing has ever been written down, all Arizapana can do is rely on his experience and sense of touch to serve as a blueprint.

At 5:30 p.m., an army of men from Huinchiri hauled the final cable down a steep, twisting flight of steps leading to the stone abutment. As the sun dipped below the mountains and cast a shadow across the gaping canyon wall, I couldn't help but wonder how on earth the Inca ever conceived this project. Believing that you can weave enough grass to walk across a canyon is one thing, but it's mind-boggling to think how many trial and errors gone wrong it must have taken to land on a coordinated plan in which entire communities cut, braid, and pull q'oya into cables weighing nearly 450 kilograms and then hurl them across a canyon. I spotted Arizapana looking down at the rushing river from the abutment and started to say as much, but before I could, he said, "Today is just the first day. The real work starts tomorrow."

———

Cayetano Ccanahuiri Puma was the last man to leave the canyon at night and the first one to arrive the next morning. As the area's head Andean priest, he is the only person who can communicate directly with the apus, and during the Q'eswachaka's construction, he and his assistants keep a constant fire burning beside the stone abutment, fueling it with offerings to the spirits. "I ask the Earth to support the bridge and the water to accept its presence," he said, as Arizapana walked down the steps and placed three coca leaves in the fire. "If the apus receive the offerings happily, they will protect us. If they reject the offerings, then they may punish us. We have to get their permission to change the Q'eswachaka."

Unlike most years, Arizapana and his team wouldn't cut the old Q'eswachaka as they built the new one this year. Three weeks before I arrived, the Ministry of Culture had determined that the circular ring holds in the stone abutment where the cables are fastened needed to be repaired, and in order to solidify them, they needed to sever the old bridge earlier than normal. So, instead of passing the new cables across the old bridge from one abutment to another, as the workers normally do, this year Arizapana had to think of another way to span the gorge, and it involved his disciple, Eleuterio Ccallo Tapia.

For the first few years after Leonardo died, Victoriano would weave the Q'eswachaka from one end to the other by himself, and it would take him until nightfall. So, just as Leonardo and the other bridge masters before him had done, Victoriano appointed and trained a *chakaruwak* (assistant bridge builder) to help him when his two sons were barely walking, and that person was Ccallo Tapia. Ever since, Arizapana and Ccallo Tapia start weaving the bridge at opposite ends and meet in the middle every year. At 64, Ccallo Tapia is four years older than Arizapana, but he has to take his orders from the lone chakacamayoc. Still, he confided in me that he hopes to one day become the bridge master if Vidal or Yuri don't accept the role, and when you look into his eyes, there is a chilling fearlessness and determination that contrasts with Arizapana's vulnerable sensitivity.

After placing his coca leaves in the fire, Arizapana peered down over the edge of the canyon to make sure Ccallo Tapia had reached his assigned position on the far bank of the Apurimac. Arizapana then ordered a man on his side of the river to find a rock, tie a piece of braided q'oya around it, and hurl the rope across the Apurimac to Ccallo Tapia. When it reached him, he and the thrower slowly carried their sides of rope back up the canyon wall to the two opposite abutments. Workers on one abutment tied this small rope to the end of a thick cable, and with Arizapana's command, 15 men on the far abutment pulled it little by little across the river until it spanned the gorge. By early afternoon, the four massive cables forming the walkway of the Q'eswachaka dangled over the Apurimac. Now, they just had to fasten them into place, which I soon learned was backbreaking work.

In order for the Q'eswachaka to remain taut and support weight, each of its 450-kilogram cables has to be twisted into a massive knot around one of six thick, circular ring holds chiseled into the floor of the stone abutment. Aside from Arizapana's and Ccallo Tapia's roles, the *tornilleros* responsible for this task have the most important job in the bridge's construction, and as one of the head tornilleros, Gregorio, told me, "It requires a lot of sweat." As the tornilleros assumed their positions under the ring holds, Arizapana stood at the edge of the abutment, facing his crew like a captain at the bow of a ship. He then screamed out, "*Uno, dos, tres . . . Tira! Tira! Tira!*" With each command, a team of 75 men in matching white sombreros and wool jackets lining the steps leading down to the abutment thrust their bodies backward in unison, pulling the cable so hard veins popped from their temples. Arizapana repeated this order dozens of times for each cable until his voice was hoarse. With each pull, the tornilleros fought to twist the cable little by little around each ring hold, and only when it had been stretched as tightly as it could go did the bridge master move on to the next cable. However, it soon became clear there was a big problem.

Each of the four communities is responsible for part of the bridge, but as the tornilleros struggled hour after hour to secure the cable made by the village of Ccollana Quehue, they realized that each of its three cords was too thick to tie around the ring hold. Arizapana shouted this news over to Ccallo Tapia on the opposite abutment, and he came over to examine the problem. "Eleuterio was responsible for that cable. It's the one that Victoriano put him in charge of," Gregorio whispered to me, dripping sweat and looking worried. "Do you see the fire? When we offer eggs to the apus [and place them in the flames], they're supposed to explode, but this year they didn't. This is not good." Tired and defeated, the men staggered up the staircase toward the road, promising Arizapana that after a long night's rest, they would return bright and early the next day to finish the job—gods willing.

By 8:30 in the morning, the rested workers began taking their positions on the abutments. Soon after, they passed the two handrail cables across the canyon and lifted them into worn grooves carved into the stone. The four communities were expecting their bridge to be renewed by dusk, and there was a palpable tension in the biting Andean air. But as Arizapana swallowed a gulp of fermented corn *chicha* and surveyed the team's progress, he flashed a cautious smile. "Everybody is working together," he said. "We can do this." He then broke off a shoot from a pine tree and told a group of men that they needed to collect 30 branches from the nearby bushes, each the exact length as his. He and Ccallo Tapia would tie them to the bridge's base as they wove, serving as crossbeams to stabilize the floor.

To pull Ccollana Quehue's thick cable into place, Arizapana ordered two dozen reinforcements who had been working on the opposite side of the river to come to his side, and as each deafening "Tira!" command echoed off the canyon, 100 men were now pulling with all their weight. When the Andean priest's two assistants placed a bloody sheep's heart in the crackling fire several hours later, it seemed like the apus were finally starting to accept the new bridge's presence: the tornilleros somehow managed to fasten the oversized cable into the circular bolt, and with the last gasps of his raspy voice, Arizapana summoned the team's remaining strength to level the four cables so they formed an even walkway.

With the handrails and base finally in position, all that was left was for the bridge master and his disciple to suspend themselves over the gorge. Ccallo Tapia was first to step off the abutment into the void. He gingerly lowered himself onto the four cables on the far side of the river and began tying a series of smaller ropes from the handrails to the outside cables to enclose his side of the bridge. Then it was Arizapana's turn. Amid the sea of sombrero-clad workers, I spotted a man wearing Arizapana's yellow-and-red chullo. He slowly stepped off the ledge, lowered himself onto the cables, and then quickly looked back toward land. But it wasn't Victoriano; it was his son Yuri.

Days earlier, Victoriano had told me that, just as his father had done with him, he would only anoint Yuri or Vidal when they had proven themselves. This was Yuri's chance. While Ccallo Tapia tied, balanced, and shuffled forward with the fluidity of a tightrope walker, Yuri struggled to reach the ropes above his head, freezing up each time the cables shivered below him. After a few minutes, several tornilleros looked back at Arizapana, who was watching quietly from the back of the abutment. The bridge master then slid on his chullo, slung a golden coil of rope over each shoulder, and walked toward the edge of the cliff. Without saying a word, he had determined that his son had had enough. Yuri's time may come, but it wouldn't be this year.

There's something truly singular about witnessing someone do something that nearly nobody else in the world knows how to do. It's like watching a secret. In one of our first conversations, I had asked Arizapana what goes through his mind when he's up there, dangling precariously seven stories over the Apurimac. After a deep breath, he said, "I'm completely focused, completely calm. I don't think about my father, or my ancestors, or the river. My duty is to make the bridge perfectly." Watching him work, I understood what he meant. There is no room for improvisation or sentimentality; it's an ancient dance that rushes through the bridge master's hands until it's second nature: reach, tie, bend, pass, fasten, repeat. This choreography is his birthright, his identity, but it doesn't belong to him. Just as every chakacamayoc before him, Victoriano's calling is to serve the community. When you're one blade of grass bound to thousands of others, you're never truly alone. Perhaps that's why the lone bridge master carries on.

It took the two weavers 10 minutes to each move a meter, and with every few scoots forward, Arizapana and Ccallo Tapia tied a wooden crossbeam to the base of the walkway. The farther they got from the edge of the stone abutments, the more the bridge swayed. No one dared to speak, and the only noise was the rush of river below. Each movement that Arizapana and Ccallo Tapia made vibrated through the cables and was felt by the other on the opposite side in perfect duality. When the wind ripped through the canyon and caused the cables to careen back and forth, the weavers even dropped their ropes and struggled to regain their balance in unison. Just as I started to look away, afraid of what I might soon see, Arizapana turned toward the nearby cliff where I was watching with the other villagers, locked eyes with me, and smiled. He lives for this.

Two hours after the weavers started, their legs were nearly touching in the center of the bridge. Before the sun receded behind the mountains, it cast Arizapana's and Ccallo Tapia's shadows on the canyon wall—two silhouettes slowly dancing toward each other under wobbling strings, like life-sized puppets. When Arizapana laid the final crossbeam, Ccallo Tapia helped him up to his feet. The bridge master steadied himself, looked up toward the heavens, and screamed, *"Hailli Huinchiri! Hailli Quehue!"* (Long live Huinchiri! Long live Quehue!), as the crowd of hushed spectators lining both sides of the canyon echoed each cry. Men from Choccayhua soon unfurled a wooden walkway made with twigs and bound with strips of cowhide across the length of the bridge's base, so that no toes or hooves could slip through the walkway. With this, the Q'eswachaka was finally complete. Women descended from the dirt road to find their partners below, and workers and their families began crossing their new bridge together.

Stars soon lit up the night sky, and amid the revelry, I spotted Victoriano standing quietly off to the side with Yuri. His hands were covered in scars. After two hours of balancing on the braided cables, he said he could barely move his legs. I couldn't help but wonder how many more years the bridge master had left in him, and I suddenly found myself overwhelmed by his sacrifice. Watching him and Ccallo Tapia risk their lives to carry on a tradition that bridges centuries, empires, and communities was one of the most stunning things I'd ever witnessed, and I told him that. When I did, he looked down, smiling somewhat sheepishly, and then gazed back up to search for someone through the darkness. Days earlier, he had told me that he'd hoped his oldest son, Vidal, would come back to Huinchiri during the bridge's renovation, and as he scanned the crowd, I saw a hint of sadness in his eyes. When Victoriano's gaze returned to mine, I asked Yuri how he felt watching his father weave the Q'eswachaka. Yuri put his arm around Victoriano and said, "I love my father. I can only hope to be the man and the chakacamayoc he is one day." I had never seen the bridge master get emotional before, but in an instant, his face broke. Arizapana's calling may be to serve the community, but I knew that the most important things left in his life are his sons and the bridge he looks after like a son.

I was the last person that night to cross the Q'eswachaka. By the time I stepped off the stone abutment, it was so black that I couldn't see the Apurimac; I just heard it, an invisible ghost rushing like wind below. I clenched the thick handrails with both hands for support and stepped onto the undulating, twig-lined path, using the glow of the moon to guide each of my cautious steps. Truth be told, I found the whole thing utterly terrifying. Not only does the bridge rock back and forth in the breeze, but the weight of each step causes the walkway to dip down and then swell back up like a wave. It felt like trying to tightrope atop a waterbed. The only thing keeping me from turning back was the knowledge that Arizapana and his Inca ancestors had been safely spanning the earth and heavens for hundreds of years.

The day after the bridge's completion each year, thousands of people from across the puna gather on Huinchiri's hillside to dance, socialize, and celebrate the renewal of the Q'eswachaka, and life itself. As I slowly shuffled across the bridge from one side to the other that night, I knew I'd probably never see Arizapana again. Every beginning in the Andes has an end, every force an opposing force. The man who brings these communities together lives all alone. There is no celebration without him, yet he can no longer bear parties. Amid the speeches, toasts, and festivities the following day, I never did find the bridge master. But I like to think that he was back in his adobe home, laughing with Yuri, waiting for Vidal, and hoping his scars would heal in time to weave the Q'eswachaka one more year.

4

The World's Rarest Pasta

We are Spaniards, Africans, Phoenicians, Carthaginians, Romans, Arabs,
Pisans, Byzantines, Piedmontese . . . We are an ancient land of long silences,
of wide and pure horizons, of dark plants, of mountains burned
by the sun and by revenge. We are Sardinians.
—GRAZIA DELEDDA, "NOI SIAMO SARDI"

The rocky path revealed itself with each new step. Brown earth deepened to night beyond the reach of our flashlights, swallowing us in a blackness so dense it seemed to hold us in place. It was 4:00 A.M. and chilly. Four hours earlier, we had shuffled out of a whitewashed church in a mountaintop town, 400 pilgrims quietly drifting through the darkness in search of the light. But after 15 kilometers, we weren't even halfway, and there was no clear sense of dark and light, earth and sky, or where we were—only shadows, silence, and an inescapable sense of Sardinia everywhere.

The murky silhouettes of stripped cork trees and splayed prickly pears lined the shepherds' trail. Gnarled juniper trees punished by centuries of mistral wind leaned sideways out of granite boulders. The air was kissed with the breath of wild fennel and myrtle growing from the Mediterranean maquis. Flowering asphodel plants stood like candlesticks, their white petals inflaming the night. Somewhere to my right, the pealing of sheep bells suggested we were being watched. I couldn't see the mountains, but I could feel them all around me, jagged limestone peaks standing guard over the twisting maze of inky chasms below. The cracked road had lost its asphalt hours ago and we navigated in hushed solitude, relying on the sound of our steps to orient us. The rasp of gravel gave way to a pattering of dirt, the dirt path dipped into the sloshing of a cold stream, and the trail then tilted sharply until we were trudging up a crumbling hillside. At the end of another switchback, I peered over my shoulder and took in the scale of our migration. We were a tiny constellation of flares moving steadily against an ocean of stars.

Just then, a hand reached out and grabbed me. It was Paolo Ladu, a 60-year-old who has plodded this trail since he was a 13-year-old boy. "I've never seen it like this," he said, clenching my shoulder for support. Several months earlier, a cyclone had ripped through the valley, dumping an avalanche of rocks and deadfall down the ridge we were scaling. The trek soon became a thrashing, branch-snapping scramble, but at least I had on shoes. Ladu winced in pain as he scissored up the mountainside, staggering barefoot from rock to root, just as he's done twice a year for the past 47 years. Those who complete this torturous trek are rewarded with a bowl of pasta—but not just any pasta. And as I scrabbled for traction on the loose knuckles of scree, the only thing pulling me forward was the promise that Ladu was leading me toward it.

"We have to pass through the darkness to receive grace," Ladu said, catching his breath. "That's what *su filindeu* is for us, grace."

Away from its cerulean seas, Sardinia's craggy interior is a rugged patchwork of deep folds and impenetrable massifs that shelter some of Europe's oldest traditions. Residents here still speak Sardo, the closest living form of Latin. Grandmothers gaze warily at outsiders from under black veils. And on the second floor of a modest apartment building in the provincial capital of Nuoro, a slight 69-year-old woman named Paola Abraini wakes up every day at 7:00 A.M., slips on an apron, and begins making su filindeu—the rarest pasta in the world. Su filindeu means "the threads of God," and there are only three other women on the planet who know how to make it: Abraini's two nieces and her sister-in-law, each of whom lives in this remote town tucked between the soaring peak of Monte Ortobene and the serrated teeth of Monte Corrasi. Su filindeu is so difficult and time-consuming to prepare that for hundreds of years, the only way you could eat the sacred dish was to complete a 33-kilometer overnight pilgrimage from Nuoro to a lonely rural sanctuary outside the village of Lula for the biannual Feast of San Francesco, which is what I had come to do.

No one can remember how or why the women in Nuoro started preparing su filindeu, but for more than 300 years, the recipe and technique have only been passed down through the women in Abraini's family—each of whom has guarded it tightly before teaching it to her daughters. But after an invitation to Abraini's home, I suddenly found myself in her kitchen, watching her transform flour into filindeu. I wasn't her first guest, though. A few years earlier, a team of engineers from Barilla, the world's most famous pasta company, had come to see if they could reproduce Abraini's technique with a machine. They couldn't. After hearing rumors about a secret Sardinian pasta, Carlo Petrini, the founder of Slow Food International, knocked on Abraini's door next. Then, celebrity chef Jamie Oliver stopped by to ask her if she could teach him how to make the dish. After failing for two hours, he threw his hands up and said, "I've been making pasta for 20 years and I've never seen anything like this . . . It's just ridiculously beautiful. It's one of the most beautiful things I've ever seen."

"Many people say that I have a secret I don't want to reveal," Abraini told me with a smile, as she leaned over her kitchen table. "But the secret is right in front of you. It's in my hands."

Su filindeu is made by pulling and folding semolina dough into 256 perfectly even strands with the tips of your fingers, and then stretching the needle-thin wires diagonally across a large circular frame in an intricate three-layer pattern. In its completed state, each frame becomes a latticework of razor-thin pasta threads so delicate and precise, so intricately interwoven, that it resembles stitched lace. Though the dish is believed to predate the biannual Feast of San Francesco (the most important events of the year in Nuoro), in the past few centuries, it has become so connected with the May and October feasts that for many Sardinians, su filindeu *is* San Francesco himself.

"Su filindeu is more than a food, it's a sacred host," said Antonio Coseddu, the priest who oversees the feast and blesses the filindeu that is offered to pilgrims in a thick soup of mutton broth and fresh pecorino.

"Just as you can't have a mass without communion, you can't have the Feast of Saint Francesco without su filindeu." When I arrived, the start of the May feast was three days away and Abraini had just finished making 100 kilograms of the stuff. To do so, she worked for five hours every day for two straight months, but it still wasn't enough filindeu to feed the 6,000 pilgrims from throughout Sardinia expected to descend on the sanctuary during the nine-day novena. So Abraini's two nieces were busily making another 100 kilograms of it a short walk away.

For all its astonishing complexity, su filindeu is decidedly simple. "There are only three ingredients: semolina wheat, water, and salt," Abraini said, vigorously kneading the dough back and forth on her small kitchen table. "But since everything is done by hand, the most important ingredient is elbow grease." With her chestnut-colored hair pulled back in a ponytail and a white-and-blue apron covering her collared t-shirt and gray ankle-length dress, Abraini patiently explained how she works the semolina flour thoroughly until it reaches a consistency reminiscent of modeling clay. She then divides the dough into smaller sections and continues working it into a rolled cylindrical shape. Then comes the hardest part, a process she calls "understanding the dough with your hands." When she feels that the dough needs to be more elastic, she dips her fingertips into a bowl of salt water. When it needs more moisture, she dips them into a separate bowl of regular water. As with so many handmade wonders, the only "secret" is in the sense of touch, an invisible instinct born from thousands of repetitions until it courses through her veins like memory. "It can take years to understand," she beamed. "It's like a game with your hands. But once you achieve it, then the magic happens."

When the semolina reached just the right consistency, Abraini picked up the cylindrical strand to stretch and fold the dough, doubling it as she pressed the heads of the filindeu into her palms like putty. She then pulled the dangling U-shaped dough down in a sweeping motion, bringing the stretched tips back up to her palm while somehow keeping the delicate threads intact. She repeated this sequence in a fluid motion eight times, and with each sweeping pull, the strands became thinner and thinner. One roll became two strands; two strands became four strips; four strips became eight threads. After eight sequences, she was left with 256 even threads, each about half as wide as angel-hair pasta. She then carefully laid the edible embroidery on a circular base, one layer on top of another to form a cross, trimming any excess from the ends with her fingers before repeating the process over and over.

After Abraini had formed three diagonal layers atop the base, I followed her past the knee-high bags of semolina in her kitchen out to her balcony, where she carefully laid the circular sheet on a table to dry in the Sardinian sun. She explained that each sheet needs to dry for at least three to four hours in the sunlight, which is why she starts making her dough early in the morning. After several hours, the layers had hardened into a delicate tapestry of white threads resembling spun silk. Abraini then broke the circular sheets into crude strips and packed them into boxes. A team of cooks appointed by the prior of the feast would place the shattered filindeu in a cauldron of boiling sheep's broth seasoned with onions, dried tomatoes, celery, carrots, salt, and generous portions of fresh pecorino to offer the pilgrims once they arrived at the sanctuary.

"Filindeu is something that exists since the dawn of time. It's something that very few of us know how to make, very few of us in the world. You'll never find a pasta anywhere else quite like it," Abraini said, her dark eyes dancing with delight. "You know, for me it's a blessing just to be able to make su filindeu. I've been in love with it since the first time I ever saw it, and I love it more each day."

But after more than 300 years in the same matrilineal family tree, these threads of God may need a miracle to survive for future generations. Only one of Abraini's two daughters knows the basic technique to make it, and she lacks the passion and patience of her mother. Neither of Abraini's daughters have daughters of their own. The three other women in Abraini's family who still carry on the tradition are now in their fifties, sixties, and seventies, respectively, and have yet to find willing successors among their own children.

"This is one of the most at-risk foods of becoming extinct, in large part because it's one of the most difficult pastas to make that exists," said Raffaella Ponzio, head coordinator of Slow Food International's Ark of Taste, an initiative that aims to classify and preserve the world's most endangered culinary traditions by "collecting small-scale quality productions that belong to the cultures, history, and traditions of the entire planet."[1] To date, the project has cataloged more than 6,300 listed items, which range from pulled *çekme* pasta made from a single mill in Foça, Turkey; to toasted *katta* strands prepared by women in Timbuktu who rub the tiny wheat-flour threads through their fingers; to Chinese *Tu zha* rice noodles, which were conceived during the Ming Dynasty and can take 20 days to make. Yet, no other pasta on Earth is made by as few producers as su filindeu—making it both the world's rarest and most endangered pasta. "Conserving su filindeu isn't just a question of a culinary artform, but also a piece of cultural identity," Ponzio said.

When you mention su filindeu to most Sardinians, a sort of quiet reverence comes over them. "This dish is so strange, so intricate, so beautiful that it's not really a pasta," said Giovanni Fancello, a local journalist and the author of several books on Sardinian food. "A pasta is something you eat regularly; this is something older and deeper, something that reminds us who we are." In fact, when you look at the long and tangled history of Sardinia and realize how much its character is bound to its pastoral roots, you realize that su filindeu isn't just the threads that hold a festival together but a symbol of Sardinia itself. And when you consider what this pasta represents and how many people it touches, what's at stake with its survival is the rugged character and unflinching spirit of an entire island.

After struggling to make sense of Sardinia during a three-day jaunt aboard a steam train that pierced its mountainous spine in 1921, D. H. Lawrence wrote that the island was "outside the circuit of civilization," a land "lost between Europe and Africa and belonging to nowhere."[2] Set 178 kilometers from the nearest mainland and slightly closer to Tunisia than Italy, no other island is as marooned in the Mediterranean as Sardinia—a fact that has historically shaped its unique character and intrigued me from the first moment I ever spotted it on a map.

When I was five years old, my family moved to a house in Maryland next door to where a Neapolitan woman in her fifties lived named Maria. She had a soft spot for young children, and I adored the way she talked, so I started inviting myself over to her small den to learn Italian. The language lessons soon morphed into cultural immersions, and I'd regularly walk back home splotched with tomato sauce stains. One day when I was eight years old, Maria showed me a drawing of Italy. It was filled with little pictures representing each of Italy's 20 regions: a pizza for Calabria, the Colosseum for Lazio, a wineglass for Tuscany. But there was one large place on the map, almost off the page, that was left blank.

"What's there?" I asked her, pointing to the unmarked, footprint-shaped island adrift in a sea of blue.

"I don't know," Maria said. "Sheep?" Even to Italians, it was a far-flung question mark.

I continued showing up at Maria's house every week until I went to college. I majored in Italian, studied sociolinguistics in Siena, and worked as a tour guide leading university students up and down the country after I graduated. Before too long, I had been to every Italian region except one—the big island that wasn't Sicily, the far-flung question mark that time and cartographers seemed to have forgotten. So I packed my journal, took a ferry to Sardinia, and ended up staying for several years to write a column about the island for a Roman magazine and a guidebook for a British publisher. I've been coming back ever since, and it turns out Maria was right: there are a lot of sheep in Sardinia (two for each of the 1.65 million residents on the Mediterranean's second-largest island, to be exact).

It doesn't take long to realize there is something undeniably distant and different about Sardinia. It's the only region in Italy whose residents are recognized as an ethnically distinct people from the rest of the country by constitutional law. It's an autonomous region with its own president, government, and official language. Residents identify themselves as Sardinian first and Italian second, and refer to the mainland as "*il continente*" (the continent). It's a place that has stood in the very center of Western civilization for millennia, yet just far enough away to remember things that the rest of the world has forgotten.

As with many things in Sardinia, Sardinia itself is very old. Geologically, it predates Italy and is one of the most ancient pieces of land in Europe, lending it a somewhat mystical, almost Tolkien-esque feel. The island is dotted with more than 2,000 Neolithic rock-carved chambers called *do-*

mus de janas (fairy houses); 800 megalithic graves known as *tombe dei giganti* (giants' tombs); and more than 7,000 massive stone *nuraghi* towers built between 1600 and 1000 BC by one of the world's most advanced, if mysterious, Bronze Age societies: the Nuragic civilization. These truncated fortresses aren't found anywhere else on Earth, and while their origin and purpose still remain largely unknown, most archaeologists think they were originally built as territorial markers between clans. By climbing one, you can almost always see another, leading experts to believe they formed an ingenious island-wide communication chain that birthed a nascent Sardinian identity. Today, these prehistoric castles are still so common throughout the island that they've come to symbolize Sardinia as much as its food, the embroidered veils and pleated-skirt costumes that are distinct to each village, and the Sardo language.[3]

By about 1000 BC, the nuraghi builders used the towers to relay an urgent warning across the island: foreign ships were approaching—a trend that has continued ever since. Sardinia's strategic position at the crossroads of Middle Eastern, African, and European powers has lured more than a dozen invaders to drop anchor in its Evian-clear bays, turning the island's coast into a cultural jigsaw puzzle. From 2007 to 2009, I lived in Cagliari, Sardinia's capital, a city that effectively tells the island's turbulent history. It was founded in 814 BC and is one of the oldest continuously inhabited places in Italy: a Phoenician settlement expanded by the Carthaginians boasting a Roman amphitheater, domed Byzantine churches that were sacked by Arab pirates, a fortified Pisan wall, Spanish watchtowers, and Neoclassical palaces built by the Dukes of Savoy. After all that, it finally fell under Italian control. As a result, while Sardinia may be best known for its Caribbean-blue beaches, thousands of years of foreign raids and rulers have led Sardinians themselves to traditionally turn their backs to the sea, fearful of those coming to exploit them. Even today, an ancient proverb still echoes across the island: *"Furat chi beit dae su mare"* (He who comes from the sea comes to rob).

Instead, the history of Sardinia is one of defiance against a constant tide of invaders. As wave after wave of conquerors washed up on their white-sand beaches, Sardinians managed to preserve their identity and retain a resolutely independent spirit by seeking refuge in the island's unyielding interior, a stark landscape of granite cliffs, hidden karsts, and boulder-strewn canyons. For hundreds of years, as Punic and Roman forces pushed farther and farther inland, the descendants of the Nuragic civilization used their castles' mazelike corridors to conduct guerilla assaults against the encroaching enemies. As a result, despite roughly 700 years of coastal domination, the Romans were never able to conquer or even subdue Sardinia's craggy core. After enduring 16 rebellions from the island's cunning mountain-dwelling warriors, the Roman orator Cicero dubbed the area *"Barbaria"* after the barbarian-like ferocity of its "rough wool-cloaked" people, and the Romans retreated.[4] Nearly 2,000 years later, the name has stuck as Barbagia, and the island's defiant character still springs from this rugged and rebellious expanse of isolated villages hemmed in by the peaks of the Gennargentu and Supramonte mountains. In many ways, the Barbagia is Sardinia's spiritual heart, and Nuoro is its geographic and cultural center. The region's imposing massifs have served as a natural bastion, effectively creating an island within an island that preserved Sardinia's ancient indigenous rites.

In the town of Desulo, people worshiped wood and stone until the Middle Ages. Until the 1950s, many villages had an elderly witchlike woman known as the *agabbadòra* (from the Sardo command *"accabbadda!"* meaning "finish it!") who was called to a person's deathbed to put them out of their misery by striking them in the head with a hammer. Across the Barbagia, I've witnessed wool-cloaked shepherds huddled tightly in a circle, their heads down and faces lit by the flames of a bonfire as they solemnly chanted *cantu a tenòre*—a series of haunting, pastoral poems sung in a deep and guttural tone, passed down from a time when all men knew were the four sounds each singer imitates: the bleating of sheep, the lowing of cattle, the sound of the wind, and the call of the shepherd. And a short drive south of Nuoro in the town of Mamoiada, I've watched as men transform into monsters each January, donning menacing jet-black masks, dark sheepskin tunics, and up to 30 kilograms of cowbells strapped to their backs. At night, they slowly drag their hunched frames forward through the streets before breaking into a series of synchronized convulsions, causing their copper bells to clang in a thunderous chorus.

These creatures are known as *mamuthones*. They've been appearing each winter for so long that no one knows what the word means or where this tradition comes from, but many Sardinians feel it harks back to some sort of prehistoric exorcism.[5]

In a way, Sardinia's long-lost Nuragic civilization never fully disappeared. The Barbagia is where the most conservative form of Sardo is still spoken, which is peppered with hundreds of words that come from the ancient nuraghi builders. Centuries of retreating inland and inward have also left the island with one of the most genetically isolated populations in Europe, and nearly 80 percent of modern Sardinians are directly related to the island's original Neolithic inhabitants.[6] People in these mountainous folds also live longer than almost anywhere else. Sardinia boasts nearly 10 times more centenarians per capita than the US, and it was the first of only five global Blue Zone regions (places "where people live the longest and are the healthiest") to be identified.[7]

Fittingly on an island with an old soul, Sardinians have long memories. Centuries of unwelcome guests treating them like second-class citizens have forced Sardinians to rely on themselves for survival, producing an introspective culture that is bound to the land and wary of outsiders. People here have never forgotten how the Romans enslaved so many coastal Sardinians that the term "*Sardi venales*" (Sardinians for sale) became a common Latin expression to mean anything cheap and worthless across the empire.[8] Or how the Aragonese imposed an island-wide system of feudalism. But most of all, many Sardinians have never forgiven their current landlords for continuing to exploit the island like a colony.

"This Italy, it has been the worst rulers we've ever had," said Sardinian journalist and documentary filmmaker Antonio Sanna, as we sat in Nuoro's Piazza Satta. He recalled how Piedmontese lumberjacks stripped the island of its forests to build mainland Italy's railroads and fuel northern Italy's industrial revolution in the 18th and 19th centuries. In the 20th century, the Italian government littered Sardinia with a series of NATO military bases and petrochemical plants that funnel most of their profits off the island. The lavish Costa Smeralda, which was developed by the Aga Khan on the island's northeastern coast in 1962 as a manicured paradise for European and Arabic multimillionaires, may have put Sardinia on the map, but it has so little to do with Sardinia that it's known locally as *La Costa Rubata* (The Stolen Coast).[9]

This explains why, when you travel anywhere on the island today, you'll inevitably see the island's Quattro Mori "national" flag hanging proudly from apartments and *"Sardigna non est Italia"* tags graffitied on walls, proclaiming, "Sardinia isn't Italy." In the Barbagia, this independent streak is even more stark, and as you drive from one town to the next, you're greeted with two street signs: one with the town's name in Italian, and another written in Sardo. In every village, without fail, those written in Sardo will be pristine, while those in Italian will be ripped through by fist-sized shotgun blasts.

"This is a government that has suppressed the story of the Nuragic civilization, denied the Sardinian language, and taken our land," Sanna said. "The Festival of San Francesco and su filindeu is a resistance against that flattening of our traditional culture by outside forces."

For centuries, personal and pastoral life in central Sardinia was dictated by a series of unwritten rules based on dignity, honor, and revenge known as the *codice barbaricino* (Code of the Barbagia) whose principle decree was *"sangue chiama sangue"* (blood calls for blood).[10] In this Wild West world, struggling shepherds would often steal sheep from rival villages but never touch those from their own towns, creating an endless loop of banditry and vendettas that foreign-ruling governments tried in vain to curb by making it illegal for Sardinians to grow beards, so that thieves could always be seen. But by the 1800s, banditry in the Barbagia transformed from personal to political, as rifle-wielding shepherds began kidnapping wealthy foreign landowners, keeping them hidden deep in the Barbagia's mountainous caves for months at a time until ransoms were met—a practice that continued until the 1990s. Far from being viewed as criminals, the bandits of the Barbagia have always been revered within Sardinia as noble guardians of the island's historic struggle against invaders, ransacking the wealthy to help the less fortunate and defying the Roman government just as their ancestors defied the Roman Empire. The threads of God pay homage to this very idea.

"The Feast of San Francesco honors a Nuorese bandit from the early

1800s who was accused of murder for a crime he didn't commit," Abraini told me, as she finished the last of her six circular sheets of filindeu for the day. She then hung up her apron with the words SU FILINDEU ANCIENT PASTA FROM THE BARBAGIA stitched in Italian, poured us each an espresso, and draped a plastic mat over the table, turning her pasta laboratory back into her kitchen. "This bandit hid out in different caves, and he invoked San Francesco, saying, 'If you can give me the grace to set me free, I will take my ox-pulled cart, and where the oxen stop, I will build a church in your honor." The bandit was freed, and as legend has it, he loaded up his wagon, set off from a church in Nuoro, and wandered through Sardinia's wild, silent interior. After 33 kilometers, he arrived at a dramatic landscape of limestone karsts and white gorges that Sardinia's official tourism website describes as "Middle Earth."

"And do you know why the bulls stopped where they did, at the foot of Monte Albo?" Paola's husband, Tonino, asked me at the kitchen table.

"How come?" I asked.

"Probably because they were tired of walking," he said, chuckling.

"Oh, stop!" Paola said, playfully hitting Tonino on the arm. "Over the years, San Francesco has become the saint of bandits here. They even say that when there's a bandit on the run, the authorities would find him in the sanctuary of San Francesco, and they wouldn't touch him because it was a sacred place."

The domed sanctuary of San Francesco is essentially an isolated ghost village. Quiet all year long, it only awakens when families from the Barbagia come together during the biannual nine-day feast to sing traditional songs, perform dances, have poetry competitions, and then sleep in the small white cottages (*cumbessias*) surrounding the rural church. The practice of Sardinian families gathering and sleeping in sacred places goes back to Nuragic times, and then as now, the highlight of these cultural and spiritual revivals has always been the communal meal.

While the Code of the Barbagia is governed by a harsh law of banditry and vendettas, it is balanced by a generous system of making and sharing food within the community (*imbiatu*). According to Cosimo Zene, a Sardinian anthropologist at SOAS University of London and the author of the research paper *S'Imbiatu: Gift and Community in Central Sardinia*, banditry may tear Sardinian families apart, but these culinary gatherings pull Sardinian society back together.[11] One of the most resounding examples of this is the Feast of San Francesco. Not only do shepherds from throughout the Barbagia donate their sheep to supply the pecorino and *su zurrette* (a type of Sardinian haggis) that accompanies the filindeu at the feast, but different communities also provide the semolina dough to make the filindeu itself.

"With the meal, people still form alliances together, reaffirm friendships, and strengthen social ties," Zene said. "In this way, the threads of God connect us as a community, as something we choose to share. It's a blessing, a communion, and also a vow—a promise to honor these symbolic codes of vendettas and strength, but also to feed each other with gifts and, in this way, to survive. If that were to ever vanish, the character, the soul of the Barbagia would be lost."

And so, for the past 200 years, every May 1 and October 4, Sardinians from all over the island with long memories come to Nuoro. The pilgrims move quietly through the darkness, past two hollowed-out fairy houses, several crumbling nuraghi, and one mammoth giant's tomb toward a ghost village. They retrace the steps of a runaway bandit they never knew, honor an ancient code that binds them, and receive a breathtaking grace to remember it all.

The world may have never known about su filindeu were it not for Sardinia's most famous writer, Grazia Deledda. A diminutive five-foot-tall woman who described herself as "bold and brave like a giant,"[12] Deledda was the first (and so far only) Italian woman to win the Nobel Prize for literature, doing so in 1926. She spent her first 29 years in Nuoro, a place she called "a Bronze Age village," where "women with eyes like Egyptians, either wrapped in their rich and thick traditional costumes or poorly dressed, carry baskets and jars on their heads."[13] Like most girls in Nuoro, her family only spoke Sardo at home, and after completing four years of elementary school, she took private lessons to learn Italian. Deledda was only allowed to leave her family's house to go to mass or wander the countryside, and she didn't see the ocean until she rode a horse to the top of Monte Bardia as a teenager, where she finally glimpsed the Mediterranean in the distance. Instead, she spent hours gazing out her bedroom window, watching the light dance across the holm oaks and towering peaks of the Ortobene and Gennargentu mountains. Her family home served as a refuge for weary travelers arriving on horseback, and from a young age, she listened to men speak of tragedy, misfortune, and age-old feuds. Against her parents' wishes, she began publishing short stories in literary magazines in her adopted Italian language at the age of 15, filling the pages with gusts of savage beauty, biblical simplicity, and the profound isolation and mystical beliefs of the Barbagia that would mark her career. When she learned she'd won the Nobel Prize for writing about "her native island with depth and sympathy," the gray-haired 51-year-old simply said, "*Già*!" (Already!) and continued working at her desk. And in what remains the shortest Nobel acceptance speech on record, Deledda thanked "the shepherds of Sardinia" and then rushed home to feed her pet crow, Checca.

Deledda's breakthrough success came in 1903 with the novel *Elias Portolu*, the story of a Nuorese shepherd who had just been released from prison in the days leading up to the Feast of San Francesco. After invoking the saint while in jail, Portolu vowed to say a prayer at the sanctuary outside of Lula upon completing the pilgrimage. It is here, at the whitewashed church surrounded by cottages, that the story's central scene unfolds. After copious amounts of wine and filindeu, Elias confronts Maddalena, the girl he had fallen hopelessly, desperately in love with.

Like Elias and Maddalena, Tonino had already fallen for Paola by the time he saw her at the Feast of San Francesco in 1969. "She was always smiling," Tonino said, looking across the table at Paola. "She was such a beautiful girl. She still is." But there was a problem: Paola was from Santu Predu, Nuoro's hilltop neighborhood where Deledda grew up, which was traditionally populated by shepherds. Tonino was from Seuna, the less wealthy neighborhood of farmers that tumbles down the mountainous crater below. Today, older *Nuoresi* still remember a time when the two rivaling groups would meet on the cobbled Corso Garibaldi that connects the two districts, and how the shepherds used to hurl stones at the farmers below. Thus, like Elias's love for Maddalena in the book, Tonino's love for

Paola was forbidden. Yet, walking for eight hours overnight without sleeping has a way of emboldening a man, and by the time 21-year-old Tonino finally arrived at the rural sanctuary, he had only one thought. "When the pilgrims first arrive, they go into the cumbessias where women wash their feet," Tonino said, with a hint of mischief showing under his thick, gray mustache. "I knew Paola would be there, and I made sure she was the one who washed mine." And so, as the purplish blaze of dawn broke against the thatched roof of a cottage on the side of a mountain, 16-year-old Paola grabbed a bucket of salt water heated by flames from crackling juniper logs and cared for the tired pilgrim. "I fell in love with him," she said, still beaming 53 years later. "He was kind and elegant and he had a lovely smile. Plus, knowing that he was the son of Rosaria made me fall in love with him even more."

Rosaria Selis was the only woman in Nuoro who knew how to make su filindeu. Today, the few women capable of making it all learned the technique from her or her daughters. When Paolo and Tonino started dating, she'd regularly come down the mountain to help Rosaria around the house. Rosaria quickly took to Paola in a way she didn't with her four other sons' partners, and as things turned serious between her and Tonino, one day Rosaria led Paola into her kitchen and placed two small pieces of dough on the table. Paola knew immediately what was happening. Rosaria wasn't just welcoming her into the family, she was untangling a sacred thread woven by the hands of countless women that had come before her so that Paola could twist her story into it.

"I wasn't nervous; I was moved. It was emotional," Paola told me. "So many years later, making su filindeu still makes me emotional."

Paola remembers carefully watching Rosaria, trying to imitate her movements as she worked the dough. But each time she picked up the cylindrical strand, she couldn't stretch it, and she would be left to knead it over and over again. "My mother-in-law finally said, 'Paola, give me your hands so you'll learn.' It took me a full year to learn how to make it properly—six years to get truly good at it where it became art. But she saw how much passion I had for this. So, after that first year, she asked me to help her make su filindeu for the feast and we made 400 kilograms of it together."

Tonino and Paola were married in 1975. A year later, Rosaria told her that she was getting too old and weak to continue making su filindeu, and she passed the torch to Paola, who has been preparing it for the feast ever since.

Su filindeu may be Sardinia's most remarkable pasta, but it's far from the island's only culinary marvel. Sardinia's tangled history and isolation have combined to preserve the most distinct cuisine in Italy, and its staples aren't found anywhere else: paper-thin *pane carasau* "music-sheet" bread, suckling *porcheddu* pig wrapped in myrtle leaves and cooked in an ember-filled pit, and digestive *mirto* liqueur made from myrtle berries, among others. But on an island that has traditionally turned its back to the sea and where many peasants couldn't afford to eat meat regularly until relatively recently, Sardinians have traditionally relied on grain to sustain them. And thanks to southern Sardinia's vast, fertile cereal fields, the island produces more types of bread and pasta than anywhere else in a country famous for its carbs.

"Sardinia is one of the richest grain cultures in the world, and each of its 377 villages and towns has their own unique type," said Michelin-starred Sardinian chef Roberto Petza, who has dedicated his career to spreading awareness of Sardinian ingredients and documenting the island's rural pasta traditions. "There are roughly 700 types of pasta in all of Italy. In Sardinia alone, there are 500, and that is a direct result of our history of invasions and mixing these influences with our own recipes." It was the Phoenicians who first introduced saffron, the secret ingredient in many of Sardinia's most famous pasta dishes. The Carthaginians then ensured that the island's golden grain fields stayed in full sunlight by threatening to kill anyone who planted a single tree near them, and the Romans exploited the land and population so much that the island's nickname was once "the granary of Rome."[14] Two thousand years later, the descriptions of many modern-day Sardinian pastas read like something from a fairy tale.

The island's most famous variety, *malloreddus*, are gnocchi-shaped dumplings rolled with your thumb around a ridged wicker basket. Even today, betrothed brides in traditional costume parade through their villages on their wedding night, wearing silver jewelry and carrying a basket full of the handmade shells to their new husband's home. *Lorighittas* are ring-shaped pastas braided into thick Rapunzel-like strands typically prepared by unmarried women. *Macarrones de busa* are slender, cylindrical strips wrapped around the underwire of a brassiere. *Andarinos* are a corkscrew-shaped pasta made in a single coastal town by twisting the dough around a reed.[15] But only one pasta in Sardinia has divine status, and we may never know where it came from.

A common legend is that Marco Polo introduced pasta to modern-day Italy following his exploration of China in the 13th century, and at first glance, there is a striking similarity between the hand-pulling of su filindeu and the stretchy, alkaline wheat noodles of southern China. But after years of research, Fancello believes the dish likely arrived in Sardinia sometime between the 14th and 15th centuries, courtesy of the Arabs.

In his book *Pasta: Storia ed Avventure di un Cibo tra Sardegna e Mediterraneo*, Fancello explains that there is an eighth-century recipe from an Arabic writer named Ishu bar Ali describing a threadlike pasta that is "woven like a fabric."[16] When the Arabs invaded Spain in 711, Fancello says they introduced a type of dry pasta called *fidaws*, whose name meant "thin as hair." In Spain, fidaws eventually became known as *fideos* (or *fideua* in Catalan), which are short vermicelli-like strands that are often simmered in a rich, flavorful broth and are still ubiquitous today. When the Aragonese arrived in Sardinia in the 1300s, their fideos became Sardinian-ized in different towns as *fideus, fundeos,* and *filindéos,* and they always referred to a "thin-as-hair" pasta that was eaten in broth. "In Cagliari's Aduanas Sardas (Customs Documents) between 1351 to 1397 and 1427 to 1429, it is reported of an important traffic of pasta 'of indigenous origin' from the island to Barcelona, Mallorca, Valencia, Genoa, Naples, and Pisa with the name 'fideus,'" Fancello said. "But only in Nuoro did this thin pasta become 'filindeu' and assume such a high, sacred value that it's no longer a pasta, but a gift."

Since Abraini became a custodian of this gift more than 50 years ago, she has dedicated her life to sharing su filindeu with the world. She has traveled around the country demonstrating the technique and explaining the history of a dish that—until recently—was completely unknown outside of Sardinia. In the last few years, Italy's premier food and wine magazine, *Gambero Rosso*, has invited her to Rome so they can film her preparing su filindeu twice. Recently, she's also begun making it for a restaurant in Nuoro, Il Rifugio, and in the process, offering non-pilgrims a chance to taste it for the first time. "I can say that I've helped make su filindeu known to the outside world. Many people even here in Sardinia didn't know about it, but I wanted others to see this marvel," Abraini said. "It's something I'm so passionate about. I put my soul into it, but I can't say it's the same right now with my daughters. This is something that takes hard work, consistency, and passion, and both of my daughters have jobs and work every day. So, how can I demand of them to come here and learn or help me?"

In light of this, Abraini once did something previously unheard of with her family's tightly guarded dish: she attempted to teach other girls in Nuoro how to make it. "It didn't go well," she admitted. "Many years ago, these two girls said they wanted to learn and asked me if I'd show them how to make it. It was during the time that I was making su filindeu for San Francesco, so I said sure. They came over for three days, and when they saw how I actually do it, how it's all done by hand, they said, 'This is too much work,' and never came back." Another time, Abraini's niece made a video of her preparing su filindeu and uploaded it on YouTube. "It showed every step of how you make it, the whole technique," Abraini said, waving the tips of her fingers. "One day this man came to the apartment, upset that his mother who had just watched the video wasn't able to do it, and said the video was purposefully wrong—that there must be other secrets. I said there are no secrets, it's all in the video, but it takes a lot of time and hard work. So, what did he do? He called me the next day, very angry, saying his mother *still* couldn't do it. That's when I gave up trying to teach outsiders. Unless someone new from the family wants to take it on and learn it, this is a pasta that is on the road to extinction."

Then, several years ago, something unexpected happened. During a weeklong return to Sardinia, I happened to learn about su filindeu from a shepherd in Nuoro. After Abraini invited me to her home, I returned a few weeks later and wrote a short article about her and this sacred Sardinian rite for BBC Travel. It was the website's most-read story of the year, an article that "introduced su filindeu to the outside world,"[17] as one Sardinian newspaper put it. Before too long, people from across the globe were descending on this hilltop town, hoping to meet Abraini and to save the world's rarest pasta from the brink of extinction.

"You don't understand how many people came looking for me!" Abraini told me, pouring Tonino and I a glass of homemade mirto liqueur. "The chef Yotam Ottolenghi came. Then Horacio Pagani, the car manufacturer, rang the doorbell with 15 members of his staff and said he couldn't leave Sardinia without meeting me. There were €2-million cars parked outside! Chefs from Canada have asked me to teach them. A woman from Greece who read your article called me and offered me €500 for a single lesson and then cried on the phone when I politely declined."

I had inadvertently become part of a story that didn't belong to me, and it made me uncomfortable. A few years later, sitting back in their kitchen, I apologized to Paola and Tonino for causing what Paola called "a stampede" of requests from would-be filindeu apprentices. "No, no! For me, it's only made me happy," Abraini said. "You have helped me introduce su filindeu to the world. In the past, if the few people who had wanted to learn had put in the work, I might have taught them. But now, at my age, I'm not willing to teach it to anyone except my family, out of respect for my mother-in-law and the traditions that were passed down to me."

Understandably, this has caused quite a lot of panic in Sardinia. "Without filindeu, there is no San Francesco, so we are worried about the future," the feast's prior, Francesco Loi, told me. "We're talking about a sacred rite that must be preserved. There are a lot of people who rely on these women's golden hands." He's right. San Francesco may be linked with a bandit, but he's venerated by an island, and almost every Sardinian you talk to today has a story of how this saint and his sacred host have somehow touched their lives.

Ladu, the shoeless pilgrim I followed from Nuoro to the sanctuary, made a promise to San Francesco when his mother was on her deathbed 47 years ago. "She had already received her last rites. The doctors told me there was nothing they could do," he said to me, an hour after trudging up the crumbling hillside. "I prayed to San Francesco and said, 'If you save my mother, I will walk in your name twice each year, barefoot.' She lived for 35 more years and died at 91, and I've maintained my promise." Hours earlier, during a mid-pilgrimage bonfire break fueled by flowing mirto and a yellowish egg liqueur called *Vov,* I had met Francesco Calledda, an 85-year-old man carrying a biblical staff who has walked 96 kilometers from his hometown of Aritzo to the sanctuary for the past 40 years because, as he said, "Filindeu and San Francesco belong to all Sardinians." And the day before the pilgrimage, I went to the home of 88-year-old Badora Piredda, a mother of 10, who started cooking the su filindeu broth for the feast after she claimed San Francesco helped her son recover from leukemia. "As a girl, I remember going to Rosaria and even her mother's to watch them make filindeu," Piredda told me, looking out the window of her Nuoro apartment and flashing a toothy smile. "I would watch them work and say to myself, 'How can this be?' I can make most every Sardinian food. Su filindeu is the only thing that always escaped me. But perhaps before I die, I will finally learn how to make it!"

Since my previous article, there have been greater calls from within Sardinia to ensure su filindeu's survival. But with the dish's primary custodian now unwilling to teach those outside her family, people have recently started looking to other women in the family to divulge the dish's secrets.

A short walk from Abraini's apartment, I met her two nieces, 60-year-old Raffaella Marongiu Selis and 54-year-old Rosaria Musina (the youngest filindeu heir). Sitting in Marongiu Selis's kitchen, I watched as the two bonnet-clad sisters shaped the threads of God from thin air, stretching and pulling the strands in a sweeping motion before laying them on the circular frame. As they prepared the remaining 100 kilograms of filindeu needed for the feast, Marongiu Selis—a soft-spoken woman with smooth olive skin, red-rimmed glasses, and short black hair—explained that she and Musina learned to make filindeu as girls from their mother, Gavina (Rosaria's daughter). Like Abraini, the sisters began by taking a small piece of dough and imitating their mother. And like Abraini, it took them years to master it.

"My daughter, Chiara, is learning, but today girls are much more busy. They're on their phones. There were no cell phones when we were kids.

At six in the afternoon, we were home. It's a different world," Marongiu Selis told me, as Musina continued weaving the circular filindeu canvas. "I've said, Chiara, you have to learn! Not just for you, but for your family. She doesn't have this great passion for it. And filindeu, for the work that it requires, you need to have a passion for it."

For years, Gavina told Raffaella that if she ever taught filindeu, it would create bad blood between her and Abraini. But as Gavina's health—and the sisters' own health—declined, Raffaella had a change of heart. "I'm 60 years old. I've survived two tumors. Rosaria has sclerosis and Paola isn't getting any younger. At a certain point, I thought, if I don't pass this on, no one will carry it," she said. Recently, Maria Antonietta Mazzone, who runs La Cucina delle Matriarche, an organization that aims to "spread awareness and pass on the ancient culinary traditions of Sardinia to avoid the extinction, commercialization, and commodification of our traditions" approached her with a proposal.

"When I contacted Raffaella, I asked her if she thought any of the daughters or nieces in her family would carry this on," Mazzone said. "I told her that this tradition would surely die if they didn't and that it would be a great loss for humanity if that happened. So, I asked her, if we were to do this in the correct spirit, would you be available to teach a few select people the secrets of filindeu in order to keep this tradition alive?" To Mazzone's great surprise, Marongiu Selis said yes. After receiving requests from all over the world and interviewing applicants to ask why they wanted to learn to make su filindeu, Marongiu Selis selected six participants that she felt would have the best chance at learning the technique and honoring its legacy—among them, an Australian chef, a cook working for the Italian food chain Eataly, and a young man from Cagliari. The participants all converged at a small farm stay in Sardinia, and after Fancello explained the dish's winding historical path from Arab pirates to Sardinian pilgrims, he handed the floor over to Marongiu Selis.

"I told the students, there was no recipe. I learned this from my mother and no recipe has ever been written down, so I will try to transmit it through my hands," she said. For the next two days, Marongiu Selis taught them what she could, and at the end of the course, she asked each participant to agree to three fundamental points: 1) every time you prepare su filindeu, you must explain that this is a sacred Sardinian dish; 2) you recount the history of where and how it was born; and 3) you must not alter the traditional preparation or recipe of it.

As Marongiu Selis picked up another cylinder of dough and whisked it through the air with the speed and precision of an orchestra conductor, I asked her, "If it took you and the other women in your family years to master su filindeu, did any of these chefs actually learn to make it in just two days?"

"Well, no," she said. "It's not that these people left knowing how to make it *well*, absolutely not. What I told them was, 'I'll show you the steps, but then it's up to you.' I did the lesson, but they need to do the work, to study it and practice it in continuation. That I know of, none of them have succeeded in mastering it, but if they do one day, I'd feel incredibly proud. Yes, I would have brought su filindeu outside the family, but I would have saved it too."

A week before I returned to Nuoro, Gavina Selis, the woman who had warned her daughter to never teach su filindeu outside the family, had passed away. With her death, the number of living filindeu makers shrank once more. But contrary to her fears, her daughter's lessons didn't create any bad blood with Abraini, who attended the funeral to console her two sisters-in-law. "Su filindeu isn't something I own. I didn't invent it, so if Raffaella wants to teach lessons, who am I to prohibit her from doing what she wants?" Abraini told me. "For me, it's a matter of principle, of tradition. What I have always said is that as a custodian of this tradition that has been passed down from mother to daughter, I will respect that. My daughters know how much of an undertaking this is for me, but they know how much I love it, so as long as the good Lord gives me health and life, I will continue to make it. I remain hopeful that one of them will one day take it on, but if they can't, then I will be sad. So many things in this world that once were no longer are."

Abraini's parting message felt like a prophecy, a pressing reminder to cherish the beautiful, gentle customs that make the world glimmer while warning us not to blink. I tried to push this idea from my mind as I walked blindly through the night toward the sanctuary, following the glint of headlamps as they rose and fell against the lush, black landscape—but it consumed me. As much as I would hate to see su filindeu fade away, I understand why Abraini doesn't want to teach it to any Canadian or Greek chef who calls her out of the blue. Sure, after several years, she may succeed in passing on the skill, but as she told me, when you take something that is so intertwined with a specific place, a specific event, and a specific pastoral code, and you present it in a different context, "it's no longer the threads of God; it's just pulled pasta." It would be like serving communion wafers at a ball game.

At the same time, I can't fault Marongiu Selis for trying to save this tradition from disappearing completely. But what feels even more devastating than the thought of these threads vanishing is the unraveling of a festival and way of life they hold together. It's one thing to put in years of practice to master this craft, but are any of Marongiu Selis's disciples willing to then travel to Nuoro twice a year to prepare hundreds of kilograms of filindeu in the name of San Francesco?

Maybe so.

Of all her students, Marongiu Selis told me that the best was a 42-year-old chef from Nuoro named Roberto Ruiu. After working in restaurants around the globe for 18 years, Ruiu had recently returned to the Barbagia when Marongiu Selis accepted him into her workshop. Perhaps because of his intimate familiarity with Sardinian pasta, Ruiu took to filindeu immediately, but as soon as the class was over, everything fell apart. "I went home and I could no longer make it. The threads ripped. It just didn't work," he told me. "So, I went back to Raffaella's home, and she walked me through it again and again. Since then, I've kept practicing and calling her. I can do it pretty well now, but I know it takes years to learn this art." Ruiu said his dream is to split his time between New York City, where he last worked abroad, and Nuoro so that he can introduce filindeu to the world while keeping it alive at home. "Food helps you learn the roots of a place. It's sharing," he said. "I've been fortunate enough to travel and have learned Mexican food from Mexican chefs and Polish food from Polish chefs. My hope is that I can introduce this food, this beautiful tradition, to those who can't travel, and in doing so, bring a little bit of my home with me."

Every food tells a story, and like any good story, it's the details that matter. There's a fine line between preserving a tradition and altering it. The engineers at Barilla couldn't commodify the secrets of filindeu, but they did succeed in mass-producing Sardinia's beloved malloreddus pasta, which they now sell across Europe with the Italian-ized name *gnochetti sardi*. For years, I felt guilty that my story had altered the natural trajectory of filindeu—that against my best intentions, I was just another outsider, coming to Sardinia and poking my nose where it doesn't belong. But I suppose Ruiu and Abraini's point is really the same: no one owns food, or filindeu, for that matter. So, if I can somehow honor it with a depth and dignity worthy of an island and its people who have forever changed me, and share this tradition with those who can't travel to an impossibly remote mountain sanctuary, then maybe that's my grace.

––––––––––

We were the last pilgrims to arrive, which made our entrance to the sanctuary all the more poetic. As we approached the final hill leading to the church and cottages, the feast's prior, Loi, descended to help Ladu. The shoeless wanderer unfurled a white banner of San Francesco that he had carried slung across his torso for the past nine hours, buried his head in it, and sobbed. Still wincing in pain with every step, he then led our small contingent up the hill toward an open green gate. The peal of a single church bell signaled our arrival. Soon, hundreds of pilgrims who had arrived hours earlier emerged from inside the reawakened ghost village. They ringed the final meters of the paved path and began chanting something old and distant in a language I didn't understand.

After an exhaustive mass and a soothing foot bath, we were led into a large dining room with wood-beamed ceilings and a framed six-stanza poem about filindeu. We lined up, one by one, to receive our pasta. As we arrived in front of a steaming metal cauldron, the women appointed by the prior presented us with a generous bowl of filindeu and proclaimed in Sardo: "For your devotion, may you be blessed by the threads of God."

Like any good soup, su filindeu makes your nose run. The mutton broth is so richly seasoned with fresh Sardinian pecorino that it's more of a stew than a soup; a meal rather than a dish. Even shattered from its circular web, the threads are so light, so subtle when swimming in the broth that the only way to capture them is to place your spoon directly under the shard-like strips and then slowly lift it up so the filindeu doesn't slip off the side. When you do manage to scoop the chunks of pecorino and threads of God in the same spoonful, the sharpness of the cheese is delicately balanced by the astonishing fineness of the pasta. On an island that produces more than 80 percent of Italy's pecorino and is renowned for its fairy-tale pastas, su filindeu is the essence of Sardinia in a bowl.

As I said my goodbyes back in Nuoro, Marongiu Selis told me she had something she wanted to give me. I went back to her kitchen, and she presented me with a specially wrapped tray full of dried, shattered filindeu, which I carefully tucked into my backpack and carried with two hands throughout the 10-hour plane ride home. When I arrived back at my apartment, I emptied out a cabinet in my kitchen and placed the threads of God all alone inside. I don't know if Ruiu will ever succeed in mastering this sacred Sardinian pasta, or in introducing it to New York, where I now live. I haven't dared try to cook my su filindeu yet, but from time to time I open the cabinet to look at it, just to make sure that it hasn't vanished.

5

The Mirror That Reveals Your Truest Self

*That in which there is this reflection of the universe,
as of a city in a mirror—that Brahman are you; knowing
this you will attain the consummation of your life.*
—ADI SHANKARA, "VIVEKACHUDAMANI"

I t was nighttime in Kerala, and everything was black. Palm trees lined
the banks of the Pamba River and stretched endlessly toward the
horizon, their tall trunks and fanning fronds shooting into the night
sky like exploding fireworks. I followed the wafting trail of smoke through
a mangrove forest and into the jungle just outside the small temple village
of Aranmula to look for a woman known as "The Secret Lady Keeper."

Coconut trees swooped low like Nike swooshes over the water's edge,
and herds of elephant ears burst from the ruddy soil. The night before, hot,
heavy raindrops the size of nickels had fallen sideways in sheets, and you
could still taste the muggy monsoon clouds that hung over India's south-
western Malabar Coast. Feeling my way through the thick, humid darkness
felt like walking inside a mouth, and whispers of cinnamon and vanilla
melted into the liquid heat in a sweet conversation. Crickets trilled in unison, their chorus broken by the clown-horn honks of wild peacocks hidden
in a chaotic tangle of green I couldn't see. Lights from a row of stilted houses
hacked from the forest soon lit the way, showing a plume of smoke coming
from inside an open iron gate.

On the other side, The Secret Lady Keeper, better known as Sudhammal
J., struck a match and lit a small brass lamp depicting Lakshmi, the wife
of Lord Vishnu. She placed the votive offering in front of her open-air
wooden shed, which stood opposite her white cinderblock home. With

the Hindu goddess of prosperity and good fortune appeased, it was time to work.

The 48-year-old pulled her long black hair back behind her gold hoop earrings, pressed her blue ankle-length kurta dress to the back of her legs, and squatted on a wooden stool a few inches off the shed's dirt floor. She then started winding a hand crank attached to an old electric leaf blower round and round, producing the rhythmic rattle of a sewing machine. As she cranked, a white PVC pipe attached to the blower fed the air into an opening at the bottom of a fireplace made by stacking five rows of bricks into a hollow, square tower. The plume of smoke soon grew into a cloud that rose to the lone light bulb dangling from the underside of the tile-topped shed. With her free hand, Sudhammal fanned the growing flame with a piece of cardboard, stopping occasionally to dab the sweat from her brow and yellow bindi. When she had turned the flames from orange to yellow to blue after 40 minutes of continuous cranking, Sudhammal got up and disappeared.

A few minutes later, she emerged from her house with two bags and slowly unwrapped them in front of me. In one were long, narrow bands of tightly wound copper, and in the other, jagged palm-sized shards of tin that glistened under the light. She placed the raw tin into a U-shaped crucible glowing atop the fire and used forceps to cover the container with a lid. She then filled the fireplace with charcoal and dried coconut husks she'd harvested from the riverbank, letting them gradually smolder to torch the tin as her 26-year-old son, Niranjan, continued cranking. An hour later, Sudhammal used an iron ladle to pour the molten metal into two rect-angular molds on the underside of an old roof tile that she'd sealed with wet clay so none of the fiery alloy would spill out. When the cast tin rods had cooled from a blazing orange to an ashy gray, Sudhammal hammered them into pebble-sized stones and wrapped a clump of the shattered pieces in a red bandana. She then hammered the copper rods she had cast in a different crucible the night before, gathered a handful of their broken bits, and looked up at me.

"Follow me," Sudhammal softly beckoned in Malayalam, a language as melodic to hear as its name is to say. She led me through piles of jute bags and ceramic bottleneck casts to a dark corner of the shed, unveiling an ancient Keralan steelyard balance rod called a *vellikol*. "Very few people outside the family have ever seen this step," Sudhammal said, flashing a tight smile. "But I won't show you all of it."

She looped a rope around the balance rod and tied the red bandana containing the tin to a hook on its bottom corner. Holding the suspended rod by the rope with one hand, she carefully inched the loop over from the balance's thinner end across its ever thicker and heavier frame with the other, like a doctor adjusting a medical scale. When the balance was perfectly horizontal, she gripped the rope with both hands, held her breath until the last hints of swaying stopped, and eyed the exact place on the scale to mark the tin's weight. She placed the tin aside and reached for a handful of copper that she would weigh and recast together with the tin. But before doing so, just to be safe, she turned away from me, ensuring that the secret formula of the sacred object she was casting stayed within the small community of alchemists who had inherited it.

For hundreds of years, under the cover of darkness, Sudhammal's family has been mixing liquid metals together to create the Aranmula kannadi: a rare and mysterious metal-alloy mirror that is believed to reveal your truest self. It is said that you have never really seen yourself until you've gazed into the polished surface of an Aranmula kannadi. In standard plane mirrors, the image you see isn't cast from the top surface you can tap with your finger, but from a silver or aluminum coating behind the glass. When light travels through the glass to this back surface and then back out again, it can cause an aberration or distortion, meaning the reflection you see of yourself isn't exactly how other people see you.[1] What makes the Aranmula kannadi so unique is that it's handcrafted using a special copper-tin mixture, which makes it front-reflecting. Because the light doesn't have to penetrate any refractive medium and change directions, what is staring back at you is a perfect reflection of who you are.

No one is exactly sure when or how this metal mirror making started, but for more than 300 years, the exact proportion of copper, tin, and trace elements like ammonium chloride that go into it have been a tightly guarded secret passed down orally from one generation to the next within a single extended family in Aranmula.[2] The keepers of this formula have always been members of the Vishwakarma community, a caste of craftsmen whose name means "all maker" and who claim to be the direct descendants of Vishvakarma, the divine architect of the universe. It takes roughly five days to mold, cast, and polish the brittle alloy in order to achieve a perfect reflection. Today, it is believed that only 26 people alive know the mirror's exact proportions. But because of the exhausting manual work involved, less than half of those who know how to make the Aranmula kannadi actively maintain the tradition. Those that do all still live in the mirror's namesake birthplace: a sleepy 16,000-person pilgrim village located midway along the Pamba River's westward journey from the spice-covered hills of the Western Ghats to the Arabian Sea. The village is clustered around a central temple dedicated to the Hindu deity Krishna that's more than 1,000 years old, and it is from here the mirror was allegedly born.

As the legend goes, the Raja of Aranmula hired Vishwakarma craftsmen from the neighboring state of Tamil Nadu to cast bronze idols for the temple sometime in the 16th or 17th centuries. The head craftsman's wife prayed that her husband would be able to impress the king, and that night, Krishna himself revealed the secret mirror formula to her in a dream. Another story says that while polishing a copper-and-tin crown for the king, the craftsmen discovered that it had an extraordinary mirrorlike reflection. The king was so pleased that he gave the Tamil artisans land to settle around the temple and offered the reflective crown to the gods. The Vishwakarma soon used this same alloy technique to create oval-shaped handheld mirrors, called *vaal kannadi,* which were reserved for royals and priests and used to conduct religious rituals.[3]

Today, these mysterious mirrors are more accessible, selling for anywhere between $40 and $350, depending on the mirror's size, but their secret formula and spiritual significance remains. For Keralites, keeping an Aranmula kannadi in your home is believed to bring prosperity and luck. It is often given as a gift at weddings, births, and housewarming ceremonies, and is also one of the eight auspicious items included in the *ashtamangalyam* set used in Hindu holy rites. And while most mirrors around the world today are simply used to gauge physical appearance, in Kerala they serve as instruments of introspection to examine one's body as well as one's soul.[4]

In 2004, the Aranmula kannadi became the second item in India to receive geographical indication status, after Darjeeling tea—meaning that only those who have inherited its patent-protected formula from their ancestors can carry on the craft in Aranmula. Traditionally, this tightly guarded formula has been passed down from father to son, but not in the case of The Secret Lady Keeper. "My grandfathers were kannadi crafts-men. My father, M. S. Janardhanan Achary, was doing this work, too, but he had four girls," Sudhammal said, as Niranjan fed the fire and her 68-year-old mother, Ponnammal, offered us saffron-spiced *kheer*. "Then in 2007, he got badly affected by a fever. I was the only daughter living here, and the day before he died, he took my hand, told me the ratio, and asked me to protect this tradition. I had seen everything since childhood, so I knew a lot of things, but girls weren't allowed to work and enter here. I decided that I will carry this on, even if women didn't do this. It was his dying wish."

Today, Sudhammal is one of the only women in history believed to have ever made the Aranmula kannadi, and she wasn't given much time to learn the craft. In the days after her father's death, just as she quit her job as a primary school teacher to take charge of the family business, she learned that her father had received an order for 2,000 mirrors from a corporation in Kerala. Recognizing that she needed help, Sudhammal recruited her mother to gather clay for the casts from nearby paddy fields; her then 11- and four-year-old sons to pack the clay into bottleneck molds; and her uncle, K. G. Mohan Achary, to mentor her and teach her every-thing he knew. The family worked tirelessly for three straight months, fulfilling as many orders as they could so that these revered items could bless Hindu homes up and down the Malabar Coast.

But while the Aranmula kannadi is believed to bring good fortune to those who keep them, that same fortune has eluded the craftsmen who toil to create them—many of whom live precariously and lost nearly everything several years ago in a once-in-a-lifetime flood. Now, the future of these sacred mirrors and the unsung alchemists who cast them remains in doubt.

Mirrors have always held a certain power over us. They can determine our happiness, influence our behavior, and frame our perception of reality.

Their name comes from the Latin *mirari* ("to marvel or wonder at"), and from the first person who caught a glimpse of themselves in a pool of water to Narcissus, so consumed by his image that he drowned gazing into his own eyes, humans have forever been fascinated by their reflections.[5] We are one of the very few species to recognize ourselves in a mirror, and no other object is as intimately tied to our own self-awareness. Peering into a looking glass allows you to simultaneously examine two things that you couldn't otherwise see: yourself and how the world sees you. Throughout history, this ability to see the unseen has lent mirrors an air of magic and mystery. As a result, people have gone to great lengths to find their mirror image and to understand its meaning.

We'll never know when we first discovered our reflections, but I like to think it was when a young hominin came upon a stream that had trickled to a rest. While bending down to drink, maybe she noticed a strange face staring back at her, and after realizing this creature was equally curious about her, she stuck her tongue out and blew raspberries. Sometime between this first encounter and the Neolithic age, when humans began settling in communities, domesticating animals, and shaping stone tools, we came to understand that these curious creatures staring back at us in the dark, still water were ourselves. By 6000 BC, craftsmen in central Anatolia (modern-day Turkey) were polishing obsidian until they could see themselves in the black volcanic glass. They attached one side of the stone to a convex surface, creating the world's first handheld mirrors. Some archaeologists think these items were simply used to examine one's appearance. But because they were precious enough to be buried alongside bodies, others believe they were used by shamans to better understand the supernatural.[6]

It took a few thousand years before our ancestors figured out how to melt and mix metals, which, it turned out, were even more reflective than obsidian. The earliest metal reflectors emerged in Mesopotamia around 4000 BC, when ancient Iraqis crafted copper mirrors. By 2900 BC, Egyptians were polishing bronze and shaping it into flat, elliptical discs supported by handles resembling papyrus stems—a design symbolizing the moment when Re, the Sun God, emerged from the primordial swamp and created the universe.[7] In the book *Mirror Mirror*, Mark Pendergrast writes, "The Egyptians believed that each person had a double called a Ka, which represented a person's essential genius, energy, and identity, as well as a Ba, the soul or consciousness." Mirrors, like mummification, were thought to preserve both Ka and Ba, and Pendergrast notes that they "were an essential element in tombs."[8] As people around the world began developing their own reflective surfaces and staring long and hard into their depths, they ascribed all kinds of mythologies to these magic mirrors.

One of the earliest-known Mesoamerican civilizations, the Olmecs, fashioned mirrors from stone as early as 2000 BC and believed they were portals to a different dimension that could be seen but not entered.[9] Their descendants, the Maya, melted globs of iron ore and polished them into shiny surfaces to communicate with the gods and their ancestors, whom they believed lived in the mirror's depths.[10] Around the same time, people in ancient China began making bronze mirrors and shaping them into round molds to symbolize fortune and reunion.[11] The Chinese believed a person's soul was contained in their reflection, so it was customary to cover or remove all mirrors from a house after a death—a practice similarly observed among many Catholic and Jewish mourners today.

In her book *The Mirror: A History*, Sabine Melchior-Bonnet explains that the ancient world was apparently as obsessed with beauty as the modern one.[12] From Egypt to Italy and Mexico to China, archaeologists have discovered hundreds of scenes in antique vessels and etchings of our ancestors gazing back at themselves in small discs of polished metal. But aside from applying makeup, fixing wigs, and admiring one's countenance, it seems one of the most common uses of mirrors in the ancient world was to see and sway the future.

Looking into shiny surfaces is one of the oldest forms of scrying, a method of divination where oracles stare into mystical mediums to see visions or reveal prophesies. Long before we gazed into crystal balls, the Sumerians, Arabs, and Magi of Persia (who gave us the word "magic") peered into water-filled goblets to see visions yet to unfold. In the book *The Ugly History of Beautiful Things: Essays on Desire and Consumption*, Katy Kelleher describes how "the ancient Greeks used a mirror to catch the light of the moon, and gazing into it, were able to see visions of the future."[13]

And in his fifth-century tome *The City of God Against the Pagans,* theologian St. Augustine wrote that in the third century BC, the witches of Thessaly wrote their oracles on magic mirrors in human blood.[14]

Perhaps no civilization was more prone to peering into mirrors to foretell the future than the Romans. In classical Rome, an order of priests known as *specularii* claimed to be able to see the past, present, and future by gazing into a metal-alloy mirror called a *speculum*—the origin of the word "speculation."[15] The Romans also employed special diviners called "blindfolded boys," who, as Kelleher writes, "could call forth images of the future from the thin haze of condensation on the surface of a mirror."[16] According to the fourth-century text *Scriptores Historiae Augustae,* the death of Emperor Julian was correctly prophesized by blindfolded boys using this technique.[17] Second-century travel writer Pausanias described how the Roman diviners also used mirrors to predict the healing of the sick, explaining that they would attach a string to a mirror, dangle it into water, and "then; looking into the mirror, [see] the presage of death or recovery."[18] Like many before them, the Romans also believed our reflections contained our whole selves, and anyone who broke a mirror was cursed with seven years of bad luck, since that's how long it took for your soul to regenerate—a belief much of the Western world still subscribes to today.

According to Pliny the Elder's *Natural History,* the first glass mirrors were made in Sidon (present-day Lebanon) in the first century. These beta looking glasses were tiny (roughly one to three inches in diameter), curved (like fun-house mirrors), and not especially useful. They were also extremely hard to make. As a result, metal mirrors remained in fashion among the world's nobility for more than 1,000 years.[19] It wasn't until the 15th century that craftsmen from Murano in the Venetian lagoon finally cracked the code to producing clear glass mirrors that didn't break. Like mirror makers in Aranmula, Venetian glassmakers jealously guarded their secret formula, and for the next 100 years, acts of espionage and bribery unfolded as craftsmen around the world attempted to imitate their methods. Nowhere was this more dramatic than in France, where it is widely believed that Louis XIV ordered the kidnapping of three of Murano's best glassmakers in the 1660s and coerced them to divulge their secrets.[20]

The "Sun King" had a special affinity for glass mirrors and wanted to start a local production of Murano mirrors in Paris. But as Melchior-Bonnet details, before the craftsmen could reveal the full formula, they started mysteriously dying. Investigators at the time suspected that Venice's infamous Council of Ten government sent spies to poison and assassinate the traitors. Yet, the one master who survived, Gerolamo Barbin, went on to contribute to the creation of Versailles's famed Hall of Mirrors in 1684, leaking Murano's secret formula to the world.[21]

Thanks to Louis XIV's industrial espionage campaign, French workshops soon began blowing, coating, and polishing their own looking glasses, making them among the first to mass-produce glass mirrors and make them affordable for the bourgeoisie. As historian Ian Mortimer explains in his book *Millennium: From Religion to Revolution: How Civilization Has Changed Over a Thousand Years*, it's hard to overstate just how much the proliferation of glass mirrors transformed the human experience.

By the 1600s, glass mirrors in telescopes and microscopes were spurring an outward and inward revolution, as humans sought to better understand our places in the universe and what makes us who we are. But as mirrors became available to the masses, Mortimer argues that human identity fundamentally shifted. We stopped viewing ourselves first and foremost as part of a community—be it a member of a village, a guild, or a church—and started to see ourselves as unique. The more we looked at ourselves and became the center of our own attention, the more individualist we became. This is when we started to value our own space and stopped sleeping in the same room as our other family members; when personal letter writing and first-person novels became de rigueur; and when the art world became saturated with haunting, existential self-portraits of people staring back at the viewer, as if to say "Look at me!" while simultaneously wondering, "Who am I?"[22]

"The development of glass mirrors marks a crucial shift, for they allowed people to see themselves properly for the first time, with all their unique expressions and characteristics," Mortimer writes. "Polished metal mirrors of copper or bronze were very inefficient by comparison, reflecting only about 20 percent of the light."[23] Yet, this wasn't the case everywhere, and while

European factories were busy smoothing and silvering their panes, a small community of craftsmen on the palm-fringed banks of the Pamba River had discovered a truer mirror image in metal alloy than could ever be seen in a looking glass.

The world's foremost expert on the Aranmula kannadi is Dr. Sharada Srinivasan, an archaeologist who did her PhD dissertation on South Indian metallurgy and has studied Aranmula's mirrors for more than 30 years. As she explained to me, from the Mesopotamians to the Mayans, the ancient world was filled with front-reflecting metal mirrors that produced a distorted image because their proportion of certain alloys was either too high or too low. Then, humans learned how to produce glass mirrors, and once we saw that they revealed a truer reflection than their metal predecessors, we never looked back—seemingly unaware that because they are back-reflecting, they still contained a slight distortion.

"What is truly unique about the Aranmula kannadi is that you have this community of artists who are continuing to manufacture mirrors in an authentic way as ancient societies would have created them so long ago, and they have managed to isolate the perfect composition of alloys to achieve this 'delta phase,'" Srinivasan said, referring to the ratio of tin and copper—to the 10th of a percent—where a metallic compound can be polished to achieve a perfect mirror image. "Metallurgists will tell you that it's very difficult to isolate delta in a lab, so these craftsmen have achieved something truly spectacular. It is one of the great metallurgical innovations in antiquity, alongside the Chinese producing cast iron, the use of glass in Iran, and the making of gold-copper alloys by the Inca."

Today, whenever we need an exact reflection, whether it's for medical lasers or space exploration, we use front-reflecting metal mirrors. But while it's one thing for biomedical and NASA engineers to design metal mirrors in a state-of-the-art optic lab, it's another for self-taught artisans to create them in the jungle.

It's hard to know how or when the Vishwakarma craftsmen stumbled upon this perfect ratio. The oldest Aranmula kannadi Srinivasan has analyzed was from the 1600s–1700s, "and it's absolutely, almost entirely pure delta phase," she said. But alongside ancient Egypt and Mesopotamia, a third Bronze Age culture, the Indus civilization, was thriving in present-day Pakistan and northwest India, and they began making bronze mirrors as early as 2800–2600 BC. These artisans made their front-facing reflectors using something called the lost-wax technique, where molten metal is poured into a mold created by a wax model.[24] This is very similar to how the Vishwakarmas make the Aranmula kannadi today. Srinivasan noted that British archaeologists have analyzed a mirror comparable to the Aranmula kannadi dating to 500 BC in Tamil Nadu, where the Aranmula artists originated. Therefore, she thinks it's entirely possible that these early Indus mirror makers may have migrated south and come up with the formula for the Aranmula kannadi long before the legend of the temple.

"This is probably the last surviving mirror-making community in the world," Srinivasan said. "To think how these craftsmen discovered this centuries ago really evokes a sense of wonder. When you watch them work, there is so much dignity in their labor—it's really very moving. Master craftsmen in much of India have usually been anonymous, so there is this profound sense of selflessness in a tradition like this. The craft is both the totality of a people and a path to salvation."

One doesn't accidentally end up in Aranmula. It isn't included in any guidebooks, there's one main homestay, and there's no sign welcoming anyone who may have taken a two-hour detour from the languid lagoons that lure most backpackers to Kerala. When I landed at Kerala's main airport and the customs agent asked where I would be staying, I said, "Aranmula." After looking at me blankly for a few seconds, he asked, ". . . What's that?"

Aranmula is best viewed by taking the 20 steps leading up to its two-storied temple. From there, you look out upon a spiderweb of drooping telephone lines that chase the village's squat terra-cotta and tin-roofed buildings out until they disappear into the jungle. Sputtering auto-rickshaws, grumbling scooters, and peckish stray dogs share the hot cement streets with vendors in open-air storefronts selling bananas, jackfruit, and mangoes cut from the forest. The name of the district that holds the village, Pathanamthitta, means "a few houses on the riverside"—an apt description for the kind of slow-stride tranquility that permeates these palm-shaded hamlets. Virtually no foreigners make it to Pathanamthitta, but South Indian travelers have been coming here for centuries—lots of them. That's because, some 65 kilometers east of Aranmula, where a series of tiny streams coalesce into coherence and form the Pamba River deep in the misty folds of the Western Ghats, there's a hill. Perched at the very top of that hill is an 11th-century temple called Sabarimala where Hindus believe the god Ayyappan (the son of Shiva and Vishnu) meditated. This site marks the culmination of one of the world's largest annual pilgrimages.[25]

Every year between November and January, as many as 20 million devotees from the Malabar Coast and Tamil Nadu place a locket with the image of Ayyappan around their necks and embark on a solemn test of austerity called *vrata* (vow or devotion). For 41 days, they abstain from intercourse, meat, alcohol, smoking, and shaving, wearing only black as they walk barefoot. They detach themselves from the material world, doing their best to transform themselves into a version of the god they hope to see once they reach the hilltop temple. Then, after draining the water of a coconut to symbolize the removal of earthly attachments, the pilgrims follow the Pamba's course through Aranmula and up to Sabarimala, where they finally glimpse the highly anticipated deity—only, it isn't a statue or avatar of Ayyappan that awaits them. Instead, as they ascend 18 golden steps to the temple, they come face-to-face with a large, reflective pillar and a message written above the entrance: "*Thathwamasi*" ("It is you"). The god they have hoped to become is within them, as it has always been. Upon seeing their mirror image and letting this truth seep in, the pilgrims shed their black clothes, descend from the mountaintop, and bathe in the Pamba to cleanse their souls.[26]

"You know, the Aranmula kannadi is much more than just a mirror," Divya Iyer, the magistrate of Pathanamthitta, told me, as local reporters snapped pictures of us. My visit to Aranmula coincided with the 75th anniversary of India's independence, and as the nation's officials ceremoniously raised the Indian flag across the country, I received an unexpected invitation from Iyer to her whitewashed palace. It seemed that not many foreign journalists venture to this corner of Kerala, and she was keen to meet me and to make sure I grasped the mirror's deeper meaning. "In the Hindu way of life, what we consider the ultimate truth, we say *aham brahmasmi*. 'Aham' is inside, and the entire universe, the entire creation, is actually within you. The process of living your life is trying to unravel the secrets of the universe through your inner self. That is a code of Hinduism. A mirror is a perfect representation of you trying to see God and the universal truth through your own image or inner self."

"How do you think the Aranmula kannadi does this better than a typical mirror?" I asked her. "Let me show you," she said, leading me away from the TV cameras and into her family's puja room—the most sacred part of an Indian home, where families keep deities, idols, and religious texts to invite positive energy inside. Iyer reached into a locked armoire and pulled out an Aranmula kannadi whose darkened brass frame suggested it was at least a century old. "Aside from searching for the ultimate truth within yourself, another core concept of Hinduism is that life is a continuity," Iyer said. "Nothing stands alone; everything is a continuance. We all carry bits and pieces of thousands of things that those who came before us did. The whole idea of life and death and rebirth, everything stems from this idea of continuance. When you are holding something like an Aranmula mirror in front of you, it is symbolic of that continuation of life and tradition—not to mention an incredibly beautiful representation of culture, science, and spirituality."

From ancient Egypt to Mesoamerica to Rome, mirrors have always bridged these physical and invisible worlds, reflecting not just how we look but what we believe. Yet, perhaps nowhere do mirrors continue to serve a more intimate purpose than in India, where they have historically been used as tools of introspection and self-realization—and this is especially true along the Malabar Coast.

As Srinivasan explained, the word "kannadi" is a Tamil word that translates as mirror, but its true meaning is more profound. "'Kannu' is eye, and 'adi' is really the full depth of what the eyes see. It's a fascinating word with lots of metaphoric layers, but it is more like the mind that determines what the eyes shall see." This symbolism helps explain the kannadi's many roles in Kerala. A mother gives an Aranmula kannadi to her daughter on her wedding day so she can see herself one last time before her soul joins her partner's. On Vishu, the Malayalam New Year, children are led blindfolded to the puja room so that their first gaze of the new year can be into the kannadi. Across Kerala, Bhagavathi (the Mother Goddess) is believed to be so powerful that her mere gaze may destroy devotees, so she is instead worshiped through the reflection of an exquisitely cast metal mirror. One of the most captivating examples of mirrors transcending worlds unfolds during *theyyam*, a sacred indigenous dance performed in northern Kerala that's believed to predate Hinduism. In the culminating act, as bonfire flames lick the sky and drums beat wildly, a performer wearing Kabuki-like makeup and an elaborate headdress several meters high peers into a mirror before transforming himself from a man into a god.[27]

Much of the modern reverence for mirrors along the Malabar Coast can be traced back to one man: Sree Narayana Guru. Born in 1855 to a poor family, the spiritual leader and social reformer would go on to lead a revolution against Kerala's discriminatory caste system, encouraging everyone to pursue enlightenment, including India's so-called "untouchable" Dalit class that was once deemed less than human. The guru consecrated more than 40 temples across Kerala and stirred those shunned by society to use mirrors to reflect inward.[28] "Lower castes weren't allowed to go to temples before. When they saw that other communities didn't want them to come in, they felt they weren't worthy enough to pray, that they were too low in stature," said 39-year-old Murukan Rajan, Aranmula's youngest kannadi maker, as prayer chants from the Aranmula temple spilled into his small storefront at the foot of its staircase. "But Sree Narayana asked every temple to have mirrors in them and encouraged people to believe that God is everywhere—even within you. So, when you go into temple, you're supposed to bow before your reflection and see the god within yourself. He awakened people to the next level."

The guru's social revolution also extended to Kerala's metal mirror makers. Despite their claim as descendants of the divine architect, the Vishwakarmas have historically been one of the state's more marginalized groups and were included in the Indian government's list of "backward classes" until the country's 3,000-year-old caste system was officially abolished in 1950. As Murukan explained to me, "This mirror-making tradition has been passed on for hundreds and hundreds of years in my family, but even those of us who made [kannadi] couldn't have one until recently because only the aristocracy were able to afford them."

Murukan then got up from his seat near a whirring fan and led me to his shop's display case. He reached in, pulled out an Aranmula kannadi, and placed it on top of the case next to a normal glass mirror. "See this?" he asked, standing his business card upright on the glass mirror's surface. I looked closely at where the card touched the glass and noticed a small space between the bottom of the card and where its reflection began. "There is a slight variation because a normal mirror isn't precise or perfect," he said. "Now, look at this. How you see yourself in this mirror is different." Murukan placed the same card atop the kannadi and stroked his black mustache in satisfaction. The gap was gone; the card and reflection were one. "This was Sree Narayana's message to the lower castes: Thathwamasi. It is you—you are God. It is all one. That is one of the reasons why we consider the Aranmula kannadi to be sacred."

Murukan explained that some of Aranmula's kannadi makers still use Ayurvedic techniques to purify the raw metals by immersing the copper and tin in a mixture of boiling water, cow urine, and tamarind leaves for several days. As I peered into the back workroom behind his storefront where two of his assistants were busy grinding clay, he explained that the entire kannadi-making process is locally sourced and waste-free, with any leftover materials fed back into the next mixture.

To make the mirror molds, artists dig for clay from nearby paddy fields or along the banks of the Pamba River. They create new mirrors by first crushing the clay tile molds from the previous crucible into a fine powder using a stone rolling pin–like grinder and slab. They then sprinkle water atop the clay powder, hack jute fiber with a machete, and mix the thin fiber strips into the clay mixture to help hold it together. An artist and his assistant—or in Sudhammal's case, her mother—will shape the clay mixture into two circular frames and leave them outside for several days to dry in the heat. Once dried, they rub both sides of the circular clay frames atop the fine powder to smooth them before applying a layer of wet coal to one side of the disc to fill in the clay's pores. There needs to be a small gap between the two discs for the molten metal to flow into it, so artists place tiny slivers of scrap metal atop the edges of one disc and then place the second on top of it, like a sandwich. The size of this gap determines the thickness of the mirror. They then use the remaining clay to seal the two discs shut and attach a second bottleneck-shaped piece of clay to the top. This U-shaped opening is where the secret proportions of hammered copper and tin shards will go. Before sealing the bottleneck shut with more clay, artists use a thin metal rod to create a tiny hole straight down from the bottleneck, so the molten metal can seep into the gap between the discs. Once these dry, the clay crucibles are ready to go into the fire.

Aside from maintaining an air of secrecy, there's a very practical reason why kannadi makers typically cast at night. "It's too hot in the daytime," said K. Gopakumar, a 58-year-old ninth-generation kannadi maker. To not waste kindling, artists typically cast as much metal as they can at once. At night in Gopakumar's open cinderblock workshop, I watched as one of his assistants placed 10 crucibles with the bottleneck face down, layered the fireplace with coal and coconut husks, and then used a similar hand crank as Sudhammal to feed a flame until it turned blue. "This is the most difficult part," Gopakumar said. "The flame can reach 1,200 degrees Celsius."

Depending on how big the mirror is, the crucible will stay in the fire for anywhere from one to five hours. To test if the molten mixture is ready, artists use iron forceps to remove it from the fire and place a thin stalk from a palm leaf into the crucible's tiny opening. If they feel the stalk vibrating, it means the mixture is boiling and is ready to be turned. They'll then carefully flip the crucible so that the metal fills the entire gap between the discs and leave it overnight. The next day, artists gently tap the top of the bottleneck with a hammer, cracking it open like an eggshell and splitting apart the two black-colored metal discs inside. Any small drop of sweat that falls onto the metal's hot surface during this phase can ruin its composition, so workers only do this after drying their brows. Before beginning the polishing process, artists use a double file to shape the cast metal disc into a circle or oval, working the file back and forth with both hands as they slowly turn the metal with the bottom of their feet—hence why Gopakumar and others work barefoot.

Once the metal disc is filed into a perfect circular or oval shape, the kannadi makers glue one side of the metal onto a wooden frame using a mixture of heated pine gum and wax. They then use wet sandpaper to slowly smooth the metal's surface. This painstaking process may take several days, but when the desired reflection is finally reached, they apply a few drops of seed or coconut oil to the metal and polish it some more with jute. They apply an adhesive mixture of sand, frankincense, and wax whose proportions are also secret to the back of the mirror and attach it to the brass frame, which is handmade using a sand-casting process. After a few final polishes with a velvet cloth and the placement of a hologram sticker to mark the kannadi's authenticity, it is finally ready to reveal the real you.

In my interviews with Srinivasan, she described the work of a kannadi maker as a Zen-like dance—a repetition of movements done over and over again until the ego dissolves and craftsman and craft unite. As Sree Narayana said, it is all one. During my time in Aranmula, I, too, fell into a Zen-like rhythm: waking up with the rest of the village as the first temple chants broadcast through the tinny speakers; gathering rice dishes and curries spiked with chilies and tamarind from banana-leaf plates with the tips of my fingers and guiding them into my mouth with my thumb, as Keralites do; shuffling out into the liquid heat, past the pile of dust-caked sandals devotees had left at the base of the temple staircase before they ascended to pray; and following the smoldering scent of coconut husks down dirt alleys and into thatched-roof workshops to watch craftsmen cast sacred mirrors from memory. In my week in Aranmula, I met as many of the remaining kannadi makers as I could, spending hours with each one, often well into the night. I'd then return to my homestay, lie down for a few hours, and inevitably be woken up in the middle of the night by a distant rush that sounded like someone shaking dried rice in a bowl. I'd go out on the balcony, and as the swell grew nearer and the birds flew away, I'd walk to the edge, look up, and stretch my arms out, letting the summer monsoon roll over me like God's greatest shower.

India is a universe. It is home to more than a billion people, millions of gods, and hundreds of languages. I had come to find one tiny star before it burned out; to see this light-reflecting wonder that had captivated me since I first learned about it years ago in a local newspaper. So, this is what I did in India, day after day after day. I can't tell you what it's like to bathe in Kerala's turquoise waters, traipse through its spice-scented Cardamom Hills, or succumb to an Ayurvedic massage. But I can still smell the woody, chocolate-hinted traces of charred coconut husks in my sleep. I remember the hollow pop a clay cast makes when it's hammered open, and the distinct plume of white that shoots up from cauldrons when alchemists add a final pinch of ammonium chloride to their alloy brew. The more time I spent with each artist, the more apparent it became how interconnected everyone's story was, and how some maintained a *Game of Thrones*–like claim to be the rightful heir of this tradition. It also became clear that while each artist's process is virtually the same, some perfume their narratives with details others in the family are quick to dismiss.

Murukan told me that the clay used to make the casts can only come from the banks of the Pamba River. In his fancy air-conditioned showroom a short walk away, Murukan's soft-spoken 50-year-old second cousin, K. A. Selvaraj Achary, told me that the clay can come from any nearby paddy field. He also suggested that he and his brother, Gopalakrishnan, whom I watched hand-chisel elaborate designs into brass frames, are in a rarified field among the kannadi makers, as they have learned the craft from a continuous line of fathers stretching back 800 years, as opposed to other artists today who have learned from more distant relatives. Yet, according to Gopakumar, the tradition is only 500 years old. He told me that the very first Aranmula kannadis were essentially ancient compacts used by aristocratic women to apply kumkum powder to their foreheads during religious ceremonies. He also told me there was a reason why this craft has traditionally been passed down from father to son and not mother to daughter. "This is too risky, too hard work for a woman to do alone," he said as his male assistants chopped jute bags with a saber-like blade.

Back in the jungle, Sudhammal told me she thought the tradition was closer to 300 years old and bristled at Gopakumar's statement. "Before, all over Kerala, the woman's duty was making food at home. Nowadays, it's changed. I'm very proud of this work and I hope other women will learn the secrets to this trade and join me in the future."

It was then that I told Sudhammal something I hadn't shared with any other mirror maker: I had a secret of my own. Over the course of my interviews, someone had inadvertently revealed the kannadi's tightly guarded formula to me. It was never something I sought out, and though I'll take this recipe to the grave with me, I told Sudhammal that the fact that this person had disclosed this to me felt like a violation of a sacred pact. As Iyer explained to me, "The secret of the Aranmula kannadi is a form of intellectual property. Who they choose to teach and not teach is a way of maintaining this tradition, but also of controlling their own destiny." But to my great relief, Sudhammal smiled and said something that each of the other kannadi makers would independently echo: there's the secret formula, and there are the skills of the craft, and it is only through years and years of experience, of watching, failing, casting, and recasting that these elements become one, like the kannadi itself. "*That* is the secret," she said.

This inherent truth bound each kannadi maker as much as blood, and while each recounted a slightly different version of when their family's centuries-old tradition started, they all shared a similar story of how it nearly came to an abrupt end. In 2018, Kerala experienced its worst flooding in a century when the summer monsoons dumped more than 240 centimeters of rainfall in the region, killing at least 480 people, displacing 1.8 million more, and causing more than $3 billion worth of damage.[29] One of the worst-affected districts was Pathanamthitta, where the water quickly spilled over the banks of the Pamba and consumed everything in its path.

On August 18, Selvaraj had just returned from Delhi, where he had presented India's prime minister, Narendra Modi, with an Aranmula kannadi. By 4:00 P.M., water started gushing inside his showroom. As he and Gopalakrishnan raced to carry as many of their mirrors as possible upstairs to their workshop to save them, a giant tree fell outside the building, effectively trapping them inside. They were some of the lucky ones.

"The flood affected everyone. People died, people lost their homes, their businesses, their animals. I lost everything," Murukan told me. "I lost tools, mirrors, frames—all swept away. There was water up to the ceiling and the entire store was filled with mud and sand. My loss was minimum to 10 lakhs [approximately $12,030]." Unable to work, Murukan took out a loan and had to sell all of his wife's jewelry and his then-six-year-old daughter's earrings in order to restart his business months later.

Sudhammal had just finished making dozens of frames in her open-air workshop when the flood started. It was just before Kerala's Onam harvest festival season—the busiest time of the year for many kannadi makers, as elders typically bestow gifts to family members. "Everything was ready, and then everything was gone: the cast metal, the boxes, the tools, everything," she said. "Then suddenly, the water started to come into the house and kept rising and rising." Sudhammal rushed her mother and two children to the second floor of the family's home. When the floodwater was nearly to the roof, the four of them leapt out of a window into the dark torrent, swimming frantically to reach a narrow flat-bottom punt boat that rescuers had somehow steered through the jungle. The family was taken to a shelter at a nearby school where they stayed for nearly a month. When I asked Sudhammal what it was like to finally return home, she placed her hand to her chest and looked down. "My heart was broken," she said. "There was so much mud, we couldn't even step foot in the house."

Kerala is the first place in India to receive the summer monsoons, and one of the most vulnerable states to flooding. Part of that is due to the state's natural geography, but numerous studies have shown that as the world continues to warm, monsoons will become stronger and less predictable. In fact, every summer since the historic 2018 floods, the Indian government has had to conduct emergency military rescue missions to save thousands of stranded Keralites. According to a 2018 government report, Kerala is also one of the least-adept states at water management, and several studies concluded that the local government grossly mismanaged the 2018 flood by releasing water from the region's 59 dams to prevent them from bursting.[30] Some dams hold as much water as 1,625 Olympic-sized swimming pools, and the opening of a single dam can cause a tsunami-like effect. In the midst of the 2018 monsoon, the government opened 34 dams in less than a week, unleashing a tidal wave that engulfed entire towns and affected the homes and property of 5.4 million people.[31]

Between her lost mirrors and flooded bungalow, Sudhammal experienced more than $15,000 worth of damage—a life-changing sum in a state where the average annual income ranges between $2,350 and $5,050. Like Murukan and most kannadi makers I met, a combination of private loans, government assistance, and support from groups like Habitat for Humanity eventually helped Sudhammal restore her house and restart her business. Yet, soon after she and her family started casting mirrors again, the pandemic hit. Sudhammal didn't receive a single order for eight months, fell behind on her loans, and was forced to take out additional loans. Because of pandemic-related supply chain issues, Sudhammal said the cost of a kannadi's raw materials is now more than twice what it was before the pandemic. But against all odds, Sudhammal continues to carry on her father's dying wish.

How any kannadi maker managed to survive two once-in-a-lifetime calamities less than three years apart is a wonder. But as I would soon come to learn, not everyone did.

During my time in Aranmula, one name kept coming up over and over again: K. G. Mohan Achary. The 77-year-old is the oldest person alive who still knows how to make the mirror, and the one Sudhammal called when she needed help fulfilling the order for 2,000 mirrors in the days after her father passed. Mohan not only taught his niece everything he knew, he gave her 10 of his finished mirrors to help her start her business. Mohan also taught his nephew, Murukan, how to make the kannadi. And when Murukan felt his 13-year-old son was ready to learn the family trade, he didn't teach him himself; he took him to Mohan. In fact, of the 26 people in the world who know how to make the Aranmula kannadi, Mohan has trained 19 of them. He has also single-handedly managed to save this craft from extinction—twice. After several days and nights with other kannadi makers, it became apparent that if there's any one person whose claim to this tradition is somehow stronger than others, Mohan's the guy. Now, I just had to find him.

I can't really say where Mohan lives—not because it's a secret, but because the car ride there was such a bumpy, dizzying blur through the jungle that I lost any sense of where I was. All I know is that when the car stopped, I had arrived at the very last house on a dead-end dirt road, and yellow butterflies were fluttering through the green thicket. Mohan lives in a small red-brick home concealed by banana and banyan trees. A blue tarp covers part of the tin roof that would otherwise let the rain in, and extends out from the doorframe like an awning, covering an outdoor rug made of six burlap coffee bags stitched together. It was too steamy for a shirt, so Mohan greeted me with a checkered sarong that was wrapped around his waist and hovered over his bare feet.

"You found it," he said, smiling with his whole face and pressing his palms together in greeting. His perfectly coiffed slicked-back hair was more salt than pepper, but turned blue as I followed him under the tarp to meet his wife, who stood clutching a cane in the doorway. When she disappeared inside to make tea, Mohan motioned for me to take a seat in a plastic chair facing him. He then introduced himself with three fundamental facts that I sensed defined him: "I am K. G. Mohan Achary, we belong to the Vishwakarma community, and the 2018 flood destroyed everything for me."

Mohan learned the kannadi craft as an 11-year-old boy from his grandfather, Krishna Achary (who is also Selvaraj's grandfather and later taught him). At the time, Krishna was one of the only people who knew how to make mirrors, so he organized a training course with 10 of Aranmula's Vishwakarma children to ensure the tradition survived. "Of the 10 students in the trade class, only I was given the complete secret," Mohan said, with a soft-spoken ease. "My grandfather trained everyone to make different steps of the mirror, but he never gave the complete recipe to any one person. A master gives hints to his disciples, and if they're really interested in learning, they go that extra mile to learn it. I was interested, so I went that extra mile, and have done my best to pass this tradition on, as my grandfather wanted."

Even after learning the secret formula, it took Mohan several years to master the craft. He made his own tools to save money and was eventually able to open a small shop outside the temple to sell kannadis. "Back then [in the 1960s], a one-inch square mirror sold for 10 rupees." He smiled. "Today, the same thing would cost 2,000 rupees." Mohan quietly carried on in his little shop for decades, but in 1990, with people seemingly uninterested in the scorching heat, long hours, and exhaustive labor required to make the mirrors, kannadi-making was again on the verge of extinction. "We understood the craft was going to disappear, so to revive it, one of us had to start teaching it to the next generation," Mohan said. "I'm the only one who took it up." Mohan selected 10 students from the Vishwakarma community, trained them, and for the second time in his life, ensured the Aranmula kannadi's survival.

In the years after, Mohan traveled around southern India, presenting the Aranmula kannadi in more than 150 exhibitions and propelling its popularity beyond Kerala, to the benefit of all Vishwakarma alchemists. Then in 2001, while heading to the market to buy metal for the mirrors, the rickshaw Mohan was traveling in flipped over, trapping him underneath, crushing his spine, and leaving him paralyzed for four months. Mohan was bedridden for three years, but he never gave up hope that he could one day return to making mirrors. After years of physical therapy, Mohan eventually gained enough strength to walk with a painful limp, and to cast, hammer, and polish kannadis on his own again. He also continued teaching others, and in the years since his accident, he's trained anyone from the extended family who has approached him with a sincere interest to learn.

Then came the rains. In August 2018, Mohan told me he was sitting right where we were, watching the paddy fields behind his house slowly flood. As the water rose, he saw his neighbors flee to higher ground, but because of Mohan's limited mobility, he was effectively trapped in his home. When the water reached Mohan's waist, two men finally came and lifted the plastic chair Mohan was bound to and carried him to a house up a hill where he stayed for eight days. When he returned home, his homemade tools and polished kannadis were so damaged that he sold some for scrap and gave the rest away to the many artists he'd trained—his life's work, washed away in an instant.

In the three years Mohan was bedridden, he had been forced to give up his shop. As a result, unlike Aranmula's other kannadi makers, he never received a penny from the government or any charity in 2018 because he wasn't operating a business at the time of the flood. Mohan told me that there had been more demand for the Aranmula kannadi in the years before the pandemic than ever before, with prices exceeding anything he ever would have earned when he worked. Meanwhile, he and his wife now survive on a monthly pension of 3,200 rupees ($38) and a government ration of 20 kilograms of rice. Only a few of his former students, like Murukan, still come around to check on him, and he hasn't taught anyone in years. Perhaps most heartbreaking of all, when Mohan and his wife returned home after the flood, they were amazed to find that a single kannadi he had made remained untouched on their wall—a glimmer of light amid the wreckage. But a few weeks before I had shown up, someone had asked Mohan if he had any mirrors left to sell. "We needed the money," he said. "I had to sell the mirror off my own wall."

I couldn't help but ask Mohan about the bitter irony of all this. He had dedicated his life to the community and the craft, saved this tradition from vanishing, taught it to others free of charge, and never benefited from the demand he helped create. It didn't seem right. Yet, Mohan views his situation with a sense of calm and karma that moved me, and reinforced everything I had learned about continuity, rebirth, and understanding the big picture through your own image. "If the kannadi had been as popular before as it is now, I would have benefitted, yes," he said, touching his thumb and forefinger together in a Hindu gesture evoking mindfulness and truth. "I am the poorest kannadi maker of them all. I don't have a proper house or a way to get around while everyone else has benefitted. But I began teaching people so this craft wouldn't die and so that others could make a living. Even if I can't benefit from it now, I am fulfilled knowing others can and others will."

That night, I was shaken awake again by the drumroll of thunder and the splattering of hail-sized raindrops outside my door. I shuffled outside to the balcony, only this time, instead of reaching for the rain, I recoiled from it and sat silently, peering through the inky black toward the banks of the Pamba. As with Mohan, the bitter irony of my situation wasn't lost on me either. I had come to Kerala to honor a tradition, but by traveling 8,500 miles in a fuel-guzzling jet to get here, I was directly contributing to the one thing that may soon wash it away. It was much easier to focus on the look of hope each craftsman cast on me when they learned that someone—anyone—from the outside didn't just want to learn their process but understand the source of their pride and the depth of their pain. But to not recognize my role in contributing to both of these things is to not see the full truth staring back at me. You can't separate the intent from the consequence; the good from the bad. It is all one. You can travel to know the world, to fall in love with it, and to urge others to care for it while simultaneously harming it.

The next morning, I received an unexpected message from the magistrate's office. India's former ambassador to the Netherlands was in town, and Iyer wanted me to meet him before I left. I quickly found the last shirt I hadn't soaked through with sweat, and 30 minutes later, we were sitting under a soaring ceiling in Iyer's palace.

In India, a district magistrate is responsible for how a region spends its money. In Kerala, they also have the unique job of managing the state's dams and deciding if or when they should open during extreme emergencies. As Iyer and the ambassador talked, it became clear that she had been under an immense amount of pressure. In the weeks before I arrived, a near-nonstop downpour had led to widespread flooding, and many people in Pathanamthitta feared they were on the verge of another catastrophe. Iyer pointed out that unlike the Netherlands, whose network of dikes and dams is a matter of national security, Kerala's combination of state- and privately-owned reservoirs makes coordinating a response nearly impossible. The two government representatives then politely asked the visiting writer what he made of all this.

I sympathized with Iyer. This problem felt much bigger than any one person—and certainly bigger than me. I thanked her for welcoming me in the midst of the monsoon season, and steered the conversation back to something I felt more sure of, and something Iyer could directly control as the district's revenue officer.

I told her that while millions of Indians may pass through Aranmula to see the god within themselves at Sabarimala, they seem to seek out Aranmula specifically for its namesake kannadi. In my time here, it had become clear that this pride of Pathanamthitta wouldn't exist without the work of one man who had twice brought it back from the brink of disappearance. I explained his circumstances, what he's given, what he lost, how he's unable to work, and how he has largely been forgotten. While I admitted it wasn't my place to poke into local affairs, I echoed a sentiment Murukan had told me one night after hours of casting: "No one here would still be doing this work were it not for him. This man deserves to be honored, but if you're going to do it, it should be while he's alive."

Iyer was gracious enough to invite me to stay for lunch, but it was getting late and I had two things left to do before leaving Aranmula. After saying my goodbyes, I left the palace and returned to the jungle. Sudhammal knew I would be coming and had placed a few mirrors on a table outside her workshop for me to see. For reasons I can't entirely explain, in all my time spent around kannadis in Aranmula, I had yet to build up the courage to face one myself. Instead, I asked Sudhammal to choose one she felt best suited me. She selected a handheld vaal kannadi and carefully packed it in a red velvet box as I handed her half of my remaining rupees. I had no way of finding her uncle again, but she did, and I just asked that she give the remainder to Mohan. I then did the same with Murukan.

I never expected that I would hear back from anyone in the Pathanamthitta government about what I had said to Iyer, but a few months later, I received an email out of the blue from the secretary of the local tourism council. It seemed the cultural minister had coordinated a fund with Iyer to help Mohan, and the tourism council was organizing several events to honor him. It felt like a sign.

That night, I picked up the red velvet box that had sat unopened under the dresser in my bedroom. As I dusted it off, I remembered something Mohan had said to me: "There is no other way than for me to believe that the kannadi is sacred. When you make a mirror, you have to be mentally and physically pure. If you give yourself to the universe and you shed your ego, you will see Him staring back at you." I slowly unlatched the box, took a deep breath, and held the kannadi up to my face—unsure where He ended, and I began.

6

Asia's Last Film Poster Painter

We are curious creatures, we Taiwanese. Orphans. Eventually, orphans must choose their own names and write their own stories. The beauty of orphanhood is the blank slate.
—Shawna Yang Ryan, *Green Island*

It was 7:00 A.M. in downtown Tainan, Taiwan, when a little man with a pink helmet arrived on his blue scooter. The 70-year-old slowly dismounted and shuffled in his sandals to an unmarked door across from the Chin Men Theater before unlocking it and disappearing inside. Moments later, he emerged, dragging six square canvases that each dwarfed his five-foot frame along the sidewalk, and leaned them one by one against the wall. He then reached into the side pocket of his paint-speckled slacks, unrolled a 27-by-40-inch poster of the movie *Top Gun: Maverick,* and brought it up to his eyes, studying it closely. After a few seconds, he nodded and disappeared back inside the dark, cramped room to fetch a ruler. It was time to begin.

The artist lowered himself onto a green plastic stool under the sidewalk's shaded metal arcade and laid the poster out on a paint-stained plywood slab that stood no more than a foot off the ground. For more than an hour, he bent over the makeshift drafting table, using the ruler and a blue pen to create a grid of horizontal, vertical, and then diagonal lines over the poster that became smaller and smaller with each pass. The aging master occasionally stopped to adjust his thick-rimmed glasses, wipe the sweat that had accumulated in the 32-degree-Celsius heat from his wispy black-and-white hair, and look up at the suit-clad businessmen breezing by him on their way to work. When he finished carving the poster into a perfectly even framework of tiny triangles, he dug into his other pocket, found a stick of white chalk, and padded back over to the canvases resting against the wall. Then, with the precision of an architect and the flair of an Impressionist, the artist patiently re-created the same line-ruled matrix across the canvases with the chalk, using the grid as a guide to sketch Tom Cruise in a startlingly lifelike scene of suspense. As the outline of the actor's furrowed brow, the swoop of his raised fringe, and the rims of his aviator sunglasses began to appear, a few passersby slowed their stride. Others stopped in their tracks, looking first at the man squatting on a tiny stool, and then up at the giant billboards displayed across the street on the theater's façade. When the lines of the scene were set, it was time to bring the image to life. The artist grabbed several brushes, six cans of paint, and laid another wooden slab on the ground, using the plywood as a palette to create a kaleidoscope of hues from primary and secondary colors.

For the next 10 hours, he toiled away in the heat, slowly mixing, brushing, and filling his six-paneled canvas with each sweeping stroke. By the early evening, the artist finally stepped back from his work, cocked his head to the side, and considered it. He regarded the power of Cruise's steely gaze, how the sun danced atop the ruffles of his green bomber jacket, and the way the shadows outlined the creases around the actor's eyes and mouth. After a few moments, a smile broke across the artist's face. "That's it," he said quietly, speaking to no one in particular, except maybe the actor staring back at him.

Yan Jhen-fa has never met a movie star, but he's painted so many he can't remember them all. Nearly every day for the last 52 years, the shy and soft-spoken artist has worked alone in Taiwan's oldest city, Tainan, immortalizing film legends in larger-than-life billboards adorning the marquees of the city's movie theaters. Day after day, hour after hour, he crouches on a slight stool, kneels on the ground, and stretches high above his head in his outdoor studios, using deft brushstrokes to depict movie icons in surreal, noir-like friezes of tension, passion, or pride. With each oil-painted illustration, Yan may fill the canvas with billowing explosions, snowcapped peaks, noble warriors, or nefarious villains. Layers of light and shadow capture Hollywood and Taiwanese actors in a glamorous glow, the vintage-style affiche evoking the golden age of the silver screen.

Behind Yan's latest portrait of Cruise, a photo collage of dozens of the artist's past works covered the wall. There was *Logan,* rendered with such clarity that the bulging veins around Hugh Jackman's bloodshot eyes reflected back in the sheen of his claws; *La La Land,* with a free-flowing Emma Stone and Ryan Gosling gliding against the Los Angeles skyline, arms outstretched in a synchronized swing; and *Seediq Bale,* where the smoldering Chih-hsiang Ma gripped a dagger as he led a legion of 1930s Taiwanese warriors into battle against the island's Japanese colonial masters. After Yan finishes each of his dreamlike portraits, he clambers up the theater's scaffolding and uses rope to hoist the six panels of his 215-square-foot billboards several stories into the air, hanging them on the theater's façade. "I've painted thousands of films in my lifetime, but my name has never been in the credits, and I've never signed my work," he said. "Still, in some small way, I feel like I'm a part of the movie production."

It takes Yan anywhere from 10 hours to three days to complete each billboard, and as he told me, "It all starts with the face." If he likes the film's digitally printed poster, he'll re-create it in a massive oil-glazed homage. If he doesn't, he'll sit in the front of the empty theater before its first screening and watch the movie. Then, he'll drag his billboard panels outside and blend his own style with the film's plot "to try to honor it in a new way."

For the past 24 years, Yan's only client has been the Chin Men Theater—the oldest theater in Tainan and the only theater left in Asia continuing the age-old tradition of displaying hand-painted film posters. In an era of digital printing and computerized graphics, Yan is one of the last artists in the world carrying on a craft that's on the verge of extinction. In fact, only two other theaters around the globe still employ a full-time billboard artist: one in Munich, Germany, and one in Athens, Greece—and neither cinema's artist has been painting the movies anywhere near as long as Yan has.

But while Yan continues to fight his lonely battle against modernity one brushstroke at a time, a lifetime of oil painting has exacted a punishing toll on his eyesight. Years ago, doctors discovered severe injuries to his retinas, and while they were able to repair his left eye, he has lost nearly all sight in his right. Little by little, his vision continues to slip away. Still, surely, if a little more slowly these days, the partially blind artist carries on.

Just as Yan reached for his brush to apply a few final flourishes to the Top Gun patch on Maverick's naval jacket, three Taiwanese fighter jets tore through the skies of Tainan in a tight V formation. They dove low and loud, shooting no more than 5,000 feet over the city's streets in a bone-rattling rumble. They then rounded back and repeated this defensive drill over and over again. With each deafening flyby, people on the streets covered their ears and cranked their heads up to the sky—except the master, who remained glued to his work.

It was a fascinating time to be in Taiwan. A few days before I arrived, US Speaker of the House Nancy Pelosi had visited the self-ruled island. Despite having its own president, government, currency, passport, and military, Taiwan only has diplomatic relations with 14 countries—many of them tiny island nations like Palau, Tuvalu, and the Marshall Islands.[1] Instead, China claims Taiwan as part of its territory and considers visits by foreign government officials as a recognition of the island's sovereignty. Pelosi's visit triggered China's biggest-ever show of military force in the Taiwan Strait. It fired ballistic missiles toward the island, ordered its warships to cluster outside Taiwan's ports, and sent fighter jets into Taiwanese air space more than 600 times.[2] As China reacted to the "wanton provocations"[3] of the US by threatening a full-scale invasion against its "renegade province," many worried that the world may soon be thrust into World War III.[4]

In many ways, the central issue in this conflict is that of Taiwanese identity. More than 90 percent of Taiwanese residents trace their roots back to mainland China, but many Taiwanese increasingly see themselves as a distinct people and culture from their Communist-ruled neighbor—a defiant, fragile democracy eager to separate itself from its big brother across the strait and chart its own course.[5]

As I turned back and forth between the fighter jets in the sky and the fighter pilot Yan was painting on the ground, I couldn't help but marvel at the fine line between life and art. But when it comes to films in Taiwan, one has always shaped the other. In fact, the very idea of Taiwanese identity and how people here have historically seen themselves is intrinsically bound with one of the island's most eye-catching traditions: hand-painted movie billboards.

As long as there have been movies, there have been movie posters. When silent films became popular in the 1910s and 1920s, theaters around the world hired artists to convey the excitement of new releases and capture an audience's attention before they stepped foot into the cinema. In an age of high illiteracy rates, some of the earliest movie posters were inspired by the bright, bold paintings used to lure people to circuses, fairs, and traveling vaudeville shows. These so-called "one-sheet" posters were hung in glass display cases inside and outside theaters and usually depicted one of the most captivating scenes from the film. The "Golden Age" of Hollywood in the 1930s and 1940s spurred the growth of movie theaters around the world, and by the 1950s, US film studios began printing and shipping their painted posters to other countries. Around the same time, the rise of automobiles created a booming industry of painted highway billboards that could be seen from great distances. Film producers recognized that the larger the advertisement, the more likely they were to draw bigger crowds, and they began to reproduce their one-sheet posters as oversized, attention-grabbing illustrations.[6]

But in many places where skilled labor remained cheaper than billboard-sized prints, handmade paintings continued to adorn cinemas for decades to come. In India, Bollywood employed 300 artists to decorate the country's theaters with vivid renderings of princesses and maharajahs for much of the 20th century.[7] In Ghana, local artists painted movie posters on flour sacks that could be rolled up and taken to the next screening until the 1980s.[8] In Poland, one of the only types of fine art not censored by the Communist government was film posters, so from the 1950s until the dissolution of the Warsaw Pact in 1991, artists hired by the state-owned Film Polski industry created stunning abstract, Surreal, and Dada-esque posters that often had almost nothing to do with the film itself.[9] And in Thailand, Myanmar, and the Philippines until the early 2000s, artists scaled bamboo ladders to paint stills of a film's most memorable scenes as tuk-tuk drivers lapped towns below announcing the latest movies from megaphones.[10]

Yet perhaps nowhere did this artistic tradition run deeper than in Taiwan, where gigantic oil-painted posters were once some of the most eye-popping sights on the island's streets. "During the heyday of kung fu movies and [Taiwanese-language cinema] in the 1970s, we had more than 700 theaters in the country, and almost every one employed its own artist," said Chen Pin-chuan, the former director of the Taiwan Film and Audiovisual Institute. "Now, Mr. Yan is the last. He is a very important treasure of Taiwanese cinema."

According to Dr. Ru-shou Robert Chen, who has authored three books on Taiwanese cinema and wrote his PhD dissertation on Taiwanese identity, the history of film in Taiwan and its film poster painters not only reflects the island's past but also reveals a deeper truth about what it means to be Taiwanese. "The idea of being Taiwanese is complicated. We are not Japanese. We are not Chinese. These two, they have been in Taiwan and occupied and ruled us. They are part of us, but they don't define who we are," Chen said. "It's not unusual for filmmakers and artists to reflect about who they are and where they come from. That happens in many countries, but especially in Taiwan because of our history and position as a castaway island—a sort of no-man's-land."

Lying 160 kilometers off the southeastern coast of China and 115 kilometers from Japan's westernmost point, Taiwan's strategic position in the South China Sea sealed its fate as a pawn in the messy tug-of-war between the two rival powers. In the 1500s, snooping Portuguese sailors spotted the uncharted enclave and dubbed it *Ilha Formosa* (Beautiful Island—a name it would retain among the English-speaking world through much of the 20th century). The Dutch followed in the 1600s, establishing a colony in modern-day Tainan on the southwest coast. This short-lived settlement was swept aside when the last loyalists from China's withering Ming Dynasty retreated to the island in 1664. They established Tainan as its capital and planned to use Taiwan as a launching pad to reclaim the mainland from the Qing, a clan who had seized all of China from the Ming. Before that could ever happen, the Qing invaded Taiwan, conquering it in 1684. Their control over Taiwan marked the longest rule of any power over the island, lasting for 212 uninterrupted years and helping to forge a shared national identity with mainland China. In 1895, the Qing Dynasty was humiliated by Japanese forces in the First Sino-Japanese War, and Taiwan became a Japanese colony for the next 50 years. The Japanese governed the island harshly, repressing its local culture and effectively forcing Taiwanese residents to become Japanese. It was during this period of colonial rule that the first films arrived in Taiwan.[11]

"By the time cinema took hold in Taiwan [in the 1920s], Taiwan had already been under Japanese control for a while and the process of Japanification was under way," said Chris Berry, a professor of film studies at King's College London and the coeditor of the book *Island on the Edge: Taiwan New Cinema and After*. "The vision for Taiwan was that it was now part of Japan. The cultural policies were for people to adopt Japanese names, speak Japanese in public, and see themselves as Japanese citizens." The colonial government wanted islanders to look, live, and think the part: they encouraged them to wear kimonos, live in Japanese-style houses, and convert to Shintoism. Berry explained that as part of this island-wide assimilation, authorities followed a strict policy of only screening Japanese films and importing the film posters that came from Japanese artists. On-site Japanese-Taiwanese interpreters even accompanied Taiwanese audiences into the island's theaters.

While all this was happening, a massive change had taken place back in mainland China: an uprising led by the Nationalist Republic of China (ROC) political party had led 15 Chinese provinces to declare their independence from the Qing Dynasty. As World War II intensified and China inflicted heavy damages on Japanese forces, Allied leaders like Winston Churchill and Franklin Delano Roosevelt began to view the ROC and its new leader, Chiang Kai-shek, as the rightful government of both China and Taiwan. The leaders decided that, should the Allies prevail, they would retrocede the island back to the mainland—which is exactly what happened following Japan's surrender in 1945.[12]

Four years after Taiwan was passed back to China, the decades-long Chinese Civil War raged into a bloody climax, and the ROC was overthrown by Mao Zedong's Communist government (PRC), leading the ROC's divisive leader, Chiang, to retreat to Taiwan. His army followed him, as did hundreds of thousands of loyalists and their families. By the end of 1948, roughly 30,000 Chinese refugees from the mainland were pouring into Taiwan every day. In all, from 1945 to 1955, an estimated one to two million Chinese Nationalists fled mainland China to join Chiang's exiled government on a mountainous island the size of Delaware and Maryland. Confusingly, to this day, Taiwan's official name remains the Republic of China.[13]

Like the Ming Dynasty before him, Chiang's initial plan was to lie low, train his troops, and wait for the day he and his soldiers could retake the mainland. That day never came, and instead of ending his government's drawn-out war with the PRC (which, technically, is still ongoing today), Chiang held Taiwan in an iron grip as he continued to proclaim he and his party were the sole legitimate rulers of "Free China." Chiang ensured his power was absolute by executing as many as 25,000 perceived Taiwanese dissenters, imprisoning an estimated 140,000 civilians, and declaring a permanent state of martial law known as the White Terror period that would endure for 38 years—the longest martial law period in world history at the time.[14]

When Chiang and his followers initially arrived on the island, they found themselves living alongside hundreds of thousands of indigenous peoples and an estimated four to six million Han Chinese. Most of these Han settlers had emigrated centuries earlier from Fujian, the southeastern province facing the island directly across the Taiwan Strait. They originally settled in what's now Tainan and called the area "Taiyuan," which later lent its name to the whole island. The Han settlers spoke Hakka and Hokkien (also called Taiwanese)—two languages that are similar to each other, and mutually unintelligible from Mandarin. But because Chiang saw his exiled government as the one true China, the autocrat imposed a series of sweeping nationalistic policies to suppress local languages and cultures and standardize Mandarin across the island, much as the previous colonial rulers had done with Japanese.[15]

In effect, Taiwan had traded one colonial power for another, both of which sought to subjugate it, strip it of its identity, and transform it into something it wasn't. The island's first democratically elected president, Lee Teng-hui, later reflected on this painful era of history repeating itself, writing: "In the period of Japanese colonialism, a Taiwanese would be punished by being forced to kneel out in the sun for speaking [Taiwanese]. The situation was the same when Taiwan was recovered [by Chiang]: my son and my daughter often wore a dunce board around their necks in the school as punishment for speaking [Taiwanese] . . . I think the most miserable people are Taiwanese, who have always tried in vain to get their heads above the water."[16]

According to Taiwanese film scholar Dr. Chen Ya-wen, just as Taiwanese audiences had been forced to watch Japanese films under Japanese rule, from 1945 to 1955, Chiang's Nationalist government imported Chinese films and film posters from the mainland, and Taiwan's film poster–making industry was "nonexistent." Since the Nationalist government had only imposed its strict Mandarin-language policy a few years earlier, almost no Taiwanese people understood the films screened on the island. But as Ya-wen explained to me, while Mandarin was the mandatory language in schools and official administrations, islanders weren't strictly forbidden from speaking Taiwanese in their homes, on the streets, and on the silver screen. And so, in 1955, the first Taiwanese-language film was released, an adaptation of a traditional Taiwanese form of opera called *gēzǎixì*, shot by a Taiwanese director, and depicted by a Taiwanese film poster painter.

It was the birth of *taiyupian* (Taiwanese-language cinema): a string of more than 1,100 largely low-budget films shot in Taiwan from 1955 to 1981 that captured the conscience and character of an island desperate to see itself in the midst of martial law.[17] Compared to the higher-end Chinese and Japanese films of the time, whose explosions, heroes, and villains offered a vision of escapism, taiyupian relied on more relatable themes of longing, lust, and adventure that reflected Taiwanese daily life. This burgeoning new film industry also saw the birth of Taiwanese hand-painted film posters, and according to Berry, the very act of Taiwanese artists depicting Taiwanese actors in larger-than-life portraits as they portrayed their struggles and joys worked to shape a nascent idea of what it meant to be Taiwanese. "Right from the get-go, the reason these films found large audiences is because local people recognized their experiences in the films and responded to them," Berry said. "At the time, the government was very much emphasizing Taiwan as just another province of China, but these films fit into the rhythms and habits of Taiwan and reflected what was going on in everyday life on the island."

As Ru-shou Chen explained, these local films and the posters that accompanied them also taught Taiwanese people about their own island. "When I was in my primary school, I had to memorize the names of mountains and rivers in mainland China, but I didn't know anything about the mountains and rivers near my own house," he said. "Those Taiwanese directors and those Taiwanese artists used those films and posters to let those people know more about Taiwan. They used film and illustrations to let the audience think about their own identity in a rapidly changing time."

According to Ya-wen, it's difficult for younger Taiwanese people today to understand how massive an impact these early Taiwanese-language films had on the island—especially in a place like Tainan, which has always been considered a bastion of Taiwanese culture and where Hokkien is still spoken most everywhere instead of Mandarin. "You have to think of the mindset of the island at the time when these films appeared," she said. "We were being suppressed and threatened with punishment for speaking our language, so going to the cinema and sitting in the theater to watch ourselves and cry along with these characters was a cathartic experience. Seeing ourselves painted on these large billboards was part of that experience."

Taiwan's tradition of hand-painted film posters can be traced back to one man: Chen Tze-fu. Hailed as a "national treasure" by the Taiwanese government, Tze-fu created a staggering 5,000 movie posters in a career spanning five decades, often with only a cursory understanding of the film's plot. His dramatic use of framing and ability to capture the essence of an idea was so compelling that from the 1950s to the 1970s, Taiwanese-language film producers would come to his studio and ask him to paint the poster before the film was even shot.[18] "He kind of preconceived the films," said Ya-wen, author of the book *Chen Tze-fu's Film Posters and the Visual Culture in Postwar Taiwan*. "He was like a creative director and artist in one, but one of the true legacies of his life and work is how he reflected Taiwanese culture as a whole."

Born in Taiwan in 1926 under Japanese colonial rule, Tze-fu—like most Taiwanese octogenarians and nonagenarians today—was raised to be Japanese by his Taiwanese parents. He fought for the Imperial Japanese Army in World War II against China (his family's ancestral nation) and then returned to Taiwan at the end of the war after his ship was torpedoed and sunk by Allied forces. "Of the 303 Taiwanese special volunteers [on board], 215 died," Tze-fu later wrote in a Japanese newspaper. "When I think of the souls wandering in the sea bottom, I cannot help but wonder which country they died for and if that was really worth it." At the end of the war, Tze-fu returned to his island home, only to be told he was now a Chinese citizen. "On my way back to Taiwan from Kagoshima, I looked up and saw the unfamiliar flag of the Republic of China, which once was said to be the enemy. Then I realized that I was like a leaf swept away by a swift current."[19]

As soon as Tze-fu arrived back in Taiwan, the Chinese navy recruited him to be a lieutenant. But during his time in Japan, he had met artists who painted film posters, a profession he had never seen growing up on the island. Instead of serving his new nation, he decided to pursue this new artform instead. The only problem was that the island's Nationalist government was importing all of its films and film posters from China. Therefore, when Tze-fu's career started in the 1940s, he was only allowed to repair Chinese posters from Shanghai. As Ya-wen explained, "In a way, [Tze-fu's] conflicting national identity was the reflection of our island for the past century."

Tze-fu's career took off with the advent of Taiwanese-language films in the 1950s. "There were no Taiwanese poster artists back then. All of the great masters, like Yan Jhen-fa, are because of him and have developed their style from him," said Dr. Chun-chi Wang, the former director of the Taiwan Film Institute. "He was so good at picking the exact moment that grabbed people's attention that all the studios wanted hand-painted posters. It was the beginning of an industry and helped popularize Taiwanese cinema." At the height of Tze-fu's career in the 1960s and 1970s, he was painting 40 posters a month, and before too long, most every theater in Taiwan employed a specialized billboard artist to reproduce his work on their façades. Ironically, as more Taiwanese children gradually learned Mandarin in school and the Nationalist government continued to sideline Taiwanese as an "uneducated" language, Taiwanese-language films disappeared and were all but forgotten. Today, less than 20 percent of the more than 1,100 taiyupian films survive, and in many cases, as Ya-wen explained, the only things that testify to their very existence—"the collective cultural memory of Taiwan"—is Tze-fu's artwork.[20]

Yet, as Taiwanese-language films began to fade away in the 1970s, Taiwan and Hong Kong began emerging as the global hubs of martial arts films. Soon, theaters were employing even more billboard artists, which spurred what Yan described as "the peak" of Taiwan's billboard painting era, beginning in the late 1960s and 1970s. It's also when Yan himself began to paint the movies.

Yan grew up the oldest of five children in the rolling farmland of Tainan County. In the mornings, he and his mother would leave their humble farmhouse to gather eggs from the family's chickens and crops from their small plot. They'd sell them in a tiny orange kiosk outside their home alongside the fish and prawns Yan's father had caught. Despite the family's meager income and daily hardships, Yan remembers his mother as a loving woman. His father, however, was anything but. "He was a very strict man. He was brutal," Yan said, as he sat surrounded by dozens of finished canvases from past billboards in his studio, directly above the outdoor area where he paints each day. "He used to tie me up and beat me. I was so scared of him that I used to hide under the bed to avoid any contact with him. Even after he passed away, I could not forgive him."

Instead, Yan found an escape in art. He studied film posters in the local paper and tried to re-create them with a pencil in his bedroom. "That's how my romance with movie posters began," Yan said, momentarily making eye contact with me before quickly returning his gaze to the ground. "I even won third place in a painting competition in third grade. I was quite talented, I guess."

Yan wasn't one for school, though, and by the time he was 12, he decided that he had had enough. Instead, he spent his days wandering the countryside, catching grasshoppers and studying the way the shifting clouds shadowed the landscape. His favorite thing to do was to sneak into the two run-down theaters showing second-run films nearby, where he'd sometimes watch as many as seven movies a day before going home to sketch his favorite scenes. "The films were so blurry you could barely see them, so I used to imagine the characters," Yan said, smiling. "Back then, all the movie theaters had hand-painted posters and each one had their own master." When Yan was 18, he finally built up the courage to tell his parents that he wanted to pursue film painting. His mother encouraged him to follow his passion. His father chased him out of the house with a broom. "He said I'd starve," Yan remembered. "And he was right."

Yan's aunt worked in downtown Tainan and knew someone in the movie poster industry who introduced Yan to Chen Feng-yun, one of southern Taiwan's greatest billboard masters. Feng-yun agreed to allow Yan to apprentice under him. For the first two years, Yan earned the equivalent of $6 per month and couldn't afford an apartment, so the homeless apprentice slept in a tiny crawl space under the theater's steps that was too small for a bed. "I could only afford to eat soup and rice. Those were the toughest days. I was down to 39 kilograms, but I never considered failing. I knew that as long as you had a specialty, you could make a living. You just had to be good enough," he said, nodding.

Like Tze-fu, Feng-yun had learned the art from a master trained in Japan, and therefore trained Yan in the traditional Japanese master-apprentice style: he never actually instructed him; he merely let Yan observe him as he worked. Yan studied how the master gripped his brushes, memorized Feng-yun's color combinations, and practiced relentlessly, using plyboard to build his grids on the back sides of old canvases the master no longer needed. Then, one day, after about two years, something clicked. "Everything has an essence, and you have to understand the subject's essence to bring it to life," Yan explained. "It's the blending of light and shadow, the person's eyes and the angles that make it come alive."

Just as Yan was honing his style and beginning to work more closely with his master on big projects, duty called. "In those days, it was mandatory to join the Taiwanese military for three years. Now it's much less," Yan said, in a quiet lull between the simulated dogfights roaring overhead.

"I was stationed at Matsu and Kinmen (two groups of islands governed by Taiwan located just off the Chinese mainland). This was when the relationship between Taiwan and China was really, really tense."

Beginning in the 1940s and 1950s, Kinmen was the scene of ferocious assaults by Communist China, which tried to invade the island but was met with heavy resistance by Taiwanese fighters hidden in cement bunkers dug into the beach. The bombarding continued into the 1970s, when the PRC fired thousands of artillery shells across the water, in hopes of rattling the island's residents enough to force their surrender. "China used to launch missiles toward us, and I'd watch them fly over my head toward Taiwan," Yan remembered. "It was mandatory to wear radioactive masks to protect us from all the smoke."

When Yan returned from the military as a 23-year-old, his former master approached Yan to ask him if he'd like to work under him. For the first time in Yan's life, he was able to earn enough money to support himself, and he was no longer tormented by his father when he returned home. "I worked under [Feng-yun] for several years. It took me 10 full years to master my technique, but once I did, I got more acclaim. This was probably the best time of my career," Yan said, thumbing through black-and-white photographs in his studio of some of the earliest billboards he painted alongside his former master—many of which were older Taiwanese-language films rescreened in Tainan's second-run theaters. The former apprentice finally stepped out of his master's shadow in the late 1970s and started working for most every theater in Tainan. From 1977 to the mid-1980s, Yan estimates that he was painting a staggering 100 to 200 billboards a month, many of which were rendered in a moody poignancy to evoke the avant-garde experimentation and anti-government views of the island's next big cinematic movement: Taiwanese New Wave films.

Taiwanese New Wave examines the dizzying sociopolitical and cultural transformations in the years before and just after the island finally lifted its martial law in 1987. The films are marked by a conscious opposition to the glossier styles of Chinese and Hollywood filmmaking at the time, and are realistic, almost documentary-style portrayals of Taiwanese daily life. Like the earlier Taiwanese-language films, New Wave captured

Taiwan at a cultural and spiritual crossroads and reflected an island increasingly frustrated with the Nationalist government, martial law, and its inability to call its own shots. And as Yan said, "I was there to paint it all."

For the 1989 film *A City of Sadness*—which portrays the pain a Taiwanese family endured during the White Terror period—the official poster shows a Taiwanese family dressed in formal Japanese clothing, as if posing for a portrait. Yan decided to ditch that version and designed his own rendering, filling the canvas with a close-up of a Taiwanese woman whose face is partly covered in a veil and her suit-clad husband bringing a white handkerchief to his eye as his face breaks. For the 1987 film *Strawman*, which portrays the final years of Japanese occupation in Taiwan, instead of reproducing the production company's poster of a woman gazing at a scarecrow in a field, Yan painted two Taiwanese peasants carrying an unexploded Japanese bomb—a nod to the many undetonated Japanese explosives that still litter the island and its waters today. And in the 1985 film *A Time to Live and a Time to Die*, about a Chinese family that migrates from the mainland to Taiwan and their son's increased isolation from his parents as he adopts Taiwanese customs, Yan ignored the cartoonish illustration of a boy on the original poster. Instead, he painted a lone boy's downcast gaze, his eyes begging for acceptance, telling me it was partially inspired by his own memories growing up.

"[Taiwanese New Wave] reflected a modern, new Taiwan, and a sense of Taiwan-ness that was in the process of becoming," Berry said. It's not hard to see how the ads for these films, often rendered with autobiographical intensity by hundreds of artists across the island, fit into this growing sense of a people whose identity was moving away from the mainland. After talking to lots of younger people over several reporting trips to the island, I've found that the murky question of what it means to be Taiwanese today tends to be divided by generations, with many born in the waning years of martial law and the advent of Taiwanese New Wave cinema viewing themselves quite differently than their ancestors.

"No one is denying that we share roots with China, but we are unquestionably Taiwanese," said William Huang, a 30-year-old I'd met in the city of Taichung. "We young people were born and raised here. We love the freedoms here and would never want to return. Just because some people escaped China and came here doesn't mean this is China." I've heard this sentiment time and again, and it reflects a growing truth that has caused tensions with Beijing to flare. According to the BBC, opinion polls show that 70 to 80 percent of the island's 23 million residents now consider themselves Taiwanese—an increase of more than three times since 1992.[21]

When Yan was stationed on Kinmen Island, he remembers the PRC shooting propaganda posters from the bustling Chinese city of Xiamen located just a few miles away onto Kinmen's low-slung villages, warning Taiwanese citizens that their perceived national existence would soon come to an end. I asked Yan if any of his attempts to "honor [films] in a new way" with original artwork were ever responses to the repeated threats he had experienced at the hands of Chinese. "When I work, my responsibility is to the film, the characters, and the plot," Yan said. "I just try to arrange and balance the elements on the billboard so they are beautiful and capture a feeling."

But in recent decades, these bygone reminders of Taiwan's past have all but vanished. At the start of the 1980s, there were more than 30 full-time poster masters employed in Tainan alone.[22] By 2000, the Chin Men was the last theater in the city maintaining the practice. The rise of DVDs, on-demand streaming, and multiplex cinema chains caused many second-run theaters across the island to shut their doors. That, along with the ever-cheaper cost of mass-produced prints, has forced those that have survived to abandon the tradition of hand-painted posters. Today, Yan insists that were it not for the Chin Men Theater and the family that has faithfully run it for more than 70 years, he would be unemployed and unknown. "There would be no me," he said.

"There has always been a hand-painted artist here, and so it's important that this culture doesn't disappear, like it has everywhere else," said the Chin Men's 70-year-old manager, Wu Chun-cheng. "In the malls now, they use computers to print posters, but it looks dull and dead. Master Yan's art is vivid and alive."

Not much has changed at the Chin Men since Wu's father and uncle opened it in 1950. Instead of computer-generated tickets, a teller still stamps each entry by hand. Inside, a sign politely asks men to remove their caps, and an arrow points people downstairs to the air-raid shelter—a relic from the days when Mao routinely threatened to invade the island, and which Wu hopes they won't have to use as tensions with China flare again. Below the theater's screen, a large wooden stage faces the audience, which used to showcase Taiwanese opera, plays, and puppetry performances. "I want to show you something special," Wu said, leading me up a staircase and into the theater's operating room, where a 1930s Rola film projector from Japan clattered to life with the flick of a metal switch. Nearby, a vintage signaling system is still used to project announcements on the side of the screen during movies. "In the days before cell phones, we would use it to help people find each other when the theater was crowded and dark," Wu said, swapping in slides of different Chinese characters to customize the projected message. "Nowadays, we use it when customers need other people to move their cars out front, and sometimes for surprise wedding proposals."

"Everything about the Chin Men is such a throwback, a reminder of past times," Ya-wen said. "Going to the theater in Taiwan used to be a very physical experience. You saw these big painted billboards, during martial law times you had to stand up to sing the national anthem before the movie, then you'd sit down and you'd hear the sound of the projector. That's been lost now, but this theater has almost all of it—minus the anthem."

Outside, Wu's brother drives an old truck through the streets once a week, advertising the Chin Men's latest second-run releases with a bullhorn. In the lobby, a concession attendant sells chips in bags designed and painted by Yan. And just outside the ticket booth under the theater's marquee, a life-sized cutout of director Ang Lee serves as a shrine to the Chin Men's most famous patron. "When Ang Lee was a high school student, he lived in Tainan and used to walk to this theater to come watch movies," Wu said. "He's always said that this theater is where he first fell in love with the cinema."

It's also where Wu first fell in love too. From his first year of elementary school until his last year of high school, Wu and his family lived on the second floor of the Chin Men in the rooms directly behind the marquee. "There were seven of us living here," Wu said, in what's now the theater's office, and where Yan climbs out a double window to tie his billboard canvases to the metal scaffolding. "This is my home. I literally grew up in this building." When Wu was a boy, he used to spend every day down-stairs, helping his father and uncle in the theater. At that time, his father employed a man named Mr. Lin to run the projector. Wu remembers Lin's daughter, Shu-hui, would come to help him from time to time. The two 11-year-olds would see each other at the theater, and continued to, week after week, year after year, as they helped their fathers—at first exchanging a few words, and later secret glances. When Wu was 19, his father sensed his son had a crush on the girl, so he surprised her family by knocking on their door.

"He asked me if I'd like to be his daughter-in-law. Can you believe that?" Shu-hui told me one night, as she looked across the dinner table toward Wu, still somewhat incredulously. "I agreed to go on a few dates, and things slowly happened."

Wu's father is also the one who first employed Yan to paint the theater's billboards back in 2000, and over the years, the artist has become an extended member of the Wu family. "We have such a long history together and a really close connection. I've watched their kids grow up," Yan said, showing me a picture of him surrounded by the Wus at a restaurant to celebrate his last birthday. "It is Mr. Wu who has helped to promote my work. It is all thanks to him that I can continue."

Having never married and with no children of his own, Yan views painting as his life partner and pours himself into each portrait. Over the years, he's acquired an intimate knowledge of how certain celebrities have aged, and has a favorite actor he likes to paint: Gal Gadot. "I am a huge fan of Wonder Woman!" Yan beamed. "She's even prettier than the other beautiful Hollywood women!" Yet, the Chin Men can only afford so many canvases, and so with most films the theater screens, Yan has to paint over his old work to make room for his new work, losing it forever. But before doing so, the artist takes out an old digital camera, shuffles over to face the marquee, and snaps a photo of the theater's façade as a final keepsake.

Ironically, while the Chin Men's paint-splashed marquee has become one of Tainan's most unique sights, for most of the past few decades, the paint-speckled artist working across the street has gone unrecognized and unnoticed. "A lot of people pass by me on the street and don't stop to look at me or watch me work. Taiwanese people are shy; they don't want to disturb you," Yan said one morning, as he spread white paint over his last billboard and began outlining a T-rex skeleton and Chris Pratt's face for the film *Jurassic World.* "Some people look up at the theater and realize I'm the one who painted these. Some even take photos of the billboards, and that makes me happy."

Yan estimates that he has painted at least 5,000 movies in his 52-year career—a number that equals the great Tze-fu and, in all likelihood, makes him among the most prolific film painters who has ever lived. Yet, it's one thing to be busy; it's another to be good.

I find Yan's work striking, especially given its surroundings. Tainan is often called Taiwan's cultural and spiritual cradle, a place home to wooden Japanese buildings and Confucian temples, and where people still cling to religious rituals from the days when the city was the last outpost of the Ming Dynasty. Yet, much of the 1.9-million-person city now has a decidedly modern feel. As in Taipei, the urban core near the Chin Men glitters with colored LED signs that adorn its tightly packed glass high-rises. Amid this backdrop, the sight of four billowing, two-story-tall oil paintings is enough to stop you cold. But since I'm not an artist, I'm really in no position to judge the master's work. So, I sent images of some of Yan's paintings to a Hollywood legend to hear his thoughts on Yan's technique.

"I am completely amazed by this man's wonderful work," said Drew Struzan, the artist behind more than 150 hand-painted blockbuster film posters, including *E.T. the Extra-Terrestrial* and the *Indiana Jones, Back to the Future, Star Wars,* and *Harry Potter* series. "The sheer scale he's working with, the energy and passion he has, it's beautiful. I've never seen anyone doing anything like this." When I shared Struzan's message with Yan, he appeared as overjoyed as I'd ever seen the artist. He was curious to know which of his paintings I had sent Struzan, so I handed him a series of postcard-sized prints of some of his previous posters I had purchased from the theater's concession stand. Yan held the stack up to his eyes, so close they were nearly touching his face, and squinted.

Fifty-two years of close contact with oil-based paint fumes has caused a number of holes to develop in both of Yan's retinas. Because the small holes in his left eye were located along the edge, doctors were able to surgically repair them. But the hole in his right eye was larger and located in the middle, "and so my right eye is now nearly blind," he said. "I can only see from the sides of my eye. The middle is all blurry." Doctors have told Yan that it's imperative he continue to come in for routine checkups every three months to prevent further damage to his eyesight, but Yan told me he can't remember the last time he went to the clinic. "I'm very busy," he said. "And I'm afraid of Covid-19."

I arrived in Taiwan expecting to find an island gripped by the looming threat of invasion. Instead, I found a people seemingly more concerned about keeping coronavirus away from their shores. Taiwan pioneered the "zero-Covid" policy China infamously adopted, and when I arrived, it was one of the last places on Earth that was still largely sealed from the outside world. Flight attendants on my China Airlines trip to the island wore hazmat suits and plastic face shields. As soon as we arrived at the Taoyuan airport, employees in full-body medical suits rushed over to douse each of us and our luggage with sanitizer from a pump sprayer before administering the first of several Covid tests. We were then whisked in a "quarantine taxi" to an officially designated Covid hotel and told not to leave our small, windowless cells for four days. Hotel employees dressed in biohazard suits left boxed meals outside my room, rang the doorbell, and then quickly scurried away before I opened the door. Everyone arriving in Taiwan was required to obtain a Taiwanese SIM card so the government could track and monitor your exact location, and there are stories of people in quarantine hotels swarmed by the police mere minutes after their cell phones died and their location could no longer be verified. I was assigned a government agent who identified himself as Mr. Lee and who checked in on me each morning with a phone call in impeccable-but-stern English, ordering me to immediately upload a picture of my hotel-issued thermometer to register my current temperature. When I'd send him the picture, his strict demeanor instantly softened, and he'd respond with emojis of dancing teddy bears or babies blowing kisses, which I found both confusing and adorable.

As a result of these measures, Taiwan reported some of the world's lowest Covid case rates for much of the pandemic.[23] But like much of the world, the pandemic had a devastating effect on the island's movie theaters—especially independent, second-run cinemas like the Chin

Men. "During coronavirus, many of the customers didn't come to the cinema, and we had to close for a few months last year [in 2021]," Wu said. "Running this theater is our family's destiny and purpose. We have been open for 73 years, and our goal is to run it for 100, but business is very bad. We are losing money."

In a way, the Chin Men is one of the lucky ones. According to Wu, of the 17 second-run theaters that were left in Taiwan in 2020, at least 10 were forced to close permanently because of the effects of the pandemic. One of these was the Zhongyuan Theater in the northern city of Taoyuan, whose billboard master, Hsieh Sen-shan, was the last remaining film painter in Taiwan besides Yan before the theater shuttered in June 2020.

Known as "Moriyama," the 77-year-old had worked for the Zhongyuan Theater for more than 60 years. Like Yan, he dreamed of painting the movies on billboards when he was a child and started as an underpaid, starving apprentice who was only allowed to watch his master. He remembers biking 25 kilometers at night from Taoyuan to Taipei's bustling Ximending cinema district as a 16-year-old, where the buildings were taller, the movie billboards were larger, and their colors more vibrant than anything he'd ever seen before. He'd shine a flashlight on their sailcloth canvases to study how the masters mixed their colors. From the 1960s to 1980s, Moriyama worked for seven second-run theaters in Taoyuan, but as digital printing became more common, his list of clients slowly disappeared until the only one left was Zhongyuan.

When I asked Moriyama how he would feel if this once-ubiquitous Taiwanese tradition were to fully disappear, there was a noticeable pause on the other end of the line. "I am quite emotional about the situation. It is such a difficult skill to acquire, but now there isn't much need for people like us. I had to retire. Mr. Yan is in his seventies, and his eyes aren't so healthy, and I worry that after he retires, there will be no one to carry it on. This beautiful tradition will be gone on this island."

Yan recognizes that Taiwan's hand-painted billboards are likely to disappear with his eyesight. So, after 52 years of immortalizing stars, he has spent the past eight years instructing aspiring artists. Now, most weekends, a group of 10 to 15 students eagerly wait under the awning across from the Chin Men Theater until their master arrives on his rattling blue scooter. Armed with easels, chalk, and paint, Yan patiently shows the group how to carve a canvas into triangle grids, how to mix six cans of paint into thousands of colors, and how to search in a subject's eyes to find their "essence." His teaching style, however, is quite different than how he learned from his master years ago.

Over several sweltering mornings, I watched as the students tried to reproduce a scaled-down version of Yan's *Top Gun: Maverick* poster. In addition to letting the group observe Yan as he worked, the master also made his rounds to watch each student work, allowing them to ask him questions and offering soft-spoken advice.

"I really admire his persistence, not just in painting, but in everything he does in life. He makes sure he will complete everything 100 percent and that it's almost perfect," said Wu Hao-ze, who started apprenticing for Yan eight years ago by carrying his buckets and now helps him paint one to two large projects a year. "When he was a teenager, he had a dream to have his paintings hung up on a theater. He worked his whole life to make that dream a reality."

RuRu Kao, another student, came into Yan's life quite serendipitously. "I live in Taipei, but I love Tainan and would visit a lot. Whenever I'd come, I would see this elderly gentleman sitting here alone, and I could tell he was a master. I majored in painting in college and was fascinated by his technique; how he creates his range of colors; and how, with a single, quick glance at a poster, he knows where the shadows and light should fall. I finally got up the courage to ask him if he was the master for the theater. He was very quiet and said yes. I asked if I could be his student, and I've been following him for seven years," she said.

Along with the Wus, Hao-ze and Kao are Yan's family. Hao-ze drops what he's doing to help Yan whenever he needs a hand—whether it's helping him hang canvases on the theater's marquee or moving items in the cluttered apartment where Yan lives alone. He told me, "I will stay with the master until he retires." Yan is so introverted that he doesn't engage with many people. Yet, Kao said that Yan calls her most days "to chat for hours" and hinted that she knew a secret about the master that he's never told anybody else.

And so, after days and days of watching Yan work, I asked him one last question: having painted so many films about love over the years, had he himself ever been in love? The master smiled and turned bright red, turning into a bashful teenager. "I have someone in mind, but it's never evolved from a friendship into a real romance," he said, chuckling lightly before looking back down. "I've never told her how I feel. I'm too shy. But maybe she knows." I came to learn that this person is Yan's hairdresser. Once a week for the past 30-some years, whether he needs a haircut or not, the timid artist will finish painting for the day, hop on his blue scooter, and go see her so that she can trim what's left of his thinning salt-and-pepper hair. Yan's even taken her to the Chin Men Theater so she can see his work, and she told him that she thinks he has a unique gift. "We get along well," he said, softly. "I think we could be happy together. Maybe one day I'll tell her."

This isn't the only maybe in the master's life. Yan isn't sure if any of his apprentices will follow in his footsteps one day—or if there will even be a theater to employ them. As he explained, it's not entirely up to him. "I am looking for someone to carry this tradition on, but it depends on luck and karma and fate. You can't force it," he said. I suppose the same is true with love.

I told Yan that I hope he chooses to tell his friend how he feels some day; that Taiwan continues to chart its own course peacefully; and that his eyesight remains steady enough so that the next time I come back to visit him, I'll be able to find him working here, quietly, if less anonymously, on the paint-splattered sidewalk. How Yan's story ends isn't entirely up to him, either, but that hasn't stopped him from picturing the final scene: "When people ask me when I'll stop, I say I will keep painting until my eyes can no longer see."

7

Where Bees Are a Part of the Family

I believe it would be difficult to meet with any cottage beekeeper who did not honestly think that his insects were endued with knowledge and sagacity beyond that of the rest of the brute creation, and sometimes beyond that of mankind.
—Beekeeper in Shropshire, England, 1883

Alison Wakeman will always remember the moment she got the call. It was January 18, 2022, and she was driving alone from her home in Telford, England, through the medieval market towns and velvety heathlands of Shropshire County, tucked against the Welsh border. Her mother had gone into the hospital that morning to receive oxygen after experiencing some trouble breathing, and Wakeman needed to run a few errands before she and her stepdad picked her up that afternoon. On the way to get her car inspected, Wakeman's cell phone rang. It was a number she didn't recognize, but she pulled off the road into the shoulder and hesitantly answered, "Hello?"

It was a nurse from the hospital. She told Wakeman that while her mother was undergoing some routine tests, she had suffered a heart attack, and the doctors were unable to revive her. She was incredibly sorry. Wakeman's initial reaction wasn't grief, but shock and disbelief. Her relationship with her mom had been quite distant, and years of heavy smoking had taken a toll on her mother's health. Still, she had told her that she'd be there to bring her back home just a few hours earlier. After composing herself, Wakeman stared silently out of her windshield at the road. It was an unusually warm January afternoon. The sun had started to sink behind the rolling hills, and rays of light streamed diagonally through the clouds.

"I just remember thinking to myself, wow, what a gorgeous day to die," she said.

Wakeman turned the car around, and on her way back home, she began compiling a list of people she had to tell. She called her stepdad, Len, first. Then her brother, the truck driver, followed by several aunts and uncles. "Someone has to do it," Wakeman said. "You go into autopilot and just get on with it. But afterward, I felt I needed to do something normal and right. That's when I went to go tell the bees."

That evening, in the soft glow of twilight, Wakeman opened the door to her backyard garden and walked somberly past her terraced rows of vegetables, her gnarled apple and pear trees, and her four clucking chickens toward a lone beehive at the edge of her property. She lowered herself onto a nearby stack of timber, and in a hushed, soothing voice, she started to tell the bees about the death that had befallen the family. Wakeman said that even though she and her mother weren't especially close, she was tremendously saddened to learn of her sudden passing. She explained that when she phoned Len, who was a year older than her mom at 85, there was a long pause on the other end of the line before he finally said, "I'm going to be very lonely." And she told the bees that if there was an afterlife, she hoped they could pass the message on to her mother that she would very much be missed.

"It was quite an emotional time. It was difficult, but it was my duty to tell them. The bees are part of my family, so it's just good manners," Wakeman said, in a mellifluous West Midlands rhythm. It was only later when she emerged from her mental fog that Wakeman realized she had forgotten something important. "When my mum died, I was in such an absolute shock and daze that I didn't even drape a black ribbon over the hive when I put the bees into mourning."

Once upon a time, nearly every household in the rural reaches of the British Isles who kept bees followed a rather strange and touching tradition. Whenever an important event occurred in the family, it was the beekeeper's job to go out to the hives and tell the bees the news. This practice, known as "telling the bees," was most often performed during births, marriages, and deaths, but families also kept their bees abreast of important household comings and goings, and even local gossip. When a family welcomed a child, it was common to carry the baby to the hive and present the newborn to the bees. Before a couple was to be wed, the new partner needed to first introduce himself or herself to the bees of the house in order to gain their approval, or else their marriage was bound to be bleak. If there was a wedding, families often decorated their hives with flowers and left slices of cake outside so their bees could participate in the celebration. And whenever a death occurred in the family, the beekeeper had to put the bees into mourning by slowly approaching the colony at night, solemnly delivering the news, and draping a black cloth or crepe above the hive so neighbors knew the insects were grieving. If the beekeeper was the one who passed, then the job of telling the bees fell to the new beekeeper, who was to knock on the hives with the key to the house, relay the doleful news of their master or mistress's passing, and seek the bees' acceptance as their new caretaker before kindly asking them to stay. It was widely believed that failing to follow this ritual would result in the colony not producing honey, escaping, or even dying themselves. For a rural household who relied on their hive, this would be a terrible fate, but there are numerous accounts of families' beekeeping fortunes linked to how closely they followed this rite.[1]

No one is quite sure where or how this custom started. Some believe it may hark back to the ancient Greeks or Romans, who believed bees were capable of relaying messages between spirits and mortals.[2] Others claim it stems from the Egyptians, who considered bees sacred beings and heirs of the world to come.[3] What is certain is that while the custom of telling the bees was practiced as broadly as in France, Germany, and the United States, nowhere was it more popular than in Britain in the 1800s.[4] Strangely, by the turn of the century, the tradition had already started to disappear, and by the early 1900s, it had all but vanished.

I first learned about this endearing observance while reporting a story for the BBC in Northern Ireland about another age-old British custom (harvesting a rare, reddish-purple seaweed called dulse). When I arrived in the sleepy coastal village of Cushendun where I was staying, there was a copy of Steve Roud's fascinating book *The Penguin Guide to the Superstitions of Britain and Ireland* placed on the nightstand by my bed. I pored over it, and among the many rituals and irrational beliefs I unconsciously subscribe to—from avoiding the number 13 and rogue black cats out of fear, to touching wood and crossing my fingers to anchor a wish—there was one shibboleth I had never heard of but found quite moving: telling the bees. Roud's brief entry on the subject is written entirely in the past tense and is filled with historical anecdotes and first-person accounts from centuries past. However, his last line grabbed me: "It would be no surprise to learn that the custom was still carried out amongst some modern-day beekeepers." I just had to find them.

It turns out that most beekeepers are a rather quiet, unfussy bunch. Compared to, say, the last Inca bridge master or Scandinavia's last night watchman, who carry on their ancient rites publicly, finding someone who softly whispers their life's most intimate details to insects in the privacy of their own backyard proved to be a real challenge. For more than a year, I reached out to dozens and dozens of local beekeeping associations across Britain, Ireland, and the US (where British beekeepers later settled and introduced the custom; specifically, New England and Appalachia) to ask if anyone knew of a beekeeper who still maintained this tradition. Many had never heard of it. Others said they knew of people who "talk" to their bees, the way you might talk to a pet, but none who "tell the bees." Most simply said, "No."

"If I went to another British association and asked them if they knew of anyone who tells the bees, they'd almost certainly say they don't," said Anne Rowberry, the president of the British Beekeepers Association, which represents more than 28,000 beekeepers and 75 local beekeeping associations across Great Britain. "You might not find more than about 150 people in the world still doing this. We don't really know—it's very hard to estimate."

Then, just as I was about to give up, I received an email from a woman in Telford. It was a month to the day after Wakeman's mother had passed, and she let me know that not only does she still quietly carry on this custom, but she knows of another custodian in Shropshire who does too. So, several months later, at the start of bee-swarming season, I drove through the rural county's castle-crowned villages and bright yellow rapeseed fields toward Wakeman's red-brick suburban home, just above Ironbridge Gorge.

After walking past a black station wagon in the driveway with a sticker over the fuel door reading POWERED BY HONEY, I rang Wakeman's doorbell and looked down to notice two decorative bee garden stones on the stoop. Moments later, a 55-year-old woman with light blue eyes, short gray hair, and a t-shirt reading KEEP CALM, I'M A BEEKEEPER appeared. I followed her through the living room, past a blanket of Winnie the Pooh with his paw in a honey jar and two throw pillows of bumblebees on the couch, and into her glass-paneled conservatory overlooking the back garden. As she poured me a cup of coffee in a bee mug, I read the temperature on her bee-shaped thermometer, eyed the time on her honeycomb-shaped analog clock, and gently petted her terrier, Bumble, who rested his head on my lap. During the next three days, Wakeman explained why she and countless people before her believe these busy little creatures are capable of inexplicable powers that transcend life, death, and logic. And as I listened, it inadvertently unlocked something deep from my own family's past that I was just starting to understand.

Humans have always had an intimate relationship with bees. They pollinate the majority of our crops and many of our trees, giving us the food we eat and the air we breathe. For much of our history, they produced our only natural sweetening agent (honey) and our longest-lasting, cleanest-burning light (beeswax candles). Bees provided humans with one of the world's first medicines, and ancient civilizations from the Chinese and Egyptians to the Assyrians and Aryans prescribed honey for everything from digestive and heart issues to coughs and skin wounds.[5] Bees also supplied the secret ingredient in the world's first alcoholic drink, a mead-like wine that originated in China 9,000 years ago.[6] The act of hunting for honey itself may be one of the oldest human activities, and archaeological evidence suggests our Stone Age ancestors were exploiting wild hives before the advent of agriculture. Rock paintings outside Valencia, Spain, show that by 5500 BC, Neolithic tribes were going to such great lengths to obtain honey and beeswax that they'd risk their lives by teetering on rickety ladders to try to swipe honeycombs from cliff faces.[7] Some anthropologists even believe the energy-rich substance may have been the superfood that helped fuel human evolution and develop our large, metabolically costly brains 2.5 million years ago.[8] It's no surprise then that these tiny, golden creatures have inspired a sense of wonder and veneration since the dawn of time.

The ancient Egyptians may have been the first to domesticate bees, at least 5,500 years ago, and they believed the insects were created when the tears of Re, the Sun God, fell from the sky and touched the earth. In his book *The Tears of Re: Beekeeping in Ancient Egypt*, entomologist Dr. Gene Kritsky explains that as early as 3500 BC, kings declared the bee as the royal symbol of Lower Egypt, a giver of life, death, and resurrection. Bees also played an important role in guiding Egyptians into the afterlife, and it was common to use honey to embalm mummies and seal sarcophagi with beeswax.[9] Honey is one of the only foods in the world that never spoils, and it was often left in pharaohs' tombs so they wouldn't go hungry on their journey to the netherworld. When King Tutankhamun's tomb was opened in 1923, jars of honey were found from 1324 BC that were still perfectly edible. A papyrus text found inside another pharaoh's tomb from roughly 1500 BC called *Amduat* (That Which Is in the Netherworld) reveals that ancient Egyptians also believed the hum of bees were the voices of dead souls.[10]

Many societies around the world shared similar beliefs about honeybees. In the creation story of southern Africa's oldest-known inhabitants, the San, a mantis was sent to find the purpose of life and asked a bee to guide him. The bee carried the mantis over a river, laying the mantis in a flower and planting the seed of the first humans within it.[11] In India's oldest sacred book, the Rig Veda (1500–1200 BC), the Hindu gods Vishnu, Krishna, and Indra are called *Madhava* from the Sanskrit word *madhu* (honey) and are represented by a bee. Vishnu is depicted as a bee on a lotus flower—the symbol of nature, life, and rebirth—and where he steps, a spring of mead appears. There is even a Hindu bee goddess, Bhramari, who emitted a beelike buzzing sound that was often imitated in Vedic chants and is believed to be the very first sound in the universe.[12] As in ancient Egypt, rulers in India collected honey as taxes, and it was thought that eating honey would make you more eloquent.[13] Similarly, the Greeks believed that any baby whose lips were touched by a bee would become a great poet and speaker.[14] It was also believed that the father of mankind, Zeus, fed on the honey of sacred bees as a child, which eventually gave him the strength to overthrow his father, Cronos. Zeus thanked the insects by making them golden in color and strong enough to resist cold and wind. The Romans renamed Zeus as Jupiter and believed that bees flew to Mount Olympus to give him the gift of honey. In return, bees asked the god to help them protect their hives. Jupiter agreed to give them a stinger, but as payment for this gift, he told them that if they use it, they would pay with their lives.[15]

Because of their harmonious example of teamwork, bees and their sugary-sweet substance have also symbolized love and marriage throughout history. In ancient Hindu weddings, it was common to smear the bride with honey, and the Hindu god of love, Kama, is depicted with a bow and arrow whose bowstring is made of bees. In ancient Greece and Rome, Eros and Cupid were also bow-wielding gods, and in Renaissance art, they were often shown dipping their fingers into honey—a tradition that dates back to an ancient Zoroastrian wedding practice and is commonly observed across Islamic traditions today.[16] Likewise, in the "Promised Land" (which is referred to as the "land of milk and honey" throughout the Old Testament) and across the Jewish diaspora, some newlywed couples spread honey on their challah on Shabbat to bring sweetness to their first year of marriage. In early Christianity, this "honeymoon" period only lasted one lunar cycle, and it is thought to date back to the fifth century, when couples across Europe received one month's worth of aphrodisiacal mead in order to spur their chances of conceiving.[17]

According to Dr. Alexandra Sapoznik, a senior lecturer in Late Medieval History at King's College London, bees in medieval Europe symbolized not only eternal unions but an ideal model of Christian society itself. It was believed that each bee worked selflessly for the benefit of the hive under one "king bee," as it was then called, or papal figure. Since bees were never observed mating, medieval Christians accepted Aristotle's famous pronouncement that bees didn't give birth, and therefore believed they were "divine" beings connected to Christ and the Virgin Mary. As a result, it became common for medieval monks across Europe to keep bees in their monasteries and abbeys, with the 13th-century Flemish friar Thomas de Cantimpré writing: "Both the unity and the virgin purity of the bees should serve as an example to the monks. Stillness should fall upon the convent in the evening, as it does upon the hive."[18] Beeswax soon became the only suitable substance for making votive candles and conducting mass throughout the Christian world, and one can't help but wonder whether the idea that bees somehow represented a model society or even divinity led some to start treating these creatures as members of their own families.[19]

As with so many myths and folkloric customs, we may never know why telling the bees evolved into a decidedly British rite. Though, if superstitions are the modern survivors of beliefs from the past, then its origins are likely found in the beliefs of a people who once flourished in the British Isles: the Celts.

The Celts arrived in Britain sometime around 1000 BC, and it's been said that they sailed to its shores specifically to exploit its many wild honeybees.[20] According to *The Triads of the Isles of Britain*, a series of medieval manuscripts of folklore, Welsh bards recorded that the first name of Britain after it was settled was *Y Vel Ynys* (The Isle of Honey), due to its sheer number of bees.[21] In Celtic mythology, the sight of a bee after a death signified the soul leaving the body, and like the Egyptians, Greeks, and Romans (whose conquest of Britain in the first century AD greatly influenced Celtic customs into the Middle Ages), the Celts believed that bees could carry messages from one world to the next. As such, the Celts worshiped bees as bringers of wisdom from the gods and those in the afterlife.[22] Bees were so hallowed that people in ancient Ireland developed the *Bechbretha*, a comprehensive 20-page list of laws dedicated to beekeeping that was first written down in the seventh century. Among its many "bee-judgments," the doctrine commanded that anyone stung by someone else's bee would be entitled to a meal of honey from that beekeeper. If the person died from their sting, then a compensation of two hives was to be paid to the family of the departed. Stealing a hive, however, was a capital offense.[23]

Bee veneration persisted in pockets of the British Isles long after the Celts converted to Christianity. The modern Scottish saying, "Ask the wild bee what the Druids knew," is a relic of a belief in the western Scottish isles that bees possessed a secret knowledge known only to religious leaders and lore-keepers.[24] An old English and Irish legend recalled that bees hummed loudly outside the Nativity to celebrate Christ's birth.[25] When Britain finally converted from the Julian calendar to the Gregorian calendar in 1752

(170 years after much of Europe did), it removed 11 days from the year to adjust for Julius Caesar's solar miscalculation in 46 BC. According to one story, the fact that the bees could no longer be heard humming on Christmas's new date was understood as a sign of God's displeasure with the new calendar.[26]

Though telling the bees has ancient and medieval roots, its traditional practice may only date back to the 17th century. As Roud notes, the earliest written reference that hives should be moved following the death of a beekeeper is in Philipp Camerarius's 1621 book, *The Living Librarie, Or, Meditations and Observations Historical, Natural, Moral, Political, and Poetical.* Yet, by the 1800s, there are so many accounts of families putting their bees into mourning in England that the practice seemed to have become commonplace. As telling the bees spread throughout Britain, spilled into Europe, and sailed over to the United States, distinct regional twists emerged.

In Nottinghamshire, whenever a beekeeper died, the "old nurse" of the house was to approach the hive, knock, and then utter the plea: "The master's dead, but don't you go; your mistress will be a good mistress to you." In Germany, this appeal was often sung as: "Little bee, our lord is dead; Leave me not in my distress."[27] In her 2005 book, *Bees in America: How the Honey Bee Shaped a Nation,* apiarist Tammy Horn noted the news of a death in New England needed to not only be sung but rhymed in verse, such as: "Bees, bees, awake! Your master is dead, and another you must take."[28] Biologist Margaret Warner Morley's 1899 book, *The Honey-Makers,* notes that in Yorkshire, bees were invited to the funeral, while in rural France, some families buried an old garment belonging to the deceased by their bees.[29] Roud cites a beekeeper from 1895 who explained that in his hometown of Derbyshire, "When a bee-master dies, tins containing funeral biscuits soaked in wine are put in front of the hives, so that the bees may partake of their master's funeral feast."[30] Whereas, in a village outside Sheffield, a beekeeper in 1869 noted that it was customary "not only to inform the bees, but also to give them a piece of the funeral cake, together with beer sweetened with sugar."[31]

In addition to verbally telling the bees—and in some cases, feeding them—some families across England and New England also lifted and turned their hives to symbolize the bees accompanying the funeral procession. In Shropshire, this was known as "heaving up."[32] In parts of the US, it was called "ricking."[33] And in Devonshire, it was referred to as "turning round," with *The Gentleman's Magazine* stating in 1884, "The custom is (or was in the year 1790) to turn round the bee-hives that belonged to the deceased at the moment the corpse was being carried out of the house."[34] For any reader who might have found this practice antiquated or unnecessary, the magazine offered this cautionary tale: "On one occasion, at the funeral of a rich farmer at Cullompton, as a numerous procession was on the point of starting, a person called out, 'Turn the bees'; upon which a servant, who had no knowledge of the custom, instead of turning the hives about, lifted them up, and then laid them down on their sides. The bees, thus invaded, quickly fastened on the attendants, and in a few moments the corpse was left quite alone, hats and wigs were lost in the confusion, and a long time elapsed before the sufferers returned to their duty."[35]

In her book, Morley cites a few dramatic accounts from 19th-century English beekeepers who failed to allow their bees to grieve. In one instance, a man in Norfolk had recently purchased a hive after its former caretaker died. When he brought it home, he noticed the bees were very sickly, and realized, "they had never been put in mourning for their late master." After fastening a piece of ribbon to the hive, "the bees recovered; and when I saw them they were in a very flourishing state." In a more somber tale, a woman in Oxfordshire recalled that when her grandfather passed, he had 17 hives, "and because no one told them of his demise, every bee died."[36]

Bees weren't only invoked in morbid times. In fact, they were considered so intrinsically bound to human rhythms and rituals that they participated in our most intimate moments. An 1893 copy of *The Journal of American Folklore* described a Massachusetts wedding from the 1830s in which "the little workers were to be informed of the event, and receive a bit of wedding-cake."[37] Morley writes that in Westphalia, Germany, young lovers were to approach the bride's hive while a family member told the bees: "Here is the young man. May he not leave her when she has children!" While in Brittany, it was customary to decorate hives with a scarlet cloth and for the newlyweds to ask the bees for their blessing before spending their first night together.[38]

Fittingly for such a personal rite, some of the most affecting examples of telling the bees come from poetry, and they offer clues about the tradition's origins. In Welshman George Edward Rees's 1917 poem "Telling the Bees," a parenthetical just below the title states, "An old Gloucestershire superstition." Rees's account describes a grieving father treading heavy and slow toward his hive to tell the bees of his fallen son's death while fighting in World War I. The bees were the first to know of the boy's birth many years ago on a much happier day, and on the father's worst, he says he "cannot choose but tell the news—the bees have a right to know," before begging of his hive:[39]

Wise little heralds, tell of my boy; in your golden tabard coats
Tell the bank where he slept, and the stream he leapt, where the spangled
*   lily floats:*
The tree he climbed shall lift her head, and the torrent he swam shall thrill,
And the tempest that bore his shouts before shall cry his message still.

The most well-known ode to this funerary rite is Quaker poet John Greenleaf Whittier's 1858 poem "Telling the Bees," in which a man returns to the home of his former lover, Mary, after a year away. The man notices a small girl approaching the family's beehives, singing a mournful tune while "draping each hive with a shred of black." He says:[40]

Trembling, I listened: the summer sun
Had the chill of snow;
For I knew she was telling the bees of one
Gone on the journey we all must go!

The narrator thinks it is his lover's grandfather who has passed, until the last stanza, where he hears the girl beg the bees to stay at home because "Mistress Mary is dead and gone!" Whittier published this poem in *The Atlantic* and included an introduction where he explained that the custom of telling the bees was brought to the United States from "the Old Country" where it "formerly prevailed"—suggesting it had already started to vanish by the mid-19th century.[41] Yet, reports of rural residents on both sides of the pond continuing to tell the bees lingered on well into the 20th century.

In 1956, the Associated Press ran a story about a bizarre incident that took place at a beekeeper's funeral in the Berkshire mountains of Massachusetts. "A strange tradition, from the forgotten rural years when almost every family kept bees, was startlingly recalled after the death of John Zepka," the dispatch begins. "When the cortege reached the grave, mourners found the funeral tent swarming with bees—on the tent ceiling and clinging to the floral sprays . . . Nothing like it had ever been seen before. Recalled was the tradition 'Telling the bees.'"[42]

Five years later, in 1961, a similarly mysterious incident occurred when another beekeeper, Sam Rogers, died in the Shropshire village of Myddle, located just 15 miles from Wakeman's home. The *Shrewsbury Chronicle* reported that Rogers' children told the bees of his passing, and at his funeral, mourners noticed that "swarm after swarm of bees were coming from the direction of Sam Rogers' home a mile and a half away." The bees settled on Rogers' tombstone, "to the astonishment of the congregation." The head of the Shropshire Beekeepers' Association reported that he "had never heard of anything like it before." Inexplicably, "by nightfall, the bees had all flown back to their hives in the cottage garden where Sam Rogers had looked after them for so many years."[43]

And in what is surely the most famous example of this intimate rite, a few months after I left Wakeman's home, Queen Elizabeth II passed away, and the *Daily Mail* broke a story that starts: "The royal beekeeper—in an arcane tradition thought to date back centuries—has informed the hives kept in the grounds of Buckingham Palace and Clarence House of the Queen's death." The article details how the royal beekeeper placed black ribbons tied into bows on the hives, and explains, "The bees have also been told, in hushed tones, that their new master is now King Charles III."

When I recounted a few of these historical incidents to Wakeman in her conservatory, it seemed to only strengthen her conviction that there exists an inherent sympathy between bees and humans. Yet, unlike so many beekeepers before her who have felt bound to this custom, Wakeman didn't start telling the bees because of a family tradition. Instead, she came into it completely by chance, thanks to an old house and an old woman.

The youngest of three children, Wakeman is the product of an unlikely relationship between a coal miner and a greengrocer. As she does now, she spent much of her childhood buzzing around her family's garden. None of her relatives kept bees, and it was only as an adult when she stumbled upon a repossessed house for sale that the thought of beekeeping occurred to her. "It was a massive house that was tumbling down. The estate agent showed me around and I asked her, 'What are those big boxes in the garden?' and she said they were bees. I said, 'Oh, well, if I buy the house, will someone take them away?' And she said, 'Oh no. If you buy the house, they come with it,'" Wakeman said, as she stitched a patch of a honeybee on her beekeeping suit. "I'd never thought of keeping bees, but that was the light-bulb moment for me. The agent explained that you don't choose the bees of a house; the bees choose you."

Wakeman nearly bought the ramshackle home, but fate intervened in the form of Kama and Cupid's bee-lined arrow. At a friend's birthday party, Alison met a man named Steve and quickly found herself enthralled by his gentleness, kind eyes, and nonjudgmental demeanor. Like Alison, Steve loved gardening, animals, and spending time outdoors. The two soon fell for each other. Then, just three weeks after meeting, Steve surprised Alison with a question. His job had asked him to relocate to Switzerland, and Steve wanted to know if Alison would join him. "He told me if I didn't go with him, he wouldn't take the job. He said he didn't want to leave me!" Alison said, blushing as she looked out of the window toward Steve tending his tomatoes in the greenhouse. "We got married in Switzerland and were there for 23 months. It was amazing, but all the time I was there, all I wanted to do was to come home and have dogs, raise chickens, and keep bees. When we finally came home and settled here, we got a dog. Then we got the chickens. And then in 2013, after years of researching beekeeping, we started keeping bees."

Like most new beekeepers, Wakeman spent much of her first year getting stung a lot. She'd joined the Shropshire Beekeepers' Association and took a theory course, but learning to actually interact with the bees proved challenging. "It's quite daunting, because in the training, we had no practical experience of being in a bee suit and handling them. The first year, you're really getting used to the bees and learning how to handle them. You make mistakes, but what I love about beekeeping is you never stop learning. At the end of the day, bees have been on this planet for millions of years. They're going to sort themselves out. It's us humans that mess things up." When I asked her if she was ever afraid of what might happen once she got stung, she brushed it off. According to studies, it turns out you're nearly four times as likely to be struck by lightning as you are to die of a hornet, wasp, or bee sting.[44]

The following year, Wakeman was asked by a teacher at a local primary school to come speak to her students about bees. "I loved it!" Wakeman beamed. "And the kids loved it too—so much so that after two sessions, the head teacher told me they wanted me to stay and they'd pay me." That school soon recommended Wakeman to other schools, and schools started recommending Wakeman to social groups. "It just snowballed," she said. "What started as a volunteer thing became a paid hobby." Today, Wakeman has spoken to tens of thousands of children in more than 50 schools about bees and their importance to the environment. Her business, Alison's Bee Class, won an award for the best educational company in Shropshire. In addition to schools, she now speaks and offers beekeeping training courses to women's groups, gardening groups, and even vintage motorcycle groups. "It's just a bunch of old boys tinkering about who happen to be curious about bees," she said.

At the end of one of her talks in 2016, an elderly woman sitting in the back of the room raised her hand and asked Wakeman a question she'd never heard before. "She said, 'Do you tell the bees?'" Wakeman recalled. "I didn't know what she meant, so I said, 'Do I tell them what?'" The old woman briefed Wakeman on the custom she learned as a young girl, and when Wakeman went home, she started researching the rite with the diligence and energy of a worker bee. "I thought it was amazing! Its origins are very old and vague that it just feels so primeval, but it makes sense: there's something quite spiritual about beekeeping. You feel a connection when you're with them," Wakeman said. "That's when I thought, you know what, if any of the traditional events happen where I could tell the bees, I was going to do it, and I did."

Wakeman's first experience telling the bees was in 2018 when her father's wife, Barbara, passed. She sewed a black ribbon, draped it over the hive in her yard, and sat on the grass to quietly deliver the news. As with her own mother's death, Wakeman said that when she told the hive, an unmistakable calmness fell upon the bees, as if they were sharing a mournful empathy between species. When she later relayed the joyful news of two family marriages, she noticed a distinct, celebratory humming noise. And when she told the bees of the birth of her two nieces, using the same soothing tone that she always uses when telling the bees, a flurry of activity erupted. "When I tell people now that I incorporate this tradition into my beekeeping, their faces scrunch up and I can tell they think it's a bunch of mumbo jumbo. It's hard to explain without sounding silly, but there's a reason people have been carrying on this custom for a long time." Today, Alison and Steve keep close to 20 bee colonies at three different locations. As we piled into their black station wagon (which Alison calls "the Bee-mobile") and headed to a nearby solar farm where most of the couple's bees live in a grassy meadow, Alison told me that her most profound experience telling the bees wasn't when her mother died, but when Covid swept across Britain and the United Kingdom issued a mandatory lockdown.

"It was surreal. I remember watching the telly when Boris addressed the nation, and it was probably the worst experience for me ever. Like everyone, I just sat there wondering, 'Is this the end of life as we know it?' The first thing that crossed my mind was, 'How am I going to get to the bees?' So, we got in the Bee-mobile, drove to the solar farm, and I sat there on the pallets by the hives just pouring my heart out," Wakeman said. Steve had just left his corporate job to help Alison with her business, and the thought of having to abandon most of their colonies devastated them. "The bees are our life. I felt a duty to tell them what was going on, and when I did, they were just really calm, as with a death. We humans were all losing our heads, but the bees were just carrying on."

As Steve unlocked the fence leading to the sprawling, grassy solar park, Alison explained that bees were eventually classified as livestock in the UK, which meant she and Steve could come here to care for them while everyone else bunkered in. "Have you told the bees any other news or gossip?" I asked, zipping up a beekeeping suit Alison lent me and wading through the park's knee-high grass toward a stack of wooden hives. "Sure," Alison said. "I told them you were coming today." She then carefully opened the lid of a beehive, revealing a hidden, sophisticated civilization inside.

Bees are one of the most adaptable creatures on Earth. Some 2,000 years after Zeus supposedly gave them the strength to resist cold and wind, they live on every continent except Antarctica, and can thrive in the tallest mountains, wettest rainforests, and hottest deserts on the planet.[45] Alpine bumblebees can fly over the peak of Mount Everest by adjusting their wing-beat patterns to survive in extreme altitudes with lower oxygen.[46] Bees in the Amazon build interwoven canopies on the rainforest floor to keep the colony dry during the strongest deluges.[47] And in 2016, a new species of bee was discovered in Death Valley that survives by quarrying nests into sandstone cliffs to stay cool in the scorching sun.[48]

To date, more than 20,000 bee species have been identified. Only 10 percent of them are social, and only two bee species are considered domestic: the Asian honeybee and the Western honeybee, which is what Wakeman keeps.[49] While much remains unknown about many of the world's wild and solitary bee species, studies have shown that, despite having a brain the size of a sesame seed, the honeybees humans have long reared and revered are remarkably intelligent creatures capable of teaching, learning, giving directions, and even holding democratic debates.[50]

A typical honeybee colony consists of one queen, hundreds of male drones, and anywhere from 10,000 to 60,000 female worker bees. The queen controls the population of the hive and has the unique power to designate the sex of her children by laying fertilized female eggs or unfertilized male ones. Meanwhile, the drone's sole purpose is to mate with the queen. Drones don't work, they don't make honey, and they can't sting. They mainly sit around and gorge themselves on honey. And because queens are only able to mate during a very brief window, most drones don't even get the chance to do their one job.[51]

As Wakeman explained, "Since they don't want to get up too early, being men, drones leave the hive each day at around 10:00 A.M. and gather in drone congregation areas, like 'man zones.'" There, they wait for virgin queens to take their nuptial flights. When a young queen flies through a drone congregation area, it's every drone for himself. Using their comically large eyes and powerful wing muscles, the fittest and fastest drones chase after the queen and try to latch on to her back while flying at about 22 miles per hour. Then, in what has to be one of the most dramatic mating rituals in the animal kingdom, as the male inseminates the female, his genitals explode in an audible pop that can be heard yards away. The drone then passes out from the excitement, flips over, and falls heroically to his death while his genitals are still lodged inside the queen's reproductive tract. "It's nature's way of making sure another drone hops aboard," Wakeman said. Some 10 to 20 other drones will repeat this epic act during the queen's maiden flight, and all of this sperm will remain viable for the remainder of her three- to four-year lifespan.

A queen may lay more than one million eggs in her life, and anywhere from 90 to 99 percent of them will be female worker bees who are responsible for the construction, maintenance, and proliferation of the nest and colony. While every bee has a specific role to play within the colony, each worker bee actually progresses through lots of jobs in her short 30- to 60-day lifespan. From the moment she's born, she starts as a janitor who cleans up the hexagonal cell where she hatched. She may then transform into a nurse who feeds the brood; a temperature regulator who waves her wings in unison with other bees to create a misting effect with the water they collect; an architect who secretes wax to build honeycomb; a general contractor who fills cracks with propolis; a bodyguard who blocks the hive's entrance from enemies; and an undertaker who keeps the hive hygienic by dragging dead bees away.[52]

In his groundbreaking book *Honeybee Democracy*, biologist and honeybee behavioral expert Dr. Thomas Seeley explains that the amount of days each worker spends doing each job depends on the hive's needs. Honeybees are incredibly sensitive beings, so when certain tasks within the colony become more pressing, a honeybee's hormones will shift to trigger a career change. As Seeley writes, a honeybee colony isn't just thousands of separate bees, but "a single living entity that functions as a unified whole."[53] In other words, much like leaf-cutter ants, termites, and human beings, honeybees are the rarest of species: a complex superorganism. "Just as a human body functions as a single integrated unit even though it is a multitude of cells, the superorganism of a honeybee colony operates as a single coherent whole even though it is a multitude of bees," Seeley writes.[54] Therefore, the common belief that the colony is governed by her majesty the queen is false. The queen doesn't rule the colony; the colony's collective coherence rules her. And like humans, when honeybees put their heads together and share this collective intelligence, they're capable of making powerful decisions that can determine the future and fate of the colony. Nowhere is this more evident than in the final and most dangerous job in a worker bee's life: the forager or scout bee.

In a basic sense, the forager or scout bee leaves the hive to go look for something—most notably pollen and nectar.[55] For much of history, it was believed that forager bees relayed the location of their food source to the hive via scent, with other foragers then going out to search for the memorized smell. But in 1944, Austrian ethologist Karl von Frisch made a startling discovery that won him the Nobel Prize. He noticed that forager bees were able to communicate the direction, distance, and quality of nectar-rich flowers to their peers in an ingenious way: by dancing. Their little shimmy is known as the "waggle dance," and it's essentially a reenactment of the bee's recent flight. In it, the bee waggles back and forth on the comb in a straight line. The angle of this line indicates the location of the food source in relation to the sun's position. The length of time she walks in the straight line represents the distance of the resource, with every second representing roughly 1,000 meters of flight. After waggling a specific distance, the bee then turns to her left or right, returns to the start of the line in a circular loop, and repeats this figure-eight boogie for a few minutes until enough bees learn the flower patch's location to fully pollinate it and bring back as much nectar to the hive as possible.[56]

In late spring, with the queen laying up to 2,000 eggs a day, honeybee hives become so overcrowded that some 40 to 60 percent of the bees will leave the hive to go look for a new home. This mass migration is known as a swarm, and it's how honeybees reproduce to form new colonies.[57] Choosing the right location for a new hive is a life-or-death matter. In his book, Seeley notes that if a colony chooses a cavity that is too small to hold enough honey for the hive to survive the winter, or is poorly insulated from predators or the elements, every bee will die. As with many human societies, whenever bees are faced with vitally important decisions that will determine their collective fate, they don't make these decisions individually, but via a unified consensus.[58]

In the case of house-hunting, a vast search committee of scout bees will go out looking for a suitable new home and relay the location of potential digs to the hive via the waggle dance. Once the other bees have visited all the different options, they will vote for their favorite by performing the waggle dance in the direction of the option they feel is the best choice. After dancing themselves into a unanimous consensus over a several-day period, thousands of bees will swarm out of the old hive in the same direction at the same time and condense in a beard-shaped cluster outside the new home. This coordinated act is emblematic of not only a superorganism functioning as an organic whole but also an enlightened democratic process. Scientists have found that the way individual bees work together in the hive is similar to how individual neurons function in the human brain, and the colony's collective decision-making has all the hallmarks of our most harmonious societies. It's therefore no wonder that the term people use to refer to both the collective, coordinated behavior of individuals within a group and also the general consensus of a group is "hive mind."[59]

"The behavior of bees gives some ideas why beekeepers have a very special relationship to them. They are insects and, in a sense, so different to us, but there is a special emotional and secret connection to how they act and how our own minds work," said Dr. Randolf Menzel, a zoologist, neurobiologist, and one of the world's leading experts on the nervous system of honeybees. "Like us, it's a bee's intelligence that keeps it alive. But unlike us, when it comes back to the colony, it gives up almost all its intelligence for the good of the group. This is a rather wonderful example of how human societies could be organized."

This special relationship between beekeepers and their bees has led to all sorts of superstitions based on the insects' behavior. As Wakeman told me, in Britain, if bees fly into a house, it means a stranger will soon call. If they rest on your roof, good luck is on its way. A bee landing on your hand means you'll soon come into wealth, whereas if it sits on your head, it's a sign of forthcoming success. Want to know if your husband has been cheating on you? Lead him past a beehive. If he's stung, it means he's been unfaithful. It's also considered bad luck to buy or sell hives, because when you sell one, you sell your luck with them. And since no bees like a quarrelsome family, you should always be careful to talk politely and quietly to your bees.[60]

It was the end of April and the start of bee-swarming season when I arrived in Britain, and Wakeman explained that there's a separate set of superstitions based on when bees navigate to a new nest. "A swarm in May is worth a bale of hay; one in June is worth a silver spoon; and a swarm in July ain't worth a fly," she said. Wakeman also explained that beekeepers don't actually want their hives to swarm, since it means they'd lose half their bees. Therefore, we'd come to the solar farm for two important reasons. The first was so that she could induce an "artificial swarm" and split her colony into two by delicately removing the queen from one hive, placing it in another with more room, and letting the old hive groom a new queen. "By splitting the colony into two, you preempt them swarming and increase your stock instead of losing your bees," she told me, closing the lid to the second hive when the deed was done. Then, as Wakeman pulled out a pink-and-white ribbon and draped it over the front of her favorite hive, I understood the other reason why she had come to visit the bees. There was news to share.

"Hi, girls," Wakeman said softly, as she took a knee on the ground beside her hive. "I've come to tell you that our next-door neighbors welcomed a little girl, Cassie, five days ago, and they're over the moon. Now, they aren't particularly close friends of ours, or else I'd have brought you cake. But I'm hoping that by sharing this good news with you, it will help you to expand your own colony to also produce lots of babies and brood. Thank you for listening."

As Wakeman delivered the news, dozens of bees swarmed out of the hive and landed on the back of her pink beekeeping suit. When she finished telling the bees moments later, they all flew off her and returned to the hive. Even eerier, the next morning when I returned to Alison and Steve's house, Alison casually mentioned something as she led me through her garden. "You know, something quite strange happened when Steve and I got back from the solar farm yesterday," she said, looking over the fence toward her next-door neighbors' house. "In two years of them living here, we've probably talked to them two times. They're quite shy, they are. But when Steve and I got back, they unexpectedly knocked on our door because they wanted us to know that they'd filled Cassie's nursery with decorations of bees."

I didn't know what to make of this. Much like with what I had witnessed when Wakeman told her bees about Cassie's birth, surely there was some logical explanation for each of these things. Maybe the bees flocked to Wakeman because it was the start of swarm season. Maybe Cassie's parents were inspired to decorate her nursery with bees because they knew their neighbors were beekeepers. I didn't know, but as I'd come to find out, the few other custodians I met who still carry out this rite each have tales of telling the bees that seem to defy logic.

While I was in town, Alison and Steve wanted me to meet their friend and fellow beekeeper Darren Williams. A tall, slender Welshman with shoulder-length brown hair, Williams and his family live alone in the graceful ruins of an abandoned 12th-century monastery called Buildwas Abbey. It's a picture-perfect scene of British medieval idyll: the family sleeps in what used to be the abbot's private chapel, they look out onto an ivy-clad arcade wrapping around a courtyard and a crumbling turreted tower, and they tend to a citrus grove in a meadow beside the River Severn. Shortly after moving in five years ago, Williams looked at his blooming apple and damson plum trees and sprawling wildflower patches and thought: "We should keep bees. Monks would have kept bees. Abbeys would have had bees. It just felt right to carry on this medieval tradition here, so I took a bee course with Alison." Through her, Williams discovered the custom of telling the bees and soon put it into practice.

When Williams brought home a New Zealand Huntaway sheepdog last year, he took her to the colony to introduce the new family member to the bees. Before inspecting the hives, Williams greets the bees in a soft, calming voice, "like you're seeing your grandma and having a chat." And as we sat on a bench in Williams' courtyard, he remembered something peculiar. "Last season when I'd inspect the hive, I'd get stung before I started talking to them. So, from my first-ever inspection this year, I talk to them right away and I've never been stung."

As with the case of Cassie, maybe this was just another coincidence—or maybe not. Aside from Wakeman, the only other beekeeper I was able to find from my more-than-yearlong search who still practices this tradition was Jacqualine Ferguson, and on my last afternoon in Shropshire, I rang her up.

Ferguson lives on a six-acre sheep farm in East Ayrshire, in western Scotland. She first learned about telling the bees from her grandfather, who lived in the Scottish Highlands and kept bees to pollinate his heather farm. As a young girl, Ferguson remembers seeing one of her grandfather's farmhands somberly draping a black strip across several hives, and she precociously asked him what he was doing. Wiping away tears, the man told her that his wife had just passed. The scene stayed with Ferguson throughout her childhood, and when she started keeping bees 18 years ago, she decided to incorporate this rite. Twelve years ago, she joyously brought her newborn daughter to her bees so they could meet her. In the years since, she's told her bees when her mother was diagnosed with dementia, when her nephew got engaged, and when the baby girl the colony had once met was old enough to start school. "All these wee things are part of our family's story," she said.

Ferguson has also had to put bees into mourning, when her beekeeper friend Jim died of a heart attack. After placing some of Jim's clothing atop his hive, Ferguson went out the evening he passed and explained to his bees that Jim wouldn't be coming to see them anymore, and that she'd be looking after them now. "You wouldn't believe it, but that summer, we got about 120 pounds of honey. In four years with those bees, Jim had never once gotten honey," she said. "Realistically, as an intelligent woman, I know it was the weather and other factors. But I can't help but wonder if the bees responded with such a lovely gesture to honor his life." Before signing off, Ferguson shared one final wish that Wakeman had also expressed days earlier. "Hopefully, when I go, someone tells my bees that I've passed away too. This is a dying art, but it's not dead yet."

In a world that increasingly relies on science over spirituality and reason over feeling, superstitions still have the power to captivate and control us. Billions of people pray, despite any definitive proof of a higher power. Others refuse to step on a crack, even though there is no medical evidence suggesting it may break your mother's back. And in a few pockets of Britain, a handful of beekeepers continue to tell their insects their deepest sorrows and greatest joys, even though, as Menzel unequivocally told me: "Bees do not hear. They cannot hear. They are extremely sensitive to vibratory signals and the velocity change of sound, but they cannot hear our voice."

Superstitions transcend science and logic. They remind us that, for all our perceived command and control, we humans remain a vulnerable, insecure lot keen to put our faith in something other than ourselves. But while we call to our livestock, talk to our pets, and may even sing to our plants, I don't know of any other relationship where we confide the most intimate details of our lives to another species out of trust and devotion. In a way, the closest analogy to telling the bees is talking to God. We are what we believe; it's what differentiates us from every other species. And from our earliest origins, we humans have recognized something special in bees that compels us to believe our lives are intertwined.

Today, with the global bee crisis reaching alarming heights, and our awareness sharpening of just how vital these creatures are to our own survival, we seem to have returned to an inherent kinship with bees. Simply put, we cannot live without them. Bees are the most prolific pollinators of the 240,000 species of flowering plants and more than half of the world's 3,000 crop species.[61] They are responsible for one out of every three bites of food we eat and pollinate 70 of the top 100 crops that feed 90 percent of the world's people.[62] More than any other creature, bees are also what make the world we live in so stunningly diverse and beautiful. Their pollination is responsible for the richness of our tropical rainforests, grasslands, and woodlands, as well as the millions of species that depend on them. In effect, modern science has proved what ancient societies understood long ago: these tiny, golden creatures are imbued with extraordinary powers that can determine our fate as a people—or in my case, as a person.

I never knew my mother's mother, but as another Quaker poet, my father, once wrote: "So many springs she knelt down on a rubber pad in dirt to mulch and prune, plant and graft, an innocent woman, loving hard at the mercy of flowers; the gift of bees."[63] One afternoon, she opened the door to her rural cottage, just as she had so many spring and summer days before, and knelt down to breathe life into dirt. As she reached for an ajuga plant with scissors, a bee landed on her finger, found a vein, and stung her as she snipped. My grandfather found her, collapsed and unconscious among the blur of color she'd created, and rushed to deliver the adrenaline injection the doctor had prescribed. Like my grandmother, he knew there was no medicine for the right sting, and by the time they arrived at the nearest hospital, it was too late.

My mother was five months pregnant with her first child when a single sting suddenly stole from her the one person who could teach her how to be a mother. It shattered her. She stopped eating, lost weight, and then somehow found the strength to give birth and raise one son and then another while still grieving. We never talked about it much growing up. But I remember when I was six years old, she picked me up from school, and as we walked past a garden, I asked her, "Mom, what would you ever do if you saw the bee that stung your mother?" A flash of heartbreak fell over her face, but she quickly forced a smile and said, "You know, it's not the bee's fault. The bee was just doing what a bee does," and with that, she reached for my hand and we bent down together to smell the blossoms. It was the only time she ever let me see the shadow she must have carried. She inherited her mother's deadly bee allergy, but also her love of flowers. She gardened each spring, filled our home with bouquets, and spread honey on my sandwiches every day before school for 12 years.

Just as I began researching this story, my wife and I were overjoyed to soon welcome our first child. In what was supposed to be a routine checkup in the third trimester of my wife's pregnancy, the doctor noticed a troubling irregularity with our son's heartbeat that quickly became a life-threatening emergency. Before I knew what was happening, I was clenching my wife's hand as she lay unconscious and convulsing on the operating table. I stared down while they carved her open, and as our son cried out to her with his first breath, I prayed that, like my mom, he wouldn't lose his mother at the exact moment when he needed her the most.

Six weeks later, on a warm spring day, my wife and I were finally able to welcome my parents to our small garden apartment so they could meet their first grandchild. We sat outside, surrounded by beds of pollinator-friendly flowers my mother had taught me to plant long ago, and a faint buzzing hiding in their blooms. As my mom cradled our son on her lap, angling him to avoid the bulge from the EpiPen she always carries in her pants pocket, I told her that I couldn't imagine what that day so many years ago must have been like for her, and all the days that came after it. For the first time, she told me.

They say grief is love with nowhere to go. Some people pour their anguish into a hobby; others share it with their bees. At her lowest point, my mom threw that love into everything and everyone around her, putting forth her most hopeful side, finding beauty in simplicity, and saying yes to the world without dwelling on what it took from her. She went back to work, kept laughing, and returned to her garden, never once waving off a bee. Like her mother, she still talks to strangers without a pause, and believes that empathy and curiosity are a practice. She accepted life's uncertainties while allowing herself to still be transformed by its wonders. In the process, she sent me out into the world with an optimism and openness that is distinctly hers. She dared me to listen, and reminded me that everyone has a light within and a story to tell. In many ways, this book is hers. I'll never know who my mom would have been were it not for a bee—and therefore, who I might have been too. But I like to think that if she ever did see the bee that stung her mother, she'd bend down, speak softly, and pass along a little message.

8

The Only Democratic Job in Cuba

To educate is to free.
—José Martí

The workers told me that the Count of Monte Cristo had been imprisoned a week before I landed in Cuba. Falsely accused of treason and jailed on a French island without a trial, the young man lay rotting away, deprived of any human contact. Day after day, page after page, the workers listened as the count begged for fresh air, prayed fervently, and threw himself against the walls of his stone cell in a fury of rage, but the only people who could hear his cries were a world away in Havana's La Corona cigar factory. Here, on the third floor of a hulking, Soviet-style compound, 335 cigar rollers sat side by side at what looked like 19th-century schoolhouse desks arranged in long rows facing an elevated platform. The air was thick with the earthy scent of fermented tobacco, and a few cracked windows let Havana's steamy humidity seep into the building, assuring the valuable leaves wouldn't dry out. As the workers busily packed, cut, and wrapped the delicate, dark leaves by hand, an eerie quiet hung over the factory floor. The men and women were clinging to every word of the story coming from the podium.

After four years on the island prison, the count had resigned himself to the fact that he'd likely never make it back to the mainland to see his father and fiancée again, so he resolved to starve himself and end his despair. Then, just as he had withered to the brink of death, he heard a faint scratching sound chipping away at his cell from the other side. The unexpected noise filled the count with a renewed hope. Upon learning this, several cigar rollers suddenly paused their hands' frenetic choreography and looked up from their wooden workbenches toward the voice captivating them from the front of the room.

"Although weakened, the young man's brain instantly responded to the idea that haunts all prisoners—liberty!" said Odalys de la Caridad Lara Reyes, seated behind a desk and speaking into a microphone. Lara Reyes turned the page in her frayed book and continued reading. "Perhaps one of those beloved ones he had so often thought of was thinking of him, and striving to diminish the distance that separated them." Lara Reyes then glanced up at the clock, placed a bookmark in the Alexandre Dumas classic, and clasped it shut. "We'll continue tomorrow," she said, smiling. As if on cue, the hundreds of *torcedores* (rollers) began banging their curved *chaveta* knives wildly against their wooden worktables in a raucous applause that reverberated through the galley.

Six days a week for the last 30 years, Lara Reyes has boarded a bus at 6:00 A.M. to get to La Corona before dawn. She then combs through half a dozen newspapers in her small office before climbing the three creaky wooden stairs leading to the rolling room's platform and taking a seat below an oversized photo of Fidel Castro in military fatigues to begin her job as a *lector*. As the official "reader" in Cuba's largest cigar factory, she broadcasts the day's news each morning to the rollers in the galley, as well as to an additional 300 leaf sorters and stemmers working on the floors below via a loudspeaker. In the afternoon, she recites new and classic novels that the workers have chosen, as a library-like silence falls on the floor. If the workers like what they've heard, the room will erupt with a cacophonous hammering of chavetas at the end of her shift. But if they're not convinced by her delivery, they'll toss the double-edged knives on the floor in protest.

Cuban cigars are renowned as the finest in the world, but one of the most important and least understood parts of their production is the role of the cigar factory reader. A unique and exclusively Cuban job today, lectores like Lara Reyes have been reading the day's news, translating novels, and reciting poems in the island's cigar factories for more than 150 years. Without any machinery to muffle noise, a lector could broadcast his or her voice to hundreds of torcedores as they rolled handcrafted *habanos* to the rhythm of the reader. The idea was initiated by political reformists as a way to increase workers' education, broaden their worldview, and elevate class consciousness while rollers concentrated on their craft. Inspired by the texts they heard, these early cigar workers founded Cuba's first trade unions, and many later rebelled against Spanish rulers while playing a pivotal role in the Cuban War of Independence. Revered by rollers, cursed by factory owners, and forcibly banned by the Spanish colonial government, the keepers of this seemingly quaint tradition served as a lightning rod in the ideological battle for Cuba's nascent identity between the 1860s and 1930s. Even the "Apostle of Cuban Independence," José Martí, gave some of his most electrifying speeches from the lector's podium to throngs of tobacco workers.[1]

Today, cigar reading has been described as "the only job in Cuba that is democratically decided,"[2] as the rollers cast their votes to choose the lector who reads to them, as well as what will be read. A good lector will help workers focus as they carefully roll a world-class *puro habano*; an unconvincing one could harm productivity; and a master lector reading a stirring work may inspire a remarkable artistic flourish. In fact, it's rumored that many of Cuba's most famous cigar brands are named after some of the rollers' favorite books over the years, from *Don Quixote*'s Sancho Panza to Romeo y Julieta to one of the world's most popular cigars, Montecristo.

Cigars and literature have long had an amicable relationship. Poet Ralph Waldo Emerson is said to have smoked a cigar after his "mid-day dinner."[3] Studs Terkel, who lionized the tradition of the lector in his 1970 book, *Hard Times: An Oral History of the Great Depression*, smoked two cigars a day and lived to be 96.[4] And Mark Twain, who started smoking cigars as an eight-year-old before burning through 22 to 40 of the things a day as an adult, once declared, "If smoking is not allowed in heaven, I shall not go."[5]

I, admittedly, had never really given cigars much thought. I've probably smoked two in my life, and I've generally associated them with the sort of gated wealth and status that just doesn't interest me. To me, cigars might as well be golf. Then in December 2019, while sifting through the racks of an outdoor flea market in Old Havana, I came across a postcard from 1902 of a man in a Havana cigar factory perched high on a chair, reading a newspaper aloud to a packed room of workers as they busily rolled tobacco leaves at their workbenches. The reader and the rollers were all wearing crisp button-down shirts and top hats, and there was a quiet dignity and simplicity about the scene that stayed with me. After learning that this tradition had since disappeared elsewhere but still lingers on in certain pockets of the island that birthed it, I vowed to come back and find out as much as I could about this curious pastime.

Three years and a pandemic later, I found myself back in Cuba during one of the most volatile periods in the country's recent history, shadowed closely by a government agent and poking at the seams of a story that I soon realized was much bigger than the readers and rollers themselves. As Zoe Nocedo Primo, the former director of Havana's Museo del Tabaco, told me: "There really is no way of explaining Cuba without first understanding the history and culture of Cuban tobacco."

When Columbus first washed ashore in Cuba's Baracoa harbor in 1492, he wrote in his journal, "This island is the most beautiful that eyes have seen."[6] After a few days, he noted that several of the native Taíno people he encountered had a "half-burnt weed in their hands" made of dried, twisted leaves rolled into a tube that was lit at one end and inhaled at the other.[7] The Taíno called their cylindrical smokes *tabako*,[8] and they offered them to Columbus as a gift. In return, he promptly enslaved the Taíno and sent a few of the dried leaves back to Spain, giving Europeans their first whiffs of the stuff.

According to Primo, early *criollos* (ethnic Spaniards born in Cuba) began farming tobacco in the 16th century, and the crop soon expanded across the rural reaches of the island as farmers sought to escape the high taxes imposed by the colonial government in towns. In 1717, the Spanish Crown ordered that all Cuban-grown tobacco be sold to Spanish agents at a low fixed rate, shipped to Spain, and rolled at Spanish factories so that they had exclusive rights to sell it abroad.[9] When criollo farmers revolted, they were brutally suppressed, sowing the seeds of tension between criollo tobacco workers and the Spanish-born *penínsular* elites for years to come.[10]

In the early 1800s, Spain discovered that rolled cigars survived the trans-Atlantic voyage better than dried tobacco leaves, and an 1817 decree finally enabled Cubans to roll and export their cigars themselves.[11] By the mid-1800s, the new middle and professional classes that were emerging in Europe and North America started to associate hand-rolled habanos with wealth and sophistication. This led not only to a surge in demand for Cuban cigars but also to a surge in the number of Cuban cigar factories. According to historian Araceli Tinajero's terrific 2007 book *El Lector de Tabaquería*, by 1865, there were more than 500 cigar factories employing more than 1,500 people in Havana alone.[12]

Much like the island today, Cuba in 1865 was a melting pot of criollo, Spanish, West African, and mixed-race people and cultures. It was also a powder keg of political and social ideas, and colonial officials were besieged by demands from Cubans to abolish slavery, create equal status among criollos and peninsulares, and improve working-class rights. As tensions bubbled up, criollo farmers formed the short-lived Partido Reformista (Reformist Party). At the time, newspapers were the front lines of Cuba's ideological and social fight to sway public opinion, and reformists had recently launched a daily paper, *El Siglo,* to challenge the colonial press and defend the rights of the working class. Yet, as Tinajero notes, in 1865, 70 percent of Cuba's white population and 95 percent of its nonwhite population was illiterate.[13] Reformists could write about revolution all they wanted, but in order to rally the masses, they needed a voice to amplify the call.

Saturnino Martínez had an idea. A cigar worker and self-taught poet, Martínez had heard that a prison in Havana had recently started reading aloud to inmates. Martínez wanted to adopt the idea, but instead of reciting religious texts as they did in the jail, the cigar rollers would select works that would broaden their worldviews and encourage them to study on their own. Martínez even launched Cuba's first workers' newspaper in October 1865 to fuel the readings. He named it *La Aurora (The Dawn),* a nod to the collective intellectual "awakening" he sought to inspire.[14] On December 21, 1865, the first reading took place amid a packed room of 300 torcedores at Havana's El Figaro factory. The rollers embraced the readings so much that after just a few months, reading aloud had spread to every major factory in the capital, and soon after, every corner of the island.[15] On January 7, 1866, *La Aurora* published an article trumpeting the success of these initial readings, writing: "Today, even in the heart of the workshops . . . imaginations are busily questioning scientific and philosophical truths meant to keep the workers abreast of the age to which they belong. They are talking and discussing; they are reading the works of good modern authors and consulting with each other about any point outside their intellectual grasp; in short, they are doing what they can to learn and to continue along the path of civilization."[16]

Cuba's initial lectores weren't professional readers but literate workers chosen from the rollers themselves who read on a rotating basis. Dressed in sharp white shirts and projecting their voices from atop a raised podium, lectores educated and entranced the rollers by reciting the day's news and delivering stirring renditions of classic literature, enticing the workers' minds to drift as they silently toiled away. "It has always been a special job, like a teacher and a journalist wrapped in one, so you needed someone with a nice, clear rhythm to their voice," Primo explained. Since each roller was responsible for producing a certain amount of cigars each day, the other rollers would give a percentage of their daily pay to compensate the lector for the wages he missed while reading. The workers even elected a president, secretary, and treasurer to oversee the process.

In addition to the reformist calls printed in *El Siglo* and *La Aurora*, readers also read regional newspapers from across Cuba. The archives of these pages serve as the best evidence of what Cuba's early lectores read to their audience—which ranged from biographies of Benjamin Franklin, Abraham Lincoln, and Bernard Palissy to novels by Victor Hugo and Miguel de Cervantes to plays by Friedrich Schiller.[17]

"Cigar factories became like classrooms where workers were sitting side by side, exchanging ideas, and being socialized," said Louis Pérez, a history professor at the University of North Carolina at Chapel Hill and the author of 12 books on Cuban history. "Before the radio, I can't think of a quicker way to disseminate information and ideas. You had hundreds of people in each factory who went home and told other people what they learned, and this is why readers and their messages were so impactful."

The rise of the reader had an immediate and resounding effect that extended far beyond the cigar factories. In his 1942 study *La Lectura En Las Tabaquerias*, historian José Rivero Muñiz writes: "Through reading, the cigar maker managed to stand out from the rest of the Cuban proletariat, serving as a mentor and guide when the social emancipation movement dawned in Cuba."[18] In June 1866, six months after the first reading took place, tobacco workers formed Cuba's first guild, La Asociación de Tabaqueros de La Habana, and elected Martínez (by then a lector himself at Havana's Partagás factory) as its president. As Muñiz noted, "the tobacco [workers] acquired a true class consciousness more quickly than any other sector of the Cuban proletariat," and this first tobacco guild soon inspired other artisan guilds and workers' unions to form.[19]

This ripple effect likely never would have happened were it not for the cigar factory readers and the newspaper specifically designed to be read to its workers: *La Aurora*. In its first few months, the paper successfully fought to extend library hours from 3:00 P.M. to 9:00 P.M. so that working-class Cubans could access the buildings. It also opened up dozens of artisan schools, which gave all workers—not just cigar rollers—access to free daily education. In less than a year, Muñiz notes that the lector and *La Aurora* had "managed to awaken class consciousness in [working-class Cuba]."[20]

Predictably, authorities tried to muzzle the reader almost as soon as he opened his mouth. Government officials feared educating the masses posed a direct threat to the colonial regime, while factory owners believed it would distract rollers from their work. Yet, most observers of the time—including US Secretary of State William Seward, who toured the Partagás factory in 1866 and noted "the profound silence of the workers listening to the reader"[21]—marveled at how the lector helped increase cigar production by fostering discipline. Some rollers were even known to work longer if it meant seeing how a novel's plot would unravel. Still, Don Jaime Partagás, the powerful Spanish owner of the Partagás factory, demanded that "all works to be read would first have to be submitted to my censorship."[22] Another peninsular, Ramón Allones, who owned the El Designio factory, told his workers that "shops were for working, not reading."[23] When *La Aurora* defended the practice from colonial criticism, it was censored, and eventually silenced altogether.

In May 1866, Cuba's colonial governor Don Cipriano del Mazo proclaimed, "newspapers and books contain certain sophisms and maxims detrimental to the weak intelligence of people who lack the judgment and education necessary to evaluate the authors."[24] Then in June, a mere six months after the first reading took place, authorities made it illegal for Cubans to gather, read books and newspapers, and have any discussion about literature that wasn't directly related to their work. The ban would last until 1868, shortly before the tinderbox of Cuban separatism ignited in the Ten Years' War (1868–1878). The decade that followed was marked by a prolonged period of Cuban repression, industrial devastation, and a mass exodus from the island. As a result, the voice of the lector wouldn't be heard again in Cuba until the 1880s. By 1869, an estimated 100,000 Cubans had been forced into exile. Several thousand of these émigrés were politically charged cigar rollers who fled just 90 miles away to Key West, Florida, passionately preserving the call of Cuban independence and ensuring the survival of the Cuban lector abroad when it was silenced at home.[25]

Key West was little more than a pirate's lair in the 1860s and '70s, but by the 1880s, Cubans had transformed it into Florida's largest city. According to George Pozzetta and Gary Mormino's research paper, *The Reader and the Worker:* Los Lectores *and the Culture of Cigarmaking in Cuba and Florida,* as the exiled cigar rollers began working in newly formed US factories, they attracted a talented cadre of readers whose influence would go on to shape Cuban identity.[26] Among them was Ramón Rivero y Rivero, who organized revolutionary clubs and founded or edited an eye-popping 14 newspapers; Fernando Figueredo, who later returned to become Cuba's first treasurer after it gained independence; and Carlos Baliño, who is often credited with introducing Marxism to the island.[27]

Another of these exiles was Vicente Martínez Ybor, a cigar manufacturer who ran afoul of Spanish authorities in 1868 for supporting Cuban independence. Faced with the prospect of death by hanging, he fled from Havana to Key West, hired as many exiled Cuban rollers as he could in his new factory, and then relocated north to Tampa in 1885—bringing scores of Cuban torcedores with him. When he showed up, Tampa had fewer than 2,000 people and no streetlights or paved roads. So, he built Ybor City, a planned industrial community that would soon go on to become the cigar capital of the world, producing 500 million hand-rolled cigars a year in more than 200 factories—each of which employed a lector.[28]

Away from the censorship of colonial authorities in Cuba, the reader's role in Florida evolved into something of a community leader and organizer. Ybor City's multiracial and working-class community displayed a fierce commitment to social justice and Cuban independence, and readers played a pivotal role in fanning the flames of the revolution. In the morning, lectores broadcast local reformist newspapers, as well as dailies arriving from Cuba and New York, nimbly translating English into Spanish and infusing emotion into the printed word. In the afternoon, they read the likes of Tolstoy, Marx, Bakunin, Flaubert, and Dostoyevsky, using their podiums as a stage as they breathed life into their protagonists. Outside the factories, they helped create social clubs that offered free night schools, libraries, and public lectures.[29]

One of the most popular newspapers the lectores in Ybor City read aloud was *Patria,* edited by José Martí in New York. A Cuban-born teacher and writer whose fiery rants against the Spanish regime led him to be exiled as a teenager, Martí went on to become the greatest revolutionary hero of Cuba—a towering figure Mormino called the country's "George Washington, Abraham Lincoln, and Thomas Jefferson rolled into one."[30]

In November 1891, a group of prominent lectores invited Martí to speak to cigar workers in Ybor City. The rollers even pooled their wages together to finance his trip. From the moment Martí set foot in Florida, he was accompanied by readers who drummed up support for his visit and introduced him in the factories where he spoke. As Tinajero writes: "Martí knew that, if he were to win over the cigar workers of Tampa, he first had to establish an extremely close connection with the lectores, because they were the linchpins of the cigar factories."[31] Martí delivered two of his most famous speeches to a packed crowd of cigar rollers from the reader's podium at Ybor's El Liceo Cubano factory. These speeches laid the groundwork for Martí's Cuban Revolutionary Party (PRC) that would eventually lead the insurrection against Spain. Lectores in attendance transcribed Martí's patriotic rhetoric and rushed to submit it to newspapers, while readers at factories in Key West and Cuba (where reading had since resumed) recited them with an inflamed passion that unified the workers and sparked Cuba's successful struggle for independence. Through the lector, Martí was able to speak to all Cubans—exiled and fighting at home. "In great measure, those lectores changed the course of history," writes Tinajero.[32]

"What has really passed by generations of scholars is that, up to 1890, the independence movement in Cuba [was characterized by] spontaneous military leaders rising up on one part of the island, declaring independence, and getting crushed," said Pérez. "What Martí does is he creates a political party, gathered resources, and developed a structured leadership to organize a war. That was a goddamn unheard of thing in 19th-century Latin American independence movements—it was a century ahead of its time. And it's not an accident that Martí takes this radical vision of a sovereign nation to the cigar workers. He has some sense of the politics of these people."

Martí went on to visit Tampa and Key West more than 20 times from 1891 to 1894, each time accompanied by lectores and community leaders who began to form his revolutionary entourage.[33] In 1893, he delivered a speech in Tampa that many historians feel led directly to war with Spain. As more than 10,000 Cuban exiles and cigar workers gathered outside the V. M. Ybor Cigar Factory to hear Martí's rousing appeal of *"Cuba Libre!"* rollers punctuated his call by raising their knives and shouting "Free Cuba!" Cigar workers soon started donating one day's pay a week to help Martí's party purchase war matériel for the coming insurrection, and hundreds of cigar rollers formed infantry companies and began preparing themselves for battle.[34]

This revolutionary fervor would culminate with the most famous cigar ever rolled. In 1895, Martí called a secret meeting of the PRC's revolutionary cabinet in New York, and they decided to launch a surprise revolt against Spain. After Martí signed an order issuing the uprising on a sheet of white paper, the party was tasked with the dangerous mission of delivering the handwritten message to Cuban leaders. The secretary of the PRC placed the note in his pocket, took a train to Ybor City, and met Figueredo at the train station. In order to smuggle the note past colonial authorities in Cuba, Figueredo suggested they conceal the insurrection order by rolling it in a cigar. Late one night, Figueredo led a group of revolutionaries into the O'Halloran Cigar Factory, where he used to serve as a lector, and they rolled five slender panetela cigars. Each was identical, except for one with two tiny yellow specks on the tobacco wrapper—the so-called "Cigar of Liberty."[35]

On February 21, 1895, a courier sailed to the seething island of Cuba with four cigars in his pocket and one in his mouth. When he arrived at the port in Havana, he calmly passed out the four panetela cigars to customs agents, kept the Cigar of Liberty in his mouth, and walked away into history. Thanks in large part to Cuba's lectores, who had passionately broadcast Martí's calls for "Cuba Libre!" from Florida to workers across the island, on February 24, the war cry of *"Viva Cuba Libre!"* electrified the nation, and Cubans embarked on their final struggle for independence, which would eventually come in 1902.[36]

———————

Today, the large rolling rooms in Cuban cigar factories where lectores read are still known as *galeras* (prison wings)—a nod to the places where reading aloud first took hold on the island. Yet, after helping to spur Cuba's sovereignty and inspiring some of the world's most recognizable cigars, this proud oral tradition is disappearing. The rise of cigarettes, machine-rolled cigars, and the Great Depression eventually silenced Florida lectores in the 1930s. In the 1920s and '30s, radios in Cuban factories began to reduce the time spent reading aloud, and eventually replaced many readers altogether. By 2009, an estimated 250 readers remained in Cuba. Ten years later, there were just 150. Now, according to numbers by Habanos S. A., the organization that oversees Cuba's state-run cigar industry, there are just 50.

In a way, what's even more surprising is that this timeworn tradition hasn't vanished entirely. But on an island whose relationship with time is complicated, its survival somehow makes sense here. From the moment you leave Havana's José Martí Airport and head toward the city, you're thrust into a parallel world where every moment that has seemingly come before in Cuba is still present. Horse-drawn carriages share the road with American Chryslers from the 1950s and Soviet Ladas from the 1970s. Crumbling Baroque palaces stand next to neon-lit Art Deco theaters and

Brutalist office blocks. Devotees of Afro-Caribbean Santería in all white wander past smartly dressed Spanish socialites talking to criollo bodega workers sporting New York Yankees hats. It's a dizzying collage of opulence and decay; colonialism, capitalism, and communism; Europe, Africa, and America.

In modern socialist Cuba, time, like most everything else, is a shared asset. Walk anywhere in Havana and you'll inevitably pass people on the street waiting in long lines to enter supermarkets, banks, post offices—anything. Gustavo García Bello, a cigar roller at the Partagás factory, told me that Cubans have gotten so used to waiting in lines that lines no longer exist. Instead, the island is filled with groups of people clustered together, texting, chatting, laughing, and otherwise going about their day as they patiently wait their turn for anything and everything. "You go somewhere, you ask '*Ultimo?*' (Who's last?), and you wait for time to pass."

I arrived in Cuba on the first of the month, the day Cuban newspapers print the locations where people can receive their monthly subsidized rations of five eggs, one liter of cooking oil, one pound of spaghetti, three pounds of sugar, six pounds of white rice, 20 ounces of black beans, two packets of coffee, and daily dinner rolls from the government. When I showed up at the Partagás factory, first-year lector Felicia Alejandra Torres Rodriguez—a watch repairer who had dreamed of becoming a lector since elementary school—had just finished reading where workers can wait in line with their official *Libreta de Abastecimiento* (supplies booklet). I later asked Bello if the queues I'd passed on the way to the factory were longer because it was the first of the month. "No, no," he said, smiling. "Every day moves slowly here." Amid this backdrop where old and new blend together and time seems frozen, the lector lingers on.

But while there were once hundreds of factories in Havana that employed a full-time reader, today there are only three: Partagás; El Laguito; and La Corona, where Lara Reyes was reading *The Count of Monte Cristo*. A short 60-year-old with graying hair, a contagious laugh, and perfect diction, Lara Reyes had previously worked as a DJ reading the daily news at radio stations. Then in 1995, her cousin, a rolling instructor at La Corona, let her know that there would soon be an opening for a new lector at the factory, but warned her she'd have to compete for the job. "It was me against two men, and they invited each of us to come in and read to the rollers for 21 days," Lara Reyes remembered, flashing an effervescent smile as we sat in her small office on the factory's ground floor, under a framed Che Guevara poster on the wall. "The hardest things for me to learn were the baseball terms in the newspaper, but the rollers were very kind and would tell me how to say them before it was my turn to read. At the end of these 21 days, the *tabaqueros* [cigar makers] voted secretly and I won!"

Now, as newer readers have recently started at Partagás and El Laguito, Lara Reyes is the last experienced lector left in Havana. As she explained, the rollers have always had the final say in who reads to them—and Lara Reyes takes her responsibility as their stentor and mentor very seriously. "I know all 300 rollers by name. For many of them, I know their birthdays and personal details about their families. Some come into my office and call me on the phone for advice," she said. "After 30 years, I still get nervous facing 300 people and reading, but that's out of respect and love for them."

Lara Reyes's first reading of the day starts at 8:15 A.M., when she recites poems she's written for rollers celebrating birthdays, reads birth announcements for families welcoming children, and requests moments of silence for those who have recently lost loved ones. She then transitions to practical advice based on topics rollers have privately asked her about, which can range from how to calm a screaming newborn to how to talk to your teenager about STDs. At 8:45 A.M., she segues into accounts of historical figures, which often relate to the novel she's reading. For instance, as she slowly works her way through *The Count of Monte Cristo,* she's reading profiles of Joan of Arc and Napoleon to the rollers. At 10:00 A.M., she turns to national and international news, reading articles she's marked with a pen from *Granma, Juventud Rebelde, Trabajadores,* and other Cuban newspapers. In all her years of broadcasting the news, Lara Reyes said two moments stick out: the first was the elation of being able to tell the tabaqueros that Pope John Paul II was coming to Cuba in 1998—a first for the nation. The second was the profound sorrow when she had to announce the loss of Cuba's titan patriarch, Fidel Castro, in 2016. "It was one of the saddest days of my career," she said. "We were crying, hurting.

There are no words to describe it." Then at 2:00 P.M., Lara Reyes launches into a novel. Since the lector was reinstated in Cuba in the 1880s, two important changes were implemented that remain in all factories today. The first is that the reader doesn't rotate from among the rollers, but is instead a professional selected from outside the factory. The second is that all books are selected by a "reading committee" consisting of workers and a few factory administrators. Lara Reyes explained that she generally presents five works she thinks the rollers will like, either from the library she keeps in her office or based on recommendations from rollers. She reads a synopsis of each, and then the workers vote by writing the name of their favorite option on a ballot. The lector then walks up and down the workbenches to collect and count the ballots to determine what will be read.

Over the years, Lara Reyes says rollers have voted for classics like *Les Misérables, Romeo and Juliet,* and *The Three Musketeers,* as well as books by Cuban authors like Leonardo Padura. She's read *The Count of Monte Cristo* more times than she can count, and she says the faded ink in the book her grandmother gave her decades ago proves it. She remembers several rollers tearing up when she read Anne Frank's *The Diary of a Young Girl,* while others inevitably try to crack the case before she can finish Agatha Christie mysteries. She adores Gabriel García Márquez's *No One Writes to the Colonel,* and calls *100 Years of Solitude* "perfect." And while she doesn't change her voice to differentiate each character in a novel, she does change her intonation "to try to capture the essence of each character."

By all accounts, the original goal of readers inspiring tobacco rollers to study on their own was a resounding success, and Tinajero notes that by the turn of the 20th century, more than 90 percent of Havana cigar workers could read and write. According to Lara Reyes, many of La Corona's workers today haven't had much formal education, and just like 150 years ago, the news and novels she recites to the rollers in the factory has a ripple effect that extends to their own families. "I never used to read at home before working here. Now, I read books at home to my children," said Ivan Alvarez, who rolls Montecristos, Romeo y Julietas, and other brands while keeping his eyes glued to the desk. "Our hands are full, they are focused, but our ears are empty and listening."

"The lector job is necessary for us, especially us women," said another roller, Idalmis Ferro Medina, who first learned to roll cigars at La Corona 25 years ago as a young, single mother. "I live very far away, so I wake up at 4:30 A.M. every day, and I go home at 5:30 P.M. and start making dinner. I don't have time to read the news. I never imagined that I'd work in a place where someone reads to you and gives you a free education. From the beginning, it was something quite new and amazing for me."

When I spoke to Lara Reyes in her office, a stream of rollers filed in and out, asking her for help with everything from their children's history homework to how to pay membership dues to a local social club. The lector gently and graciously greeted each one, offering a kiss on the cheek, inquiring about their families, and patiently addressing their requests. When the last roller exited, Lara Reyes lowered her red-rimmed glasses, leaned across her desk, and explained to me how these relationships are reciprocal.

"The reader and the rollers have always been one big family. I recently got coronavirus and was hospitalized and on oxygen for 11 days. It became very bad. I can't explain the sentiment I felt when these workers came to visit me. They called me, they checked in on me with heart, and they helped me as I help them. We're bound together, as perfectly as this," she said, sliding a masterfully rolled, torpedo-tipped Montecristo No. 2 cigar across the table to me.

Even for a nonsmoker like myself, it's hard not to marvel at the craftsmanship of a hand-rolled cigar, or the staggering amount of work it takes to produce one. According to cigar journalist and master blender Nicholas Syris, who graciously accompanied me to Cuba, cigars pass through 300 sets of hands before they're finally ready to be sold and smoked. Considering that not a single tobacco leaf is chemically treated, that its sweet or spicy flavors are naturally occurring, and its brown coloring is achieved through an organic process, a finished cigar isn't just the culmination of a massive human effort, but a natural expression of the terroir where it was grown. Many countries, such as the Dominican Republic, Nicaragua, and Honduras, make quality cigars. But what makes habanos so highly coveted is an ingredient that no other nation can claim: the rust-red soil of Cuba's fertile Pinar del Río valley, which produces the finest tobacco in the world. So, after several days inside Havana's cigar factories, I headed to Cuba's westernmost province to learn about tobacco's astonishing journey from seed to cigar, and some of the many readers who help shape it along the way.

As you rattle west out of Havana along the national Este-Oeste highway, a more pastoral portrait of Cuba emerges. A rolling canvas of copper-red fields unfurls toward conical limestone boulders that rise and fall in sharp angles. We swerved to avoid sombrero-clad tobacco farmers riding side-saddle on donkey-drawn buggies, narrowly missing campesinos on the shoulder hawking whole, still-feathered turkeys hanging upside down by their legs. Men and women huddled in any shade they could find to avoid the midday sun—be it under a banyan tree or a roadside billboard declaring CUBA CONTRO EL US BLOQUEO (Cuba against the US blockade).

If Cuba's Pinar del Río province is considered the pinnacle of the tobacco-growing world, then the mineral-rich Vuelta Abajo region near the towns of San Juan y Martínez and San Luis is the holy grail. Here, a combination of sandy, well-draining soil and warm days and cool nights that help "stress" each tobacco plant has combined to turn this pancake-flat farmland into the Champagne of cigars. Of the dozens of high-quality *vegas* (plantations) and thatched tobacco-drying houses dotting the landscape, one stands out: Finca El Pinar Robaina. Tended by the same family since 1845, the 40-acre vega's reputation as the world's greatest tobacco farm is a testament to the late Alejandro Robaina, a grower and cigar maker so beloved that the Cuban government issued a stamp in his honor.[37] While every other Cuban plantation produces tobacco for one or more of the nation's state-owned cigar brands, like Cohiba, Montecristo, and Romeo y Julieta, Alejandro was the only farmer allowed to grow the crop under his own name. Since his passing in 2010, his nephew and grandson, Francisco Jesus and Hirochi (the fifth and sixth generations, respectively), have steered the family business.[38] After Hirochi showed me framed blessings to the Robaina family from two popes and a signed thank-you note from President Obama—who acquired the family's signature Vegas Robaina cigars during his historic 2016 tour of the island—Francisco Jesus explained what makes this region so perfectly suited for tobacco.

"There are four elements to quality cigars: soil, weather, experience, and seed variety. Two of these elements can be transferred anywhere in the world—seeds and experience. What makes this area so unique is the pH level of the soil and the microclimates," he said, looking out at his field of swaying tobacco plants from his porch while a peep of free-range chickens clucked by our feet. "This area also has soil classifications and microclimates that are so localized that one side of the road will produce different flavored tobacco than the other side of the road."

Just as fluctuating weather and growing conditions mean that no two wine bottles taste exactly the same, no two cigars do either. But compared with winemaking, which has five basic steps (harvesting, crushing and pressing, fermentation, clarification, and aging), each tobacco plant is examined an average of 170 times before it's even ready for its first fermentation. It starts by hand-selecting seeds that are planted in nurseries. After 35 days, the sprouts are replanted in plowed burrows whose soil has been irrigated and whose chemical components analyzed to ensure optimal conditions. After another 35 days, the plants reach full height, and they're ready to be picked. Farmers start by picking the bottom leaves, which are thinner and have less nicotine, in a series of six passages—each of which takes about seven days. They then pick the middle leaves, and finally those closest to the top of the plant, which are the thickest and contain the most nicotine. The leaves are then taken into a nearby wooden curing barn, pierced with long needles to form a sort of tobacco-leaf kebab, and hung from the roof for about seven weeks to dry. Once the leaves turn golden brown, they're ready for the first fermentation. Unlike with grapes in winemaking, no alcohol is produced when you ferment tobacco leaves. Instead, fermentation reduces the leaf's tar and nicotine and makes it less bitter while heightening its more floral, nutty notes.

Roughly six months after the seeds are planted, the fermented tobacco leaves are ready to leave the farm and head to a local *escogida* (sorting house). Here, specialized workers in brightly lit rooms carefully analyze the leaves against a stark-black background, rejecting any with cracks or blemishes and grouping the leaves together in as many as 20 color gradients in preparation for a second fermentation. Interestingly, these workers are almost always women, as they're thought to possess a keener eye for detail and color than their male counterparts.[39]

As with rolling tobacco leaves, sorting them for eight hours a day can be monotonous, repetitive work, so many escogidas hire a lector to stimulate their employees. This is the case at the largest sorting house in the area: Pinar del Río's V13 Escogida. After a winding two-hour search down rutted dirt roads, I finally found Bernardo Campos Iglesias, the factory's former reader, living in a humble cinderblock house at the end of a spidery lane. At 87 years old, Iglesias is the oldest living lector in Cuba, and the only one to have worked before and after the Cuban Revolution (1953–1959). As he swallowed my outstretched palm in a two-handed vice grip and swiftly ushered me into his ochre-painted living room, it was clear he hadn't lost a step.

"I was born under a tobacco plant in 1935 and have never been sick a day in my life," Iglesias said. A mountain range of sinewy veins ran up his brown, brawny arms, and he didn't look a day over 65. "I've never smoked a cigar, I don't drink, and I exercise every day. You have to be well-prepared, mentally and physically. If not, you are lost. That's what I always told my students, both in the school and the factory."

Iglesias has a bachelor's degree in philosophy and worked as a teacher for 33 years. As a child, he loved to read and started working as a lector in a local escogida when he was just 17. "At that time, Cuba was capitalist, and before the Revolution, the lector still collected money from the workers, just as had always been done since the tradition started. Since the Revolution, it's become a job with a set salary. The reading also isn't the same. In the capitalist system, the factory's owner told me I shouldn't speak wrongly of a capitalist society. In a socialist system, you can't speak wrongly about socialist society," Iglesias said. The factory's owner was Jose Padrón, a staunch opponent of the Revolution who would eventually flee Cuba and survive four bomb attacks after Castro seized his family's land in 1961.

That same year, Iglesias was ordered by Castro's new government to join a combat battalion fighting off the island's remaining counter-revolutionaries in the western Sierra de los Órganos mountains. "I worked under a commander who was very close to Che Guevara. The commander knew that I liked to read, so I was selected to read the *Revolución* newspaper to the battalion every day at noon. This was during the period of the Bay of Pigs attack. We knew it was coming, but we didn't know where, so we had to mobilize and be ready. When it finally happened, the battalion learned about it because I read the newspaper to them."

After two years working in the USSR as a Russian translator and a long teaching career, Iglesias returned to Pinar del Río to serve as the lector at the V13 Escogida from 1998 until 2011. "A lector has always played a very important role, and that's to defend the working class while educating them. I want the best for Cuba, but the situation is difficult, economically. The problem is you. Because of the US's aggressive blockade, we are like *this*," Iglesias said, staring me in the eyes as he slowly dragged a finger across his neck, as if slitting his throat. Though no longer a lector, Iglesias told me he's never stopped reading, and he offered to see me off with four of the day's different Cuban newspapers, which he'd already read, front to back, earlier that morning. A cloud of dust kicked up from the car as I slowly drove away from Iglesias's country home, clutching the day's news. When I glanced up at the rearview mirror, I saw the Revolutionary veteran standing at attention, and still staring back at me.

After leaving the sorting house, the color-coded leaves make one more stop before heading to the rolling factories in Havana: the *despalillo* (stripping facility), where workers carefully remove the fermented tobacco leaf's central vein. The main stripping facility in the Vuelta Abajo region is located in the provincial capital of Pinar del Río, a quiet, 125,000-person cluster of crumbling colonial villas and colonnaded Neoclassical buildings painted in cheery pastel colors. It was here, at the Niñita Valdés Despalillo, where I met the country's longest-serving lector, María Caridad González Martínez, a woman whose story is unlike any other reader's in Cuba.

González Martínez grew up just two blocks from Niñita Valdés, where her mother worked as a leaf stripper. Many days after coming home from school, González Martínez would stand outside the window of the factory, waiting for her mother to finish, while listening to the lector,

Esperanza, reading novels. "I was enchanted by it—the different tones, the dramatizations, the voices for every character," said the 58-year-old, brushing her short, dyed-blond hair from her tinted sunglasses and smiling. "I started working in the factory in 1986, and after about five months, I heard Esperanza was going to retire. I had been attracted to this job since I was a little girl, so when I heard there was an opening, I decided to go for it!"

González Martínez competed against five other applicants during a monthlong trial period before the head of Niñita Valdés informed her that the workers had chosen her to be their lector. "I guess they liked my voice," she said. Then in 1989, after reading to the tabaqueros every day for three years and getting a sense of what they liked, González Martínez went home one night, took out a notebook, and started writing. When it was time for the workers to vote for the next novel several weeks later, they chose *Oscuridad y Destino,* a story about a blind girl in an orphanage who grows up to find her long-lost father. "I remember when I was reading it, I put so much passion into it. I knew every twist and turn, every up and down, and how every character feels in a way that I didn't with any other book—and that's because I had written it myself. No one knew it, though," she said. "At the very end, when I told the workers that I was the author, they were shocked. Some people even cried. It was very emotional for me, and they encouraged me to keep going."

Over the next 14 years, González Martínez would go on to write 18 more novels in notebooks and stationery, just so she could read them aloud to the factory's 130 workers. None of them are published. Instead, after cooking dinner, cleaning the house, and putting her daughter to bed, the reader would get to work writing in longhand until 2:00 A.M. and then recite each chapter to her audience later that day before she'd finished writing the book. "Based on their reactions as I read it, I'd change the plot to surprise them or create an ending I thought they'd really like," she said. "In a way, the workers became like my editors."

In the early 1990s, the collapse of the USSR, which had propped up Cuba economically for decades, triggered an era of extreme shortages on the island. During this so-called Special Period, González Martínez sometimes struggled to find enough paper to finish her novels, so she'd resort to ripping out blank pages in her daughter's school notebooks, looking for loose-leaf paper, or "anything I could find." These days, she still keeps a few of her handwritten novels stashed away at home. They include *Secretos*, about a family that pretended to be wealthy until one of its members exposed their deep, dark secret; and *Tallando Sueños*, in which a poor carpenter pines for the girl he grew up with and searches for her in Havana. Then in 2003, after 14 years of only sharing her writing with her colleagues at the leaf-stripping factory, the lector learned that one of her books was finally going to be published. "It was truly overwhelming. Everyone at the factory celebrated," she said. González Martínez has since gone on to publish nine children's books in Cuba, winning four national awards for her work.

"People sometimes ask me, 'Why don't you leave? You could get a job as an editor somewhere else.' And I say, 'Why would I?' I love it here," she said. "I always say that my first job is as a lector. The workers here were the ones who inspired me to become a writer. Were it not for them, I never would have had the courage to show anyone my work." As González Martínez walked me outside by the loading dock where the de-stemmed leaves head for Havana, I asked her if she misses reading her own handwritten work to the tobacco workers. "Oh no, I've never stopped!" she shot back. "I'm working on three new novels for the workers right now. I still work late into the night, except these days, it's when my granddaughter is asleep, not my daughter."

When the leaves finally make it to the factories in Havana, master blenders in a tightly sealed room sort them according to a secret formula that corresponds to each cigar brand and size. The blended bunches are then delivered to the rollers, who transform them into about 100 cigars a day.

"Rolling a cigar is more of an art than a science," said Leopoldina Gutierrez Espinosa, one of the most renowned torcedores in Cuba. "It takes a nine-month apprenticeship to become a Cuban roller, and like all craftsmen, we draw inspiration from many sources—including the lector." Known across Cuba as La Chinita (The Chinese Girl) because of a hint of Asian ancestry in her West African roots, Gutierrez Espinosa rolled for more than 40 years at Havana's H. Upmann factory. For many of those years, as she sculpted the wrapper leaf into a rounded or torpedo shape with the chaveta, stretched it over the filler and binder, and guillotined it to size with the knife, she listened to the soothing voice of Gricel Valdés-Lombillo. A former history teacher with a mother's warmth and a shock of bright yellow hair that falls in curls to her dark shoulders, Valdés-Lombillo served as H. Upmann's reader for 27 years. But as I'd soon come to learn in her Havana home, she was forced out of the job in 2020 under rather suspicious circumstances.

"I miss it. I miss everything about it," Valdés-Lombillo said, sitting under a large framed photo of her reading at H. Upmann that dwarfed the photos of her grandchildren and Jesus crucifix hanging in her living room. "After 27 years, we were like a family, and it feels like I've lost a member of my family." With this, the lector's eyes welled with tears, and as she looked across the room to the man watching us, she started to sob. "Why don't we take a minute?" the gentleman said, before stepping outside to smoke a cigar.

Since I arrived in Cuba, a government agent had followed me to every official interview I had arranged. Sometimes he would stand over my shoulder taking notes, other times he'd sit off to the side. But he was always there, watching, listening, lurking. He told me he was a representative from Tabacuba, the holding company that oversees Cuba's tobacco production (all Cuban cigar factories are state owned). When I mentioned this to ordinary Cubans, they each let me in on a little secret: "Yes, he works for Tabacuba," a taxi driver told me, turning up the radio as he spoke. "But he likely reports to G2 [the Cuban state intelligence agency that was modeled after the Soviet KGB]. They're keeping a daily file on you, and just because you don't see someone doesn't mean you're not being watched."

The agent's presence didn't bother me, but it seemed to make a lot of readers and rollers I interviewed nervous, like Valdés-Lombillo. When the man was out of earshot, I offered Valdés-Lombillo a tissue and asked if everything was okay. "There are certain things that I cannot say," she said quietly, keeping her eyes on the agent outside. "But things have become much more censored. We lectores no longer have the same freedom to read what we want, or what the workers want to hear." Through a series of head nods and coded responses to my questions, Valdés-Lombillo explained that as the coronavirus pandemic spread and the economic situation in Cuba grew more dire, frustration among everyday Cubans—including tobacco workers—intensified. Around this time, a new manager started at the H. Upmann factory who not only told Valdés-Lombillo she couldn't read anything political, but stripped her of any autonomy by telling her what she had to read. Soon, one of Havana's most beloved and longest-serving lectors was pressured to retire, citing "concern for coronavirus." Several years later, H. Upmann, which had employed a lector since 1866, had yet to hire a replacement and had no plans to.

"You can silence the reader, but that doesn't solve the problem," Valdés-Lombillo said. She's right. In July 2021, during Cuba's toughest phase of the pandemic, the same tensions that were bubbling to the surface among tobacco rollers when Valdés-Lombillo was forced out boiled over, as a rare and astonishing wave of anti-government protests swept across the island. In the country's largest political demonstration in 30 years, thousands of Cubans took to the streets, some screaming, "You're starving us to death!" as they denounced the widespread food and medicine shortages, frequent power outages, and rampant inflation crippling the island. In response, the Cuban government quickly shut down the internet, rounded up hundreds of protestors, and charged many with sedition—sentencing some to as many as 30 years in jail. In the time since, tensions in Cuba had remained on a knife's edge, which likely explained why I was being watched.

The official line about the uprising from Cuba's foreign minister was: "There is no popular uprising."[40] Instead, the nation's rulers and its state-controlled media alleged that the "riots" and "disorder" were the result of a "perverse" coordinated attempt by the US, "laboratories," and "technological platforms" to overthrow the Cuban government.[41] Versions of this claim went out in each of the country's two main daily newspapers: *Granma,* which is published by the Cuban government, and *Juventud Rebelde,* which is published by the Young Communist League. Each lector I spoke with revealed that they're only allowed to read the news from Cuban newspapers or state-approved websites, so if they were allowed to say anything about the demonstrations, this is the message that echoed through the galleys. Lara Reyes explained the rules of reading to me like this: "In the morning when I arrive at La Corona, I look at outside web-sites to know what is happening in the world, for my own interest—like El Pais or the BBC, but I only read those articles to the rollers when they're more neutral human-interest stories."

"Are you able to read news stories from El Pais or the BBC aloud to them?" I asked her. She laughed nervously and then responded, "I wouldn't dare." Instead, if Lara Reyes wants to offer workers an international per-spective, she's encouraged to read from the website Russia Today, which is funded by the Russian government. The USSR was Cuba's closest comrade throughout the Cold War, and Russia remains its largest creditor today. My visit to Cuba unfolded as Russia intensified its full-scale invasion of Ukraine. While every Cuban I spoke with expressed concerns about the violence that was taking place, they were careful not to call the invasion an "invasion" or a "war." Rather, Cuban authorities, the state-run media, and everyday Cubans have adopted the official narrative of its ally by calling it a "special operation." When I asked Torres Rodriguez, the new lector at the Partagás factory, if she reads news reports to the rollers about what is happening in Ukraine, she paused before carefully saying, "This place is not mine. I am a worker and I accept that. I try to be as professional as possible, so I won't read anything controversial."

Within this context, it's hard not to sympathize with Cuba's last lec-tores or ignore the paradox of their role: How are you supposed to inform workers about what is happening in Cuba and the wider world when you can't say what is happening in Cuba or the wider world? Granted, the seemingly simple task of reading aloud in Cuban cigar factories has been unnecessarily difficult since its inception. Lectores have been censored by colonial authorities, monitored by factory owners, told what to read by committees, and forced out by workers if their delivery wasn't believable. But through no fault of the readers themselves, I couldn't help but feel that a tradition that was started to broaden workers' worldviews when Cuba wasn't free has morphed into a tool to restrict workers' worldviews now that Cuba is free.

This inherent contradiction is by no means limited to lectores. The more you talk to everyday Cubans, the more it becomes clear that there's a certain impossibility to life itself on the island that has only grown sharper in recent years. "You've come at the worst time in the history of my country. Everyone is desperate. Everyone is leaving," a Cuban journalist told me over dinner in Havana. Data from the US Customs and Border Protection showed that Cubans were fleeing for the US in the highest numbers since the 1980 Mariel boatlift, when drastic shortages led Castro to encourage any Cuban who wanted to leave the country to board a boat and go. Many Cubans are now trying to get to the US via Nicaragua, which dropped its visa requirement for Cubans shortly before I arrived, and signs of this mass exodus were everywhere.[42]

At the Havana airport, a line of Cubans waiting for a flight to the Nicaraguan capital of Managua streamed out the door. In light of the demand, authorities had been gouging Cubans with $3,000 tickets, and some families appeared to be carrying little more than a backpack after selling their belongings to afford the trip.[43] "Going to 'see the volcanoes'?" I quietly asked one man, using the coded term that Cubans had adopted to explain they're going to Nicaragua, migrating north to the US, and never coming back. He looked down and nodded. Others, like the tobacco blender I met in Havana's Miramar neighborhood who spoke five languages, started to tell me about his plan to hire a man in Mexico to smuggle him across the border into California. Then, when he noticed a camera over his shoulder in the state-owned cigar lounge where we were sitting, he quickly changed the subject and left.

"There's no food. Everything we eat is imported," the journalist continued at dinner. "On a normal salary, I couldn't afford to send my son to school." He explained that he earns 6,000 CUP (roughly $250) a month—a good salary on an island where the average monthly wage is roughly 4,000 CUP (which is what the lectores I spoke with earn). While many nations have low wages, the prohibitively expensive cost of everyday supplies in Cuba is maddening. As an example, most Cubans don't drink the tap water. But since a bottle of water costs 80 CUP—or roughly two percent of the average monthly salary—most Cubans don't buy water either. "So, how do you drink water?" I asked the journalist. "You boil the tap water," he said. As the 2,000 CUP ($83) bill arrived for our dinner of two orders of chicken and rice, two beers, and one large bottle of water, the journalist explained what he meant by "normal salary."

"When you get hired for a job, the first question you ask yourself is, 'What is the salary?' and the second question is, 'What can I steal?' Unless you have family in Florida sending you money—and even if you do—the only way you can live in Cuba is to creatively 'take' from your job. Company drivers use the cars as taxis at night. Cigar rollers take home their five earned cigars a day, save them until they have enough for a bundle, and sell them to tourists on the street. And me? I act as a middleman selling cigars to the Canadians. Otherwise I couldn't survive."

In Pinar del Río, as the third power outage of the day blanketed the town in blackness, Carlos, the 50-year-old museum curator whose home I was staying in, took me up to his rooftop to escape the 33-degree-Celsius nighttime heat. As we peered up at the stars, I asked him how he felt about the state of things in Cuba. "The system is broken. Nothing works," he said. "Fidel was a leader. When there was a hurricane, he would be there the next day with the people. Now, we're in the eye of the hurricane, and there's no plan, no leader." I asked him, "If you were to talk to a leader and say, 'The monthly salary in Cuba is this, the rations are this, and other basic necessities cost this—how are Cubans supposed to survive?' What would they say?" Carlos replied, "They'd say it's enough."

I then asked, "What if you were to tell them that when a bottle of water costs $3.35 and a bag of rice $3, it's not enough?" Carlos smiled and said, "I wouldn't get to say that, because I'd already be in jail."

After a long silence, Carlos asked me what I thought of Cuba, so I told him. I said that it's easy to romanticize Cuba—to marvel at the parade of Plymouths you see plying the cobblestone streets, the swinging neon signs glistening at night, the make-do-and-mend vintage appliances you glimpse getting hammered back to life through an open doorway. However, it's much harder as an American to reconcile how this retro reality came to be. In the US, we're told that it's due to an economic "embargo," a term referring to one nation's choice to ban commercial trade with another. But I explained that few Americans understand that the US heavily penalizes many foreign businesses or governments that trade with Cuba—in some cases prohibiting them from doing so altogether if they also want to trade with the US. I said that it's impossible for us to fathom how these sweeping global sanctions affect daily life for Cubans. They restrict access to food, building supplies, and medicine, and have cost Cuba more than $130 billion since they were implemented in 1962, according to the United Nations. Whether you call this an "embargo," as Americans do, or a "blockade," as Cubans do, to me, it's a relentless act of war designed to smother the Cuban economy, starve its people into submission, and collectively punish the island for spurring US control 60 years ago. It's inhumane.

The bitter irony of all of this is that much of the reason that the US upholds a policy every other UN member state except Israel has voted to repeal over the last 30 years is because of the voting power of Florida's Cuban community. Several generations after the first wave of politically charged cigar readers and rollers helped build Florida and propel the revolutionary cause against Spain, their descendants are some of the most vehement opponents of the Cuban Revolution and the staunchest supporters of Cuban sanctions. Many Cuban Americans see the egalitarian dreams of Martí crushed under the grip of Castro's socialist regime. And so, six decades after President Kennedy ordered a shipment of 1,200 Cuban cigars to the White House just hours before authorizing an economic policy specifically designed to "bring about hunger, desperation, and overthrow the government," as a leaked memo later revealed, the sanctions live on, as does the pain, separation, and ideological chasm between Cubans and Cuban Americans living just 90 miles apart.[44]

When Lara Reyes finished her day's reading of *The Count of Monte Cristo* at the La Corona factory, a middle-aged roller with a spider's web of wrinkles around his eyes and a shy smile slowly approached the podium. He asked the lector if she could reveal a spoiler and tell him what happened to the count. Did he ever make it off the island prison, he asked? Was the faint scratching sound he heard in his cell really from a long-lost loved one from the mainland, striving to diminish the short distance that separated them? The reader shot the roller a coy look and said, "I guess you'll have to wait until tomorrow."

9

The Man Trying to Save Japanese Food

花より団子
(Food over flowers.)
—Japanese proverb

Yasuo Yamamoto has a secret—or, more accurately, 87 of them. As the sun rose over the Japanese island of Shōdoshima, the 49-year-old shuffled out of his 19th-century wood-paneled home at the foot of a mountain, walked across a gravel driveway to his family's storehouse, and slipped off his sandals before stepping into a pair of rubber work boots. Using both hands, he slid open a massive charred-black door and disappeared inside the dimly lit warehouse. I followed his slender silhouette into the dirt-floor barn and was engulfed by a yeasty, caramelized aroma. Moments later, Yamamoto flipped on a lone light bulb dangling from a 300-year-old wooden rafter high above, revealing a two-story laboratory lined with 87 hulking cedar barrels caked in so much fungus-filled crust they each looked like they were growing beards.

While my eyes adjusted, Yamamoto gripped a bamboo railing and led me up a creaky staircase from the base of the barrels into the warehouse's dark, cobwebbed loft. Streams of morning light poured in through the small square windows, landing atop the 2.5-meter barrels and illuminating a narrow wooden walkway separating each vat's gaping circular opening. I looked down, around me, and above my head. Every inch of the barn's planked passageways, tree-trunk beams, and ceiling slabs was covered in centuries' worth of black bacteria, causing the thick brown goo inside the three-ton barrels to bubble and pop. The entire building was alive.

Yamamoto carefully threaded the slick, mold-glazed walkway, silently examining the dense pinto bean–like texture of the fermenting slurry inside each vessel. Then, when the fifth-generation soy sauce brewer came to a cedar barrel covered in an especially chaotic tangle of cobweb-like bacteria, he crouched down and fanned the air coming from the blend up toward his nose. As he did so, the brew inside the mammoth cauldron oozed more actively, as if responding to his presence. "This is what gives our soy sauce its unique taste," Yamamoto said, lightly tapping the top of the 150-year-old wooden barrel and its forest of microorganisms. "Today, less than one percent of soy sauce in Japan is still made this way."

Until 75 years ago, almost all Japanese soy sauce was made this way, and it tasted completely different than what the world knows today. But despite a government ordinance to modernize production after World War II, a few traditional brewers continue to make soy sauce the old-fashioned way in *kioke* cedar barrels, and Yamamoto is the most important of them all. Not only has he made it his mission to show the world how real soy sauce is supposed to taste, but he's leading a nationwide effort to preserve the secret ingredient in a 700-year-old recipe before it disappears.

Shoyu (soy sauce) is the single most important seasoning in Japan's UNESCO-inscribed *washoku* traditional cuisine. It's found in every kitchen, used in nearly every meal, and placed on every table in Japanese restaurants from Tokyo to Texas. More than just a flavor, its signature umami savoriness is an entirely different dimension of taste—so much so that umami was added as one of the five basic human tastes alongside sweet, sour, salty, and bitter by scientists in 1990.[1] When it's aged and fermented in a wooden barrel, soy sauce can be as sophisticated as a fine wine, but today, most of the world dips its sushi in the equivalent of a boxed rosé. That's because, in order to increase production during the country's postwar recovery, the Japanese government encouraged brewers to ditch the traditional wooden barrels used to ferment food, adapt stainless steel vats, and cut the customary multiyear fermenting process to just two months. According to Yamamoto, a kioke isn't just a vessel, it's *the* essential ingredient needed to make soy sauce, as the porous grain of the wood is home to millions of microbes that deepen and enrich its umami flavor. Because this bacteria can't survive in steel tanks, many commercial companies pump their soy sauces full of additives. So unless you've visited an ancient craft brewer or artisanal store in Japan, you've likely only ever tasted a thin, salty imitation of a complex, nuanced brew.

For the past 150 years, the Yamamotos and their millions of microbes have been making the family's Yamaroku soy sauce by mixing soybeans with wheat, salt, and water and letting it ferment in a four-year process. But as more and more of Japan's soy brewers have swapped their wooden barrels for steel tanks, a big problem has occurred: the country is running out of kioke, and almost no one still knows how to build them. In the last 10 years, Yamamoto has set out to learn this ancient craft and teach it to as many people as possible to try to ensure its survival.

What's at stake is something much bigger than just soy sauce. Until a century ago, Japan's five main fermented seasonings (soy sauce, miso, vinegar, mirin, and sake) were all made in kioke. Today, only about 4,000 kioke are still used in Japan to make soy sauce, and far fewer are used to ferment the country's other seasoning staples.[2] When these natural fermentation chambers are replaced with steel vats, the authentic taste of traditional Japanese cuisine is lost. And if they were to vanish completely, an irreplaceable part of Japan's cultural and culinary character would disappear with them.

––––––––––

Soy sauce is one of the oldest condiments in the world. We humans have been adding salt to our food for at least 5,000 years, but around 2,500 years ago, Chinese chefs discovered that if they fermented their salt-cured meat and fish, they could extract a savory paste, which they called *jiang*.[3] By about 200 BC, these hard-to-come-by fermenting agents were replaced by soybeans, which were much easier to harvest than animals were to catch, and didn't smell nearly as bad as they gradually decomposed. By the Tang Dynasty (618–907), Chinese families were fermenting soybean-based jiang in clay jars, and this early version of soy sauce became a common seasoning in dishes across the country. In fact, were it not for a wandering Buddhist monk, the world may have forever associated soy sauce with China, not Japan.[4]

When Buddhism started to spread to all social classes in Japan during the 12th and 13th centuries, more and more Japanese started following the emperor's edict forbidding them from eating meat—a practice they would faithfully continue for the next 700 years.[5] As a result, many farmers began cultivating soybeans as a protein-rich meat substitute. Then in 1249, a monk named Shinchi Kakushin set sail from Japan to study Buddhism under a famous Zen master in China. Unfortunately, by the time he arrived, the master had died, so Kakushin did what any good traveler would do whose best-laid plans had changed: he rolled with it. The monk set off on a five-year pilgrimage, walking up and down China's Zhejiang province and absorbing as much as he could from Buddhist temples and Chinese culture. When Kakushin returned to Japan in 1254, he became an abbot near the town of Yuasa and brought back the recipe for *kinzanji* miso: a sweet and chunky side dish made by fermenting soybeans, barley, and vegetables.[6] Legend has it that while Kakushin was teaching this miso-making method to his fellow monks in Yuasa, he noticed that the heavy stones pressing down on the fermenting mixture created a small pool of viscous liquid at the bottom of the vat. Not one to waste anything, the frugal monk dipped his finger in the solution, became captivated by the taste, and started cooking with it. Before long, every household in Yuasa was using the liquid as a seasoning, and as this miso by-product (called *tamari*) spread to neighboring villages, the basis for soy sauce as we know it was born.[7]

By the 1300s, Yuasa's brewers had ditched the clay vessels they'd previously used to make kinzanji miso and started brewing their early soy sauce in the same wooden kioke barrels used to ferment sake, which gave it a smoother, more aromatic taste. Unlike Chinese soy sauce, which was traditionally made with 100 percent soy, Japanese brewers blended an equal mixture of wheat and soy, which gave their variety a sweeter, more nuanced, and less salty taste. This remains the main difference between Chinese soy sauce (*jiàng yóu*) and the Japanese shoyu most of the world consumes today.[8] "The essence of soy sauce came from China, but the way of making it has been perfected here, to the point that soy sauce as we know it today is undeniably Japanese," said Keiko Kuroshima, who wrote the definitive tome on Japanese soy sauce, *Shoyu Hon,* and is one of only three soy sauce sommeliers in Japan (certified inspectors who visit breweries and report on their products).

Word of Yuasa's savory seasoning eventually reached the island of Shōdoshima, which was one of Japan's major salt producers throughout medieval times. Located in the center of the Seto Inland Sea, it served as a natural bridge before the advent of roads, connecting Japan's southern islands with the country's bustling central ports. The island's salt workers sailed over to Yuasa to learn the village's slow fermentation technique in the late 1500s, and when they returned, they realized that Shōdoshima's dry, Mediterranean-like climate was well suited for yeast fermentation—and therefore, to soy sauce production. As households across Japan began acquiring a distinct taste for kioke-brewed shoyu during the forthcoming Edo period, Shōdoshima (fittingly: Small Bean Island) would play a pivotal role in feeding the nation's growing appetite.[9]

The Edo period (1603–1867) formed the building blocks of modern Japan and Japanese identity. After 150 years of near-constant civil war and social upheaval during the preceding Sengoku (Warring States) period, the Edo era was marked by more than 260 years of calm and stability. The country unified under a central shogun commander, relocated the capital from Kyoto to Edo (modern-day Tokyo), and transformed the once-sleepy fishing village into the world's largest city by 1721. The government also adopted a policy of national seclusion, effectively closing its borders and banning trade with every nation except the Netherlands—and to a lesser degree, China and Korea—for more than 200 years. Left to its own devices and relishing its newfound serenity, Japan became a sealed-off incubator of ideas, which allowed the country's culture to flourish.[10]

"The great majority of what we consider to be 'Japanese' came into a recognizable form during those two and a half centuries—sushi, Kabuki, haiku, and so much more," said Dr. Andrew Gordon, a professor of modern Japanese history at Harvard University and the author of several books on Japan. "The creation of a national road network, the increase of trade across the country, and the blossoming of print culture all helped create a shared culture too."

One of the most quintessentially "Japanese" things to spread throughout the country during this period was soy sauce. By the early 1600s, thick kioke-made soy sauce from Yuasa was being shipped across the country and sold in markets. As people grew fond of the seasoning, local variations developed. In western Japan, craftsmen used roasted barley to make their lighter-colored *tamari shoyu*. In eastern Japan, a darker wheat-fermented variation simply known as shoyu emerged. Some families offered the seasoning to samurai leaders as tribute taxes. They, in turn, served it to their armies who couldn't get enough of it and helped spread the word of the salty-sweet seasoning. In places like Osaka and Nagoya, local industries began to emerge in the 16th and 17th centuries to feed the soy sauce–crazed workers hired to build the cities' new castles.[11]

The growing popularity of shoyu in Japan was directly linked with the rapid Edo-era urbanization of Japan. As Gordon noted, "So much of the so-called 'Japanese culture' and sense of being Japanese that crystallized in this time happened in cities, for the simple reason that it was easier to share goods and ideas." According to early census records, less than two percent of Japan's population lived in cities before the 1600s, but by 1725, roughly 20 percent did.[12] During this time, two major soy sauce–producing hubs emerged: one was in the Kansai region—specifically the cities of Kyoto and Kobe—which tended to produce a lighter, thinner, and saltier shoyu called *usukuchi* (pale mouth). The other was in the cities of Noda and Chōshi, near the burgeoning new capital, Edo, which leaned toward the richer and more robust *koikuchi* (dark mouth) that most of the world knows today. Since they had to house hundreds of large kioke barrels, these soy sauce breweries were among the largest structures in Japan at the time, rivaled only by Buddhist temples.[13]

During the latter half of the Edo period, the expansion of sea salt production across the Seto Inland Sea caused demand for Shōdoshima's cash crop to wane.[14] To fill the void, the island's producers shifted their focus to shoyu, which had previously just been produced in small batches for local consumption. Thanks to Shōdoshima's central location along Japan's main shipping line, the small, mountainous holm was able to easily acquire high-quality soybeans and wheat from Kyushu to the south, and wheat from Hyogo to the north. The only other ingredients needed to make soy sauce were both things the island had in abundance—water and salt—so brewers incorporated Shōdoshima's prized, pure white *shima-shio* (island salt) into the mixture and fermented it for several years in old kioke they purchased from sake producers.[15]

The result was a bold, creamy shoyu so striking and refined that as soon as it began to be shipped to Kyoto, Kobe, and Osaka in the late 1700s, so many orders flooded in that the island had to open more and more shoyu breweries to keep up with demand. According to the Shōdoshima Shoyu Association, by the 1870s, the 24,000-person island was home to 400 soy sauce brewers—more, per capita, than anywhere in Japan at the time.[16] "Shoyu became part of everybody's diet in Japan in the 18th and 19th centuries, when Japanese culture developed in full bloom, and this island played a major part in that," said Kuroshima, who grew up in Shōdoshima. "Up to that point, food had been a means of survival, but in the Edo period, it became a source of fun and experimentation. People started realizing how good everything tasted with soy sauce."

As we sat outside Yamamoto's living, breathing fermentation barn, Kuroshima explained why shoyu became such an indispensable staple in Japanese kitchens, and why koikuchi (which has traditionally been brewed in Shōdoshima) eventually became Japan's most popular variety. "Compared to salt (which doesn't have fragrance or umami) or miso (which takes an extra step to melt the paste into a liquid), shoyu is incredibly easy to use: you just pour it over food and it goes well with almost any Japanese dish. Of all the different soy sauce varieties, koikuchi, which tends to be thicker, contains elements of all five human tastes. It also has a deodorizing effect that masks the 'fishy' smell of raw fish while also killing bacteria. It's a great preservative and an incredibly versatile, all-purpose seasoning."

Residents in 19th-century Japan seemed to agree, and by the end of the Edo period, records show that the country's roughly 35 million people were each consuming an average of more than one gallon of the stuff each year.[17] The first edition of the *Japanese Encyclopedia of Food and Drink (Inshoku Jiten)* states that, "Shoyu surpasses other seasonings in its ability to make each dish unique by evoking the complex and delicate flavors in the food itself."[18] Japanese cuisine has always been marked by simplicity and an emphasis on light and natural flavors. Kuroshima even hinted that the nation's adoration of and reliance on shoyu may explain why it never developed a wide range of sauces (as happened across Europe and Latin America) or incorporated an extensive use of spices and herbs (as so many other East Asian countries do). What's certain is that, as soy sauce spread from Buddhist temples to urban markets and became the workhorse of Japanese kitchens, its role in shaping the country's cuisine has been immense. "There are many Japanese foods that would not exist today without shoyu; for example sushi, sukiyaki (a meat and vegetable hot pot–style dish), and tempura," said Masaharu Morimoto, an Iron Chef and owner of 19 Japanese restaurants around the world. "It's an essential ingredient."

According to Yamamoto, since soy sauce can either be used as a topping or to enhance a food's natural flavor, many of Japan's most iconic regional dishes trace their roots back to how local brewers adapted their shoyu to fit the local diet. From Tokyo's traditionally deep and intense shoyu came the briny *unagi* eel and salty *yaki onigiri* (grilled rice balls). Kagawa's signature *sanuki udon* noodles and chilled *somen* noodles are textured by Shōdoshima's creamy shoyu in its dashi broth. Around Kyoto and Osaka, the lighter and saltier "pale mouth" shoyu makes its way into ubiquitous dishes like *yudofu* (hot tofu), *akashiyaki* (round dumplings made from an egg-rich batter), and *kabayaki* (grilled fish). In Nagoya, whose regional dishes are so unique that it has its own name—*Nagoya-meshi* (Nagoya cuisine)—one of the key ingredients is tamari soy sauce, which flavors dishes like *kishimen*, a type of flat udon noodle that's often referred to as "the soul food of the Aichi prefecture."

In some cases, the history of local Japanese soy sauce tells the history of Japan itself. The Portuguese were the first Europeans to arrive in Japan in the early 1600s, but their efforts to convert the population to Christianity soon drew the ire of the ruling Japanese shogun.[19] The military dictator eventually kicked them out of the country, expelled every other Western nation who had aided Portugal's conversion efforts, and initiated Japan's self-imposed isolation in the 1630s. The lone Western trading partner Japan allowed was the Dutch East India Company, which had proven to be a valuable commercial ally and generally minded its own business. Dutch ships were only allowed to enter the country in the Kyushu region near the port of Nagasaki, and one of the most coveted things they supplied was sugar. "Because Nagasaki was the only place where sugar could come in during our isolationist period, brewers there started mixing it with their shoyu," Yamamoto explained. "Even now, the shoyu and much of the food made down in Kyushu is still much sweeter than in the rest of Japan."

Today, regardless of the region, Yamamoto maintained, "There is not a day that goes by that a Japanese person wouldn't use soy sauce." In fact, after three trips up and down the country, I can't think of a single meal I've had that hasn't had a trace of shoyu mixed into it. In the classic breakfast trio of rice, miso soup, and dried fish, the fish is usually seasoned with shoyu and the rice is sometimes topped with *nattō* (fermented soybeans infused with shoyu). The ever-present lunch bowls of ramen, soba, or udon noodles each feature a soy sauce–based broth; while popular on-the-go bento boxes often contain either fish (which Japanese people dash with shoyu), chicken or beef (often cooked in shoyu), or meat glazed with teriyaki (whose signature ingredient is shoyu). Dinner is typically the biggest and most important meal of the day in Japan. While sushi and sashimi (which are always paired with soy sauce) may be among the nation's most famous culinary exports, most Japanese only eat them on rare occasions. Instead, many dinners follow the classic meal plan of *ichiju-sansai* (one soup, one bowl of rice, and three side dishes). The soup is often miso or *suimono* (which contains shoyu), and the sides are often vegetables simmered in mirin and soy sauce with a protein flavored by shoyu. As Kuroshima told me, "Of Japan's five traditional fermented seasonings, shoyu is the one we can't live without because it's the key ingredient of washoku."

In a simple sense, washoku is Japan's traditional cuisine. It has historically been used to differentiate what people in Japan ate before the country finally opened its borders and absorbed more influences from the West in the final years of the Edo period. But just as the Mediterranean diet isn't strictly a "diet" and embodies a broader way of life, washoku encompasses a range of principles, social practices, and values that have been passed down over generations. "Washoku is a combination of the characters 'wa'

(和), meaning 'Japan' or 'harmony,' and 'shoku' (食), meaning 'food.' Literally, washoku is the harmony of food, and at the heart of this indigenous food culture is a harmonious balance of elements that are nutritious, beneficial, and presented in an aesthetically pleasing way," said Elizabeth Andoh, a graduate of Tokyo's prestigious Yanagihara School of Japanese cuisine and the author of six books on Japanese cooking, including the renowned English-language cookbook *Washoku*. "But washoku is much more of a philosophy. It's a way of thinking about the food we eat that is very compatible with the value system most Japanese have, and a real window into Japanese culture." At the center of this philosophy is an emphasis on simple preparation of local, seasonal ingredients; an inherent respect for nature and the sustainable harvesting of crops; and a balanced preparation of foods and presentation of dishes. Each meal should feature a variety of textures, an attractive and intentional palette of colors, and a full range of flavors. But like a set of nesting dolls, even the precepts of washoku have an interlocking symmetry: there are five overarching principles of food preparation, and each principle contains five points.

First is the aforementioned ichiju-sansai, in which each meal is built around the structure of five elements (rice, soup, and three sides), with more elaborate versions—such as *ichiju-rokusai* (rice, soup, and six sides)—stemming from this core quintet. Then, there's *goho*, the five cooking methods (simmering, searing, steaming, frying, and leaving food raw), where each meal should contain one component prepared each way. Next, each meal should also contain the five basic human tastes, called *gomi*. Finally, each meal should include five colors (black, white, red, yellow, and green), called *goshiki*, which not only make a meal aesthetically pleasing but also suggest each dish's nutritional benefit. The culmination of this effort is that each meal should appeal to the five senses, or *gokan*. Essential to this "principle of fives" is the order in which you should apply the five seasonings that serve as the foundation of every washoku meal: sugar, salt, vinegar, soy sauce, and miso. This formula is so ingrained into the head of many Japanese people that most children memorize the expression "*Sa-Shi-Su-Se-So*" (which corresponds to each seasoning's name in Japanese) before they're tall enough to reach the stove. "It's our ABCs," said Misao

Sugibayashi, an instructor at the Tsukiji Cooking school in Tokyo. The basic idea, she explained, is that the ingredients whose flavors are most susceptible to being changed by heat are added last. "Except for salt and sugar, the other three seasonings are traditionally fermented in kioke. Nothing is more important than shoyu, though. If I have shoyu, I can make Japanese food anywhere in the world."

Beyond the meal's preparation and presentation, one of the most fundamental elements of washoku is a deep sense of gratitude for family and nature that is rooted in the ancestor worship and animism of Japan's indigenous Shinto faith. Before every meal, those sitting around a table will start by saying "*itadakimasu.*" Though the word translates as "I humbly receive," Sugibayashi explained that it's really a heartfelt thank you to everyone and everything that participated in preparing the meal: the family members who passed down the recipes; the cooks, farmers, and fishermen who provided the food; and the animals and plants who sacrificed their lives so those eating can live. At the end of the meal, diners will then say "*gochisousama,*" which means "It was a great feast," but is really more of an appreciation of the effort and care it took for the host to serve you.[20] "Washoku both embodies and encourages Japanese identity. It shows that harmony and balance are very important, and discord is unwelcome. It values the natural world, respects rules and structure, and focuses on community good over individual desire," Andoh said. "The five traditional fermented seasonings are the backbone of this practice. Without these, you don't have washoku as we know it today." And therein lies the problem.

After the US dropped atomic bombs on Hiroshima and Nagasaki and effectively ended World War II, the situation in Japan was one of "complete and utter devastation—materially, socially, psychologically, and emotionally," Gordon said. Allied bombings had decimated every major city besides Kyoto, ruptured the nation's transportation network and power grid, destroyed a quarter of its residences, left two and a half million Japanese dead, and spurred a national food shortage that would last for years. In an effort to suppress Japan's "militaristic nationalism," a US-led coalition of Allied forces (referred to as GHQ in Japan) occupied the nation from 1945 to 1952 and imposed a series of sweeping changes as part of Japan's surrender. Under the direction of US General Douglas MacArthur, the GHQ introduced popular sovereignty, placed Japan's military under civilian control, and effectively wrote the constitution that Japan still uses today.[21]

"The two bywords from the get-go were 'demilitarize and democratize.' That was the agenda. Helping Japan flourish economically was not there at the start—but then the goals shifted," Gordon said. "What really changed things was the hardening of the lines of the Cold War in 1947 to 48. The Republic of China was losing [its civil war] to the Communists, and the US had a great fear that Japan would cast its lot with China. The US realized it needed to not just make Japan democratic, but to help it rebuild with a thriving, capitalistic economy so it could be an anchor and partner to the US." One of the ways it did this was by urging Japan to enhance its manufacturing systems. Gordon explained that Japan's postwar government was "desperate" to rebuild its economy and modernize its production, so it offered incentives like subsidies, tax breaks, and loans to companies to jump-start its lifeless industries, and many of these companies used the funds to adopt American technologies. The Japanese government also encouraged its industries to share new patents and production techniques so that everyone would thrive, essentially muting competition in a sort of "managed capitalism." These elements—along with a broader series of land, labor, and economic reforms—are what led to the Japanese Economic Miracle: the nation's booming period of growth between the end of World War II and the end of the Cold War that saw Japan transform from atomic bomb victim to economic giant. From 1950 to 1973, Japan's economy grew at twice the rate of Western Europe's and more than two and a half times faster than that of the US.[22] In just 30 years, it would catapult to become the world's second-largest economy and the envy of much of the modern world.[23] This is also what led to the beginning of the end of traditional shoyu and washoku cuisine.

In 1917, three of the largest shoyu-producing families outside Tokyo merged their businesses to form Noda Shoyu Co., Ltd.—the company that would eventually become Kikkoman, the world's largest soy sauce brand. According to Kikkoman's corporate website, when the Japanese government started rationing soybeans and wheat during World War II, Kikkoman engineers coped with the lack of raw materials by developing the Semi-Fermented Soy Sauce Manufacturing Method: a way of making soy sauce using a variety of chemically hydrolyzed soy and wheat proteins "that is alternative to soybeans." When the government further rationed supplies after the war, Kikkoman created a second method in 1948 that heated the fermenting mash to increase its nitrogen rate and sped up the natural fermenting time from more than one year to just two months. Kinichiro Sakaguchi, Japan's leading authority on the biochemical process of fermentation at the time, called this creation a "revolution of soy sauce," and in 1951, the Japan Institute of Invention and Innovation awarded the modified method with the Imperial Invention Prize.[24]

At the government's encouragement, Kikkoman opened the patents for these new fermenting formulas to its competitors, and shoyu companies across the country quickly adapted it.[25] This radical, industry-wide shift in shoyu production aligned with the GHQ's recommendation to abandon wooden kioke and adopt massive stainless steel tanks in order to feed more people quickly. By all accounts, the shift worked, and today Kikkoman boasts that this "revolution" is what encouraged the GHQ to increase the distribution of soy sauce across war-torn Japan.[26] Yet, the advent of chemical shoyu in Japan had another, more permanent effect.

Kikkoman is largely responsible for transforming soy sauce from a Japanese staple into a global seasoning. The company has swallowed up dozens of competitors and operates in more than 100 countries.[27] Since it opened its first overseas base in 1957, Kikkoman's international success has inspired countless competitors around the world. While the company discontinued using chemically modified ingredients in 1970, many of its competitors have not and use wheat bran or flour instead of wheat while dumping additives like caramel, sugar, and preservatives into their vats. Kikkoman also continues to brew its soy sauce in modern steel tanks with a heated, six-month fermentation time—effectively inspiring a global model of soy sauce production that yields an inherently different taste than true soy sauce.

Today, there are only three national cuisines inscribed on UNESCO's list as an Intangible Cultural Heritage of Humanity: French cooking, Mexican cooking, and Japanese washoku. According to Andoh, who played a role in washoku's UNESCO nomination, the goal in inscribing it was to preserve the traditional production methods that had birthed Japanese cuisine from continuing to be altered by industrialization and modernization. Central to this effort is the preservation of the kioke themselves. As Yamamoto told me, real, authentic Japanese food started with the first kioke; and it could end with the last one.

"Japanese base seasoning is mostly mass produced. [There are] hardly any real products left," Yamamoto said. "When the ability to produce kioke barrels disappears, the main ingredients will also disappear. There is a need to preserve the real thing and pass it on to my children and grandchildren's generations. That's our mission."

———————

Shōdoshima residents are quick to tell you that their 155-square-kilometer island is shaped like a cow. To find Yamamoto, you follow the road north from the cow's udder through a cluster of centuries-old wood-paneled warehouses exuding the unmistakable whiff of fermenting shoyu known as Soy Sauce Village, turn right at one of the island's only stoplights, pass two Shinto shrines, and take the narrow one-lane road toward the mountain. At the end of an alleyway lined with stone walls and gabled tile-roof houses, look right, and you'll see two mammoth kioke sitting in a gravel driveway surrounded by a two-story home and storehouse wrapped in charred-wood cladding. There, on a spring-fed plot in the shadows of Mount Hoshigajo, is where Yamamoto's family and their millions of microbes have been living for the past 300 years.

As a child, it never occurred to Yamamoto that the men in his family brewed soy sauce. While his father and grandfather mashed, mixed, and measured their shoyu in the dimly lit barn, Yamamoto and his friends often played baseball in front of the family's storehouse. By the time he was 10, he realized that his friends' houses smelled differently than his, and none of theirs was filled with large cedar drums. "My friends' fathers usually went out to work, and I always wondered why my father and grandfather stayed home," Yamamoto said, showing me a collection of faded black-and-white photographs of Yamamotos from generations past dwarfed by the towering kioke in the family's fermenting barn. "It's not that we were all that different; there [have] always been a lot of brewers on the island."

What is different is how many of Shōdoshima's brewers have continued to make their shoyu the old-fashioned way. As Yamamoto explained, one of the main reasons this small island once had 400 soy sauce brewers is the tight-knit nature of the island itself. Compared to bigger cities, Shōdoshima's soy sauce companies paid their workers good salaries and allowed each of their employees to purchase kioke from their companies at discount prices. That way, if they wanted to branch off and start their own businesses, they could. As a result of the companies' focus on community over capital, while the rest of Japan was adopting stainless steel tanks and modernizing its shoyu production at lightning-fast speed, many of the island's smaller, family-run companies—like Yamaroku—couldn't afford to purchase steel vats as quickly. "I suppose we were behind schedule," Yamamoto said, chuckling. Instead, the island's brewers held on to their wooden barrels, and as they saved enough money to eventually add steel tanks to their factories, they adopted the newer, shorter fermenting times and dumped in the same hydrolyzed proteins, additives, and preservatives into their kioke as the big guys. Today, Shōdoshima's once-bustling Soy Sauce Village is still home to 15 shoyu companies, and while all of them now use stainless steel containers to brew the majority of their blend, each also maintains a collection of aging, fungus-filled kioke to brew authentic Japanese shoyu. According to Yamamoto, of the roughly 4,000 kioke still used to ferment soy sauce across Japan, more than 1,100 are found here on Shōdoshima.

Like most families on the island, the Yamamotos never ate at restaurants when Yasuo was growing up. It was only when he left Shōdoshima for the first time to study economics in Nagoya that he first tasted shoyu that hadn't been brewed for years by his father. "I thought, 'What on Earth is this salty soy sauce? How could anyone eat this?'" he recalled. After graduating, Yamamoto returned to the island and asked his father if he should carry on the family business. He remembers that his father looked down and said that after four generations, there was no real family business left. "He told me there was no money and no future," Yamamoto said, running his hands through his floppy, middle-parted black hair. Times had changed; the market had shifted away from locally made artisanal products toward bigger brands. And for all his brewing expertise, Yamamoto's father wasn't a savvy businessman or marketer. "There was nothing to inherit. My family had only managed to survive by eating the rice and vegetables they planted."

Dejected and unemployed, Yamamoto took a job selling the traditional Japanese condiment *tsukudani* (nori simmered in shoyu) in supermarket chains across Tokyo and Osaka. "I hated it," he said flatly. "For seven years, I went to supermarkets with high-quality tsukudani made with real shoyu and mirin. Everyone turned me down because they only wanted to buy cheaper things made with unnatural ingredients." Then one day, while scanning aisle after aisle of mass-produced washoku seasonings made with artificial flavors, Yamamoto had an epiphany. Instead of begging customers who wanted cheaper, mass-produced food to buy traditional Japanese ingredients, why not help his father sell his traditional shoyu to customers who were tired of only seeing cheaper, mass-produced shoyu in supermarkets?

Yamamoto promptly quit and came home. But a few months after returning to what was left of the family business, he found his father collapsed and vomiting blood outside the fermenting barn. Yamamoto's father had never been to a hospital in his life. "He absolutely hated them," Yamamoto said. Yet, at Yamamoto's insistence, he rushed his father across the island to a doctor who discovered an ulcer in his stomach. Diabetes developed soon after, and the doctor told the family to prepare for the worst. "He somehow hung on for 20 years and only died earlier this year," Yamamoto said, lowering his glasses. "But ever since the illness, he stopped working." So, in 2003 at the age of 31, Yamamoto became responsible for the future of the family business.

Yamamoto's father never had enough money to acquire steel vats. Instead, like many of the island's other brewers, he used most of his kioke to brew the cheaper, salt-paste shoyu the government had encouraged alongside his traditional soy sauce. Using his newfound marketing experience, the first things Yamamoto did after taking over the company were to dump out the modern soy sauce that hadn't sold as well, double down on his family's traditional four-year formula, and start shipping directly to customers instead of wholesalers. Early one morning, Yamamoto showed me what goes into this centuries-old four-year formula.

It was 5:00 A.M. and pitch black when Yamamoto met me in his white minivan outside the family-run *ryokan* where I was staying. We slalomed south through the island's narrow one-lane roads until we reached a nondescript factory near Soy Sauce Village. Inside, the rattling whirl of machinery echoed throughout the metal cathedral as roasted wheat slid down a conveyor belt toward a press. Once crushed, the wheat was mixed with steamed soybeans that dribbled out of a giant cauldron in a cloud of vapor. The combination was then fed onto a second conveyor belt and sprayed with *koji-jin*, a fungus that kick-starts the fermentation process of the wheat and soybeans that had been slowly growing in a giant vat nearby. Yamamoto comes here 16 times a year to collect enough raw ingredients to keep his kioke barrels full after he bottles the mash—and always before sunrise. "I start working at 6:00 A.M. every day, so if I come here early, I can make it back in time," Yamamoto said, as he and two of his employees loaded dozens of burlap sacks filled with the mixture into cars. Back in his fermenting barn, Yamamoto angled a forklift down the dirt aisle separating the cedar kioke and raised the burlap bags to the loft's wooden walkway. As Yamamoto's employees dumped 1,110 kilograms of soybeans and 1,000 kilograms of wheat into a newer wooden barrel, a hose pumping 3,500 liters of salt water filled the bottom of the kioke while Yamamoto stabbed the dark-brown slush with a long bamboo pole to aerate it. This mixture, called *moromi*, ages for 24 months as the microbes in the barrels, the bacteria in the warehouse, and the enzymes in the moromi all work together as secret fermenting agents. In the spring, the shed becomes infused with a fruity citrus aroma. In the summer, yeast causes the mash to bubble vigorously. And in autumn and winter, the spores fill the air with an intoxicating liquored fume.

After two years, Yamamoto will remove the mash from this newer kioke barrel and use an antique press to squeeze out every drop of flavor. Later that day, I watched as he emptied the thick, soupy sum from another kioke onto the top of the press and cranked a metal lever to gently squeeze it. As the fermented moromi dribbled down the press, Yamamoto caught a small pool of the black shoyu in a white saucer and let me taste it. What had trickled out was pure liquid umami, with sweet and nutty hints of all five flavors, just as Kuroshima had explained. But instead of bottling this right away, Yamamoto pours this robust shoyu back into an older kioke to ferment and intensify for two more years. Like cigars or wine, no two barrels of shoyu taste exactly the same, and by the time Yamamoto eventually bottles his blend, larger brands will have cranked out anywhere from eight to 24 steel vats' worth of the mass-produced stuff.

Yamamoto may be the only brewer at Yamaroku, but he's not working alone. The way he sees it, his role is to care for the millions of microbes that are hard at work. "The soy sauce is not made by me, but by the bacteria. I only help out," he said, looking up at the black, moldy spores covering the fermenting barn like a Jackson Pollock painting. "My job is to maintain this ecosystem. That way, the bacteria is at its happiest and makes great soy sauce." This is the fundamental difference that separates Yamamoto from Japan's other soy sauce manufacturers. Not only does he believe you can't control the natural environment for the bacteria that flavors shoyu to thrive; he's convinced his microbes are alive and fully aware. "I believe they have a consciousness," he said.

So twice a day, the shoyu alchemist clambers up to his loft and gingerly walks across the narrow planks to smell the moromi and "talk to the bacteria from deep inside my soul." According to Yamamoto, the bacteria talk back by bubbling louder. "Some researchers would laugh at me, but the closer you get to it, the louder the popping gets. I think they know when I'm closer. They seem to work harder as more people come in—especially women. I think the kioke are probably male." Yamamoto also revealed a secret that Kuroshima would later share with me from her experience meeting hundreds of brewers and tasting their shoyu: over time, each soy sauce takes on the personality of the person who creates it. "In my generation, the taste is richer and more profound with a hint of sweetness compared to my father's generation, and people tell me I'm that way," Yamamoto said with a smile. "I think it shows that [the bacteria] is happy. When the bacteria is happy and works hard, it creates fantastic soy sauce."

Yamamoto speaks of his shoyu as though it were a loved one, and in many ways, it is the past and future of his family. In addition to passing down the knowledge of shoyu brewing, the most important thing

Yamamoto's ancestors did was to pass down the actual bacteria needed to brew it. Yamamoto's century-old storehouse was built using bacteria-filled beams that have been in his family for 300 years—the very foundations of the Yamamotos' former Edo-era house on this land. This, together with the family's 150-year-old kioke, is how the Yamamotos have created and maintained their two distinct shoyu varieties over generations: the robust, creamy, and intensely rich *Tsuru-bishio*, and the lighter and more delicate *Kiku bishio*.

Today, there are roughly 1,140 shoyu manufacturers in Japan,[28] and Yamaroku is one of fewer than 10 to use only kioke. While this distinction has helped Yamamoto revive the family business in a more craft brew–friendly era, it also means that his family's fragile ecosystem faces an uncertain future. Because kioke can only last about 150 years, Yamamoto's ancestors never had to make new ones. Now, many of his barrels are on the brink of becoming unusable. Before World War II, hundreds of companies across Japan built kioke for Japan's five fermented washoku seasonings. Decades later, there was only one: Fujii Seiokesho, located outside Osaka. When Yamamoto contacted them in 2009 to build three new barrels, he discovered that they hadn't received an order for a new kioke since before the war and had spent the past 70 years repairing the country's aging wooden barrels. He also learned the youngest cooper at the three-person company was 68 years old, had no successors, and was planning to retire in 2021. So, while Yamamoto could order these new barrels, soon no one would be available to fix all his old ones.

Recognizing that the future of his family's company and all authentically fermented Japanese foods depended on the continuation of this craft, Yamamoto and two carpenters traveled to Fujii Seiokesho's workshop in 2012 to learn the ancient art for themselves. After three days of instruction and a year and a half of practice, they made their first barrel in 2013. Making these mammoth 3,600-liter barrels is a team effort requiring five people to work over a 10-day period. More than 40 planks of 100-year-old Yoshino cedar are rounded and laid vertically to form a cylinder. To lock the planks into place, Fujii Seiokesho's craftsmen told Yamamoto not to use glue, but bamboo. By talking to an elderly neighbor who worked for the family in the 1940s, Yamamoto discovered that his grandfather had planted a secret bamboo grove before World War II for exactly that reason, knowing that one of his descendants would one day need to build more barrels. Yamamoto's father didn't even know about the grove, so the elderly man took Yamamoto up the mountain to show him where it was.

On our last morning together, Yamamoto and I twisted and turned up a narrow lane, past a staircase of terraced rice fields, to a thicket of bamboo a kilometer from his home so dense it was more wall than woodland. I followed Yamamoto as he wove through the forest, stopping at a clearing to stare up at the soaring stalks as they rustled, creaked, and knocked together in the mountain breeze, like swaying skyscrapers. "This place brings me to tears," he said, sniffling and wiping his nose on the sleeve of his sweatshirt. "Without it, I wouldn't have been able to make my first barrel. My grandfather was thinking about the future and his family. This was his gift." For each kioke, Yamamoto searches in the grove for just the right shoots to harvest. He taps the bamboo above the joint with a pen and listens closely for a sturdy, high-pitched sound. If the hollow shoot produces the right echoey pitch, he'll cut it at the base. Back outside the fermentation barn, I watched as he and several assistants shaved the cut shoots down to make elastic strips that he wove into braided bamboo hoops by beating them with a wooden mallet to make the rings more elastic. He and an assistant then climbed atop a ladder and hoisted the cylindrical hoop around the barrel, carefully hammering it into place like a belt across the kioke's midsection to prevent any liquid from seeping out.

Since 2013, Yamamoto and his colleagues have constructed 62 barrels, but he hasn't kept all of them. As word of his quest to revive kioke craftsmanship spread, Yamamoto has started receiving orders from other fermented food producers across the country. "The Fujii Seiokesho business stopped in 2021. [The youngest cooper] couldn't physically carry on. Now, we are one of the last places left who can make kioke," Yamamoto said, as he hammered the final of seven bamboo hoops around the barrel with a rubber mallet. Yamamoto knows that if he doesn't find a viable successor, the secret ingredient behind Japanese washoku could die with him. So, every January since 2013, he has hosted a free 10-day kioke-making workshop at his brewery where he teaches fellow craftsmen the essentials of kioke construction. Since the first workshop, thousands of shoyu brewers, carpenters, and other fermented food makers from across Japan have descended on the island to learn from Yamamoto. The group typically makes three or four new barrels together in each workshop, and while Yamamoto keeps some of these, he gives many away to other companies. As he sees it, the only way authentic washoku can survive is to build more kioke, reacquaint the world with how Japan's fermented seasonings are supposed to taste, and drive up demand. To do this, he's proposed an ambitious goal to other shoyu brewers: to increase the market for kioke-brewed shoyu from less than 1 percent in Japan to 1 percent in the world—a leap that will likely require the construction of hundreds of additional kioke.

"It's hard to put into words how much Yamamoto-san has helped Japan and this island. He's showing us the proof of what we can do with the old traditional brewing methods. He's a big inspiration," said Kohsei Takebe, the head of one of the Shōdoshima's largest soy sauce companies, Takesan. "In reality, without Yamamoto-san's project, real soy sauce wouldn't survive. My company wouldn't survive. Our [new] kioke come from him. If we try to compete against the big companies like Kikkoman, we wouldn't win."

Ironically, several years ago at one of his January workshops, Yamamoto remembers that a man attended who revealed that he worked for Kikkoman. The gentleman was especially keen to learn how to repair old kioke instead of making new ones. I asked Yamamoto why Kikkoman, the company that pioneered mass-produced, stainless steel shoyu, would want to know how to repair wooden barrels, and he let me in on a little-known secret. Despite the Japanese government encouraging brewers to modernize production, Kikkoman maintains several old kioke that it uses to supply authentic shoyu to the Japanese emperor and imperial family.

"Everyone knows that kioke shoyu tastes better—even the government!" Yamamoto laughed. In a way, the fact that more than 99 percent of Japanese shoyu companies would willingly comply with an unwritten rule to make their shoyu worse makes no sense. But in a nation famous for its conformity, where those caught jaywalking and littering are often shunned, it makes perfect sense. "Deviance in Japan is met with resistance," said Haruko Hosokawa, a local guide, as we looked down toward Yamamoto's fermenting barn from a lookout high atop Mount Hoshigajo.

"A popular Japanese proverb says, 'The nail that sticks out gets hammered down.'" And while the size and attention of Yamamoto's kioke workshops have grown over the years, so have the whispers of those who have started to question his push to change the status quo. "He's the odd one," said Yosuke Shiota, the president of the Shōdoshima Shoyu Association, inside his brewery located in Soy Sauce Village. "There isn't anybody left in Japan who can make kioke, so it's a wonderful thing what he's doing, but he's running fast and alone while the rest of us are left behind."

A short walk away, I found Fujii Yasuto, a fourth-generation brewer who heads up Shokin Shoyu, which is home to 110 kioke. When I asked him why he felt it was important for Yamamoto to save these barrels, Yasuto chose his words carefully. "A kioke is simply a tool. It's like a knife or bowl for a chef, and no chef is going to boast, 'Look at my pots and pans!' I'm not putting Yamamoto-san down, but it's hard to just talk about shoyu brewing by only focusing on these barrels. There are other aspects to it." Yet, when I asked Kuroshima to give me her professional opinion of Yamamoto's four-year fermented product compared to the hundreds of other blends she's tasted in Japan, the shoyu sommelier lit up. "It's very bold, very forward," she said. "If you have a deep-fried pork, or even a simple tofu, pouring his soy sauce on it transforms it into something magical."

To date, of the thousands of washoku brewers and craftsmen who have attended his workshops, Yamamoto said only about five are capable of building a proper kioke. Like brewing authentic shoyu itself, it's a slow and strenuous process. That's what led so many people to give up long ago. And while Yamamoto will likely never be able to make enough kioke to save traditional soy sauce and washoku cuisine in his lifetime, there are three main reasons why he presses on: Kozo, Kosuke, and Emi—his children.

In the past, Yamamoto's daughter, Emi, used to run into the family storehouse to ask if she could taste her father's shoyu. His oldest son, Kozo, whom he hopes will one day take over the family craft, would eagerly lead him into his great-grandfather's bamboo grove to search for shoots. Now, all three are teenagers with lives and interests of their own. "When they were little, they always wanted to help me. Now, they're always on their phones," Yamamoto joked, showing a hint of regret. "They know the importance, but they're not interested in taking it over right now. Kozo is really into IT, and he's going to vocational school. I told him, go learn the job, and before you're 30, maybe you can come back to the island to help me run the business. Kosuke is also eager to leave Shōdoshima."

This is an all-too-familiar story in Japan. Because of the nation's rapid rural migration, aging population, and anemic birth rate, more than half of the nation's 1,718 municipalities are now classified as "depopulated areas" by the Japanese government. But on Shōdoshima, the situation is especially dire. The island's population has shrunk by nearly half since 1990, and today, 43 percent of the island's estimated 13,870 people are aged 65 and older (compared to 29.1 percent nationwide).[29]

Signs of Shōdoshima's aging, shrinking population are everywhere. The island is scattered with pyramid-shaped *muen-san* tombstones of deceased souls who have no descendants left to look after their graves. Its elementary schools are half empty, and many working residents I encountered were well past the country's legal retirement age of 70—from the octogenarian owners who ran my ryokan to the 90-year-old waitress with a cane-shaped spine who served Yamamoto and me one night at dinner. In an effort to halt the local youth exodus and inject new energy into their vanishing communities, Shōdoshima and 11 neighboring islands in the Seto Inland Sea have launched a once-every-three-years art exhibit called the Setouchi Triennale, which transforms abandoned homes and rural landscapes into modern, Instagram-friendly art installations.

Shortly after Yamamoto and I were quietly staring up at the swaying bamboo stalks in his grandfather's grove, I was shoulder to shoulder with a line of iPhone-clutching tourists, looking up at a giant geodesic dome made from 4,000 bamboo shoots stripped from the island by a foreign artist. As I left the installation and headed toward the port to catch my ferry off Shōdoshima, I couldn't help but wince at the thought of how Yamamoto would feel if the bamboo grove his grandfather left for his family to save authentic soy sauce was one day used as a backdrop for a selfie.

Only time will tell if there's a sixth generation of Yamamotos using the family's bacteria to brew shoyu, but as Yamamoto told me while the bamboo stalks rustled, creaked, and knocked together in the breeze, as much as he wishes his children would carry on after him, ultimately, it's their choice. Still, with every new kioke that he makes, he writes his name and the names of his three children on an inner panel of the cedar wood before sealing it shut. By the time Yamamoto's newest kioke are fully caked in the family's centuries-old bacteria, he will likely be gone. By the time they finally split apart to reveal the names written inside, his children and grandchildren may be too. But Yamamoto hopes that whoever discovers them in the future realizes something he learned long ago: "The reason I can consume this soy sauce today is because somebody I didn't know hundreds of years ago made it."

10

The Most Romantic Job in Europe

Mit den ersten Bäumen, die gefällt werden, beginnt die Kultur.
Mit den letzten Bäumen, die gefällt werden, endet sie.
(With the cutting of the first trees, culture begins.
With the falling of the last trees, it ends.)
—GERMAN PROVERB

On a crisp autumn afternoon, deep in northern Germany's Dodauer Forest, I sat alone on a fallen log's mossy fleece. Streams of sunlight filtered through the thinning canopy, dappling a carpet of yellow and brown leaves at my feet. Save for two frolicking squirrels, a determined woodpecker, and a pair of flirting songbirds volleying chirps back and forth, there wasn't another soul in sight. Moments later, a lone postal carrier wearing a bright yellow-and-black uniform came crunching through the woods. When she reached a clearing, she rummaged through a bag slung over her shoulder and carefully climbed a three-meter wooden ladder to deliver a thick stack of letters to a 500-year-old oak tree. Then, just as quickly as she appeared, she hiked back through the forest and disappeared toward the next mailbox on her route.

One of the letters was tucked into a bright green envelope. It was from Jan. He's 35 years old, a Taurus, and wants children someday. He likes long walks through the woods, and while he doesn't mind taking them alone, he's wondering if there's a woman out there—preferably aged 30 to 35 with medium-length hair and "free space in her heart"—who would want to join him. If so, he hopes that she, too, is looking for love inside the knothole of this oak tree.

Known as *die Bräutigamseiche* (the Bridegroom's Oak), this ancient timber outside the town of Eutin has been matching singles long before Tinder and is rumored to be responsible for more than 100 marriages. Today, people from all over Germany write letters addressed to the tree, hoping that for the price of a postage stamp, they may find a partner. There's Daniela, a mother from Rödinghausen who's looking for someone who can make her laugh; Stefan, a 31-year-old techno lover from Hamburg who wants to share his life with someone who allows him "the freedom to read many books"; and Selena, a "funny, authentic, and empathetic" woman from Wittichenau who just wants to know "if there's anyone else out there who believes in destiny."

"There's something so magical and romantic about it," said 79-year-old Karl-Heinz Martens, who delivered letters to the tree as its postman for 20 years, starting in 1984. "On the internet, facts and questions match people, but at the tree, it's a beautiful coincidence—like fate." Though retired now, Martens still keeps several scrapbooks filled with photographs, letters, and newspaper clippings from his time as love's official messenger, which he happily showed me over homemade apple cider and marzipan cookies at his spotlessly clean ranch-style house, just outside Eutin. In his two decades of service to the oak, Martens delivered letters from every region in Germany. As we sat down at his small kitchen table, Martens explained that while many people know about the tree today, back in 1890, it was a secret shared by two young lovers.

"Once upon a time, in the deep, dark Dodauer Forest, there lived a girl named Minna," Martens began, lowering his voice as his eyes twinkled behind his black-rimmed glasses. Minna was the daughter of the Dodauer Forest keeper, and she had fallen in love with the son of a chocolate maker, named Wilhelm. Minna's father disapproved of the relationship and forbade her from seeing Wilhelm, so the two started secretly exchanging handwritten letters and leaving them in the hollow of the oak's trunk. A year later, Minna's father finally granted her permission to marry Wilhelm, and the two were wed on June 2, 1891, under the 26-meter-tall tree's sprawling branches.

As Martens turned a page in his scrapbook, he showed me a faded black-and-white photograph of the wedding party beneath the towering oak. "It seems this was printed in the local paper," he explained, stroking his short white beard. The story of the couple's fairy-tale courtship spread, and soon, hopeful romantics throughout Germany who had had no luck finding partners in biergartens or ballrooms began writing love letters addressed to the Bridegroom's Oak. But because postal carriers didn't know which of the Dodauer's thousands of oak trees was *the* oak tree, they dumped these love letters at the nearest address—the forest keeper's house. By 1927, the tree was receiving so much mail that the forest keeper marched letter carriers out to the correct oak and convinced the German postal service to assign it its own postman and address: Bräutigamseiche, Dodauer Forest, 23701, Eutin, Germany. The post office even placed a ladder up to the fist-sized mailbox, so that anyone who wanted to open, read, and respond to the letters could. "You see, the 'secrecy of the post' is lifted at the oak." Martens smiled. The only rule, he explained, is that if you open a letter you don't want to answer, you should place it back in the tree for someone else to find.

According to Stefan Laetsch, a spokesman for Germany's national Deutsche Post mail service, the tree receives about 1,000 letters a year. "The busiest months are April and May," he told me, peering up at the oak's gnarled branches. "It seems everyone is searching for love in the springtime." For those pining for someone specific, Martens explained there's a legend that says if a woman walks around the oak's five-meter trunk three times under a full moon while thinking of her beloved, without speaking or laughing, she'll marry within the year. Today the Bridegroom's Oak remains the only tree in the world with its own mailing address. Six days a week for the past 97 years, a postman has walked through the forest—rain, snow, or shine—and climbed the ladder's eight rungs to stuff letters from starry-eyed singles into the tree. And in those 97 years, no one has delivered mail to the oak nearly as long as Martens.

"It was my favorite part of the day," Martens said, handing me a photo of himself wearing a brimmed cap and bifocals as a clean-shaven 45-year-old, smiling as he dropped letters into the oak from atop the ladder. "People used to memorize my route and wait for me to arrive because they couldn't believe that a postman would deliver letters to a tree." But despite holding the most romantic job in Germany for 20 years, Martens had given up on love when he first took the role. In 1984, he was a recently divorced 40-year-old who lived alone with his black cocker spaniel–lab mix, Meica. He spent his days diligently delivering mail and splitting custody of his son, Olaf, and his nights watching sports at home and bowling with the guys from the post office. "I had no interest in dating again," Martens said, bluntly. "None." Still, something from Martens' past subconsciously drew him to this magical tree in the woods, and as he closed his scrapbooks and clasped his hands, he began to tell me a remarkable tale of luck and circumstance as gilded as any German fable.

Martens' ex-wife, Jutta, also worked for the postal service, and a year before Olaf was born in 1972, Martens followed her to Eutin, a quiet town of 17,000 people located 90 kilometers northeast of Hamburg, where she was from. Bound by lakes on two sides and dense forests on another, Eutin is a paean to German preservation. It's one of the last places in Germany that's home to a royal family, and its hulking, moat-wrapped castle is still privately owned by the dynastic House of Oldenburg. The town is clustered around a 12th-century Romanesque church whose sharp Gothic spire lists slightly to the side after nearly 900 years upright. Cobblestone streets thread red-brick, half-timbered homes dating to the 1600s, and a five-story windmill from the 1850s with a thatched roof still towers over the town. For years, Martens would steer his yellow mail truck through Eutin's narrow streets on one of the most coveted—and compact—postal routes in town. Then one day when one of his colleagues called in sick, Martens was asked to fill in and work one of the network's least-coveted routes. "It was a 20- to 30-kilometer drive around the outside of Eutin, primarily to farms and neighboring villages," Martens recalled. "Right in the middle, there was a two-kilometer detour where you'd need to get out of the truck and walk through the woods. From that day, I requested it to my boss repeatedly."

Martens continued to request the route—month after month, year after year. Even as his marriage began to crumble and he started swearing off love entirely, he inexplicably sought out a job that would extend his workday and force him to play matchmaker for lonely-hearted singles. But why? "It is unbelievable that the secrecy of the post is lifted here," Martens explained. "I had already received one happy accident in my life because of this coincidence, so I felt a duty to the tree."

———

Martens was born in Gelting, a 2,000-person fishing hamlet facing Denmark across the Baltic Sea on Germany's northern tip. He was raised by his father and paternal grandparents, and the only things he knew about his mother, Yvette, were through the hushed details he'd overheard growing up. Yvette's parents had owned a laundromat in a small village near Cognac, France. In 1943, a year before Martens was born, his father served as a parachutist in the German army and was stationed in France. When he wasn't dropping into Allied territory on reconnaissance missions, it was his job to wash the other soldiers' linens. So, one day he wandered into the closest laundromat, where he spotted the owners' three daughters. He pointed to the youngest one and said, "She will be my wife." He asked the girl's father if they could see each other outside of the laundromat, and the two ended up sneaking off one night to lie together under the moonlight. "My mother was only 17 or 18 at the time," Martens recalled. Shortly thereafter, Martens' father was sent from France to Italy, and he never learned that Yvette had become pregnant. Before he had a chance to write Yvette, he was shot in combat. Since he and Yvette weren't married, the German army never informed her of his whereabouts, and she presumed he was either missing or dead.

Yvette named her son after his father, Karl Martens Sr., and she was sure she'd never see or hear from her lover again. More than a year passed, the war ended, and Yvette tried her best to move on. Then, at the end of 1945, she got word that Karl Sr. had miraculously reappeared in an Italian military hospital. After Karl's father had healed enough to safely transfer back to Germany, Yvette reunited with him in Gelting and introduced him to the infant son he never knew he had. The two married, but Yvette soon found that life in Germany was lonely. She didn't know anyone, didn't speak the language, and was so homesick that she begged Karl Sr. to return to France with her to raise their baby. His parents insisted that their grandson would have a better upbringing in Germany, surrounded by the extended family who was already raising him. So, when Martens was just two years

old, Yvette returned to France all alone. She and Karl Sr. divorced shortly
thereafter, and he soon married a woman Martens described as cold and
distant. For years, Martens' father and grandparents never talked about
Yvette, and it was only when he was 11 that he learned he had a mother.
All he knew was that she was an attractive woman with black, curly hair,
and that she was somewhere in France, but he had no way of finding her.

When Martens turned 16, his father told him it was time for him to
choose a career. "At that time, the only choices you had in Gelting were
to be a fisherman, a bricklayer, or a construction worker," Martens said,
resting his brawny hands on his paunch. "I couldn't fish and didn't want to
lay bricks, so I became a postman, like my father." By the time he was 25,
Martens was working in the small town of Kappeln, just south of Gelting.
His job was to deliver letters door to door, but one day, he was ordered to
sort through the piles of misplaced packages and letters that had been left
in the post office.

Back then, Martens explained, the West German Bundespost had a
rule that if a recipient was either unavailable or if their name and address
were illegible, instead of returning the letter to the sender, it was protocol
for a postman to open it, read it, and try to determine where the letter
should go. "This was the only time in Germany the secrecy of the post
was lifted," Martens explained, sternly. "And we postmen were to take
an oath and swear to not reveal the personal information inside." The
Bundespost actually changed this rule in 1970, but on this chance day
in 1969, Martens was handed several stacks of undeliverable envelopes
and told to go through them. At the very bottom of the pile, Martens
came across a letter addressed to his grandmother in Gelting, who had
since passed. The sender's surname was Fuss, which he didn't recognize,
but the postage was French. Martens opened the letter, read the first few
lines, and nearly fainted. It was from his mother. She was alive, had remarried—a Frenchman named Fuss—and had learned enough German
to pen a letter explaining that she was desperately looking for her long-
lost son. But she wasn't the only one: the French military was looking
for him, too, as they'd taken him for a deserter. Yvette was hoping Karl
Jr. could find it in his heart to forgive her for leaving, and invited him
to come to Mulhouse, just over the German-French border, where she

was living. After steadying himself, Martens went to his superior and requested special permission to keep this undelivered envelope himself, a strictly verboten offense for a postal carrier. The head of the postal service granted Martens a rare exception, and after taking some time to process it all, Martens replied to her. "I had never written a letter that long in my life before," he recalled.

After a few more exchanges, Martens loaded up his Volkswagen Beetle and anxiously drove toward the French border to meet a woman he had no memory of ever knowing. When the two met outside of Yvette's home, all of the anger and resentment from Martens' childhood washed away, and he wept for the first time in years. Over the next few days, Martens met two stepsisters he never knew about, and his relationship with his mother quickly blossomed. He identified in her a certain gregarious streak and love for storytelling that he'd long recognized in himself but could never place, and he began traveling to France three times a year with Olaf to visit her. "We just fit," Martens said, showing me a framed picture of he and his mother together in Mulhouse. "It might be fate, call it what you want, but were it not for the happy accident that, on this day, the secrecy of the post was lifted for me, I never would have met her. And that's why I love the Bräutigamseiche so much. I felt a special connection to it from the first moment I laid eyes on it."

By 1984, Martens' boss wanted a postman to not only deliver letters to the oak, but to reeducate residents in the surrounding Schleswig-Holstein area about its history. "For many decades after the war, we Germans were ashamed of our past. My boss wanted someone to help reacquaint them with it—someone social. Of course, coming from France, that is my nature," Martens said, chuckling. No longer tied to a partner, Martens devoted himself to the tree. When he wasn't working his route, he made it his "duty" to pore over crumpled documents at local *heimatverein* (heritage societies), where he found not only photos and records of Minna and Wilhelm's wood-bound wedding but also the romantic legend surrounding the oak's origins. "Ahem," Martens said, lowering his voice again as he leaned toward me from across the kitchen table. "There once was a prince of a Celtic chieftain who was tied to a tree in these forests. A young maiden with long blond hair came along on a white horse and rescued him. To thank her, the prince planted a sapling where this mighty oak now stands, and the two lived happily ever after."

Martens also interviewed elderly area residents to ask what they remember of the oak, and in doing so, he started hearing story after story about lonely hearts who had met their soulmates through the oak's matchmaking powers long after Minna and Wilhelm. One was Frau Sörnson. In 1970, her brother confided to her that he had recently ventured into the woods and left a hopeful note for a woman in an oak tree's hollow. After laughing this off, Sörnson eventually followed her brother into the forest to try her luck as well. When she arrived at the oak, she realized that the only piece of paper she had on her was an old gas receipt, so she scribbled her name and address on it and placed it into the knothole. A week later, she received a response from a man who would eventually become her husband. Shortly thereafter, her brother also married a woman he met through the oak. Another couple was Peter and Marita Pump. In 1958, he was a young German soldier stationed in Plön, 14 kilometers west of Eutin. One day during training, a military instructor took Peter and other recruits into the forest and told them about an oak with its own address. Peter reached into the oak's hole, felt several letters, and pulled out a piece of paper that had just a name and address written on it. Back in the barracks, he responded, addressing his note, "To the Honoured Miss Marita," the 82-year-old told a German newspaper. "It was something of a joke."[1]

"Naturally, I was quite surprised when he responded, because I hadn't written to the tree in the first place," Marita is quoted as saying. "My friends at work had done it, because I was too shy." Marita didn't respond to Peter at first, and it was only after her mother found the note and remarked how "clever" it was that she convinced Marita to write back. "It's her fault that I wrote him," she said.[2] The two corresponded for a full year before Peter built up the courage to meet her. Soon, he was traveling several times a month from Plön to Marita's house 27 kilometers away in Haffkrug. "Back then it was half a trip around the world by bus," he told the newspaper. The two were married in 1961, and still travel 47 kilometers from their home in Neumünster to visit the oak every few years. "We have to check to see whether it is still there," Peter said.[3]

After meeting as many couples as he could who had met through the oak's knothole, Martens followed his orders and did what he could to spread the tree's story. At first, he would park his yellow mail truck at the nearest road and wander through the thicket of oak, beech, and chestnut trees on his way to the Bridegroom's Oak. If he happened to see anyone else on the way, he'd launch into the legend of how a prince planted it for his princess and how two young lovers later wed under the oak's branches. Before too long, curious onlookers began plodding through the woods to wait for Martens at the tree. In a nation renowned for its order and efficiency, many people didn't believe that the Bundespost served a postbox in the forest or that Martens was even a real postman. "People would be open-mouthed when I got there, as if to say, 'Is this right? It can't be true.'" So, for a few years starting in 1986, Martens convinced his boss to let him drive his yellow mail truck through a clearing in the woods, right up to the tree. "That's when things started to take off," Martens said, sliding a series of local newspaper clippings across the table to me, one showing a salt-and-pepper-haired Martens atop the ladder in 1989 with the headline, "Problems of the Heart? Write to This Oak Tree." "Of course, there were many postal workers who delivered to the tree before me, but the oak's popularity grew from my compost."

Martens arrived at the tree every day at noon on the dot. At first, those waiting for him were generally from Eutin. Then, as word spread and regional and national papers began printing the story of the Bridegroom's Oak, people from across Germany started showing up. Soon after, tourists from neighboring Austria would hike through the Dodauer to hear the tree's tale and try their luck at love in the knothole too. "I told the story of the tree with pleasure, but not endless time," Martens said. "Post office work is precise, and I had to finish my route by 1:30 P.M." After the Goethe-Institut published a short story about the tree in a German-language textbook,[4] international journalists started waiting at the oak for Martens too. Before long, he was delivering love letters in languages he didn't understand. "Africa, America, Russia, Japan, Scandinavia," Martens said, counting on his fingers. "The next day, they would always be gone." In 20 years, Martens said there were only two days when he called in sick, and 10 days when no one wrote to the oak. And while he'd occasionally deliver as many as 50 envelopes a day, not all of them were love letters. "Before unification, people from the DDR [East Germany] who had no contacts in the West used to write to the tree and ask what kind of cars and music we had," Martens remembered. "Some ladies would even ask if I could send them some women's tights."

"Did you ever respond?" I asked.

"To send tights? No, I'm a postman, I wasn't paid for that. Then they may have asked me to send bras as well!" Martens said.

"I mean to those curious about life in the West," I said.

"I wanted to write back, but my boss recommended me not to. I made copies of the tree's history that my chief approved, and I sent that to the East Germans instead."

As the tree's popularity increased, so did the number of marriages Martens helped forge. He recalled the story of a man who had traveled alone from Germany's North-Rhine Westphalia state near the Dutch and Belgian border to Eutin on a holiday. One day when it was raining, he decided to hike through the woods and pull an envelope from the oak. He found a letter Martens had delivered several days earlier from a woman who was also visiting Eutin on vacation. The two discovered they lived just 19 kilometers away from each other, halfway across Germany, and soon wed.

Then there's the story of the Christiansens. In 1988, Claudia Meier was a 19-year-old nurse living behind the Iron Curtain in East Germany's Ore Mountains. Because her family's home sat at the top of the mountain, they were one of the few households in her village that got TV signals from the West. One night, her mother tuned in to a West German quiz show featuring the story of the Bridegroom's Oak, and at the end of the program, the oak's address appeared on the screen. Claudia's mom grabbed a pen, jotted it down, and encouraged her daughter to send a letter. "I only wrote to it looking for a pen pal," Claudia told me in her dining room. "I was curious about life in the West." Martens delivered the letter in January, and a few days later, Friedrich Christiansen, an agricultural mechanic from Malente who had had "trouble finding girls," reached into the knothole and discovered it. "I was struck by how beautiful the handwriting was," he said, delicately unfolding a sheet of orange paper containing

Claudia's original note and placing it on the table in front of me. "It was so precise. I thought, 'This woman must be perfect.'" He wrote back. One letter turned into 40, and the two started cautiously calling each other at night. "It was so difficult, because the Stasi police were always listening," Friedrich said. After a year of furtive phone calls, the two made a plan to meet in the Ore Mountains in early 1989. But with Germany still cleaved in half and travel between the nations risky, the couple devised a secret plan, hashed out through coded letters the Stasi wouldn't crack: Friedrich drove 10 hours from his home near the Bridegroom's Oak to the border, and then snuck into the East by pretending to be Claudia's cousin.

During a four-day period, Claudia proudly showed Friedrich the softer side of her East German state—her father's accordion factory, the spires of Dresden, the towering sandstone pillars of Saxony. By the end of Friedrich's stay, Claudia realized she had romantic feelings for him. "I guess you could say it was love at second sight," she said. The two continued to exchange letters and coded calls across the border for nearly a year with a newfound longing. When the Berlin Wall finally came down in November 1989, they met for only the second time and were married in Claudia's village in May 1990. Today, they live just six kilometers from the oak and remain happily married, never forgetting that their storybook ending is thanks to a special tree in the forest. "The oak is magical for us," Claudia said, reaching for Friedrich's hand. "It's like a German fairy tale."

It's easy to see how the Bräutigamseiche fits within German folklore. From *Little Red Riding Hood* to *Snow White*, German fables are filled with stories of enchanted forests and longing lovers. The forest is where Prince Phillip and Princess Aurora meet for the first time in *Sleeping Beauty*. It's where the prince first hears Rapunzel singing from atop the tower. And in the German version of *Cinderella*, she doesn't meet Prince Charming at a ball, but in the mist-shrouded woods. Yet, while it's tempting to chalk up the oak's matchmaking powers to chance, or a sweet coincidence of life imitating art over and over again, to do so is to miss the forest for the trees. The more time you spend in Germany, the more apparent it becomes that the story of the Bräutigamseiche is something that could only happen here—and that's because, in many respects, the Bräutigamseiche reflects the story of Germany itself.

Despite the fact that Germany is one of the most modern, industrialized nations on Earth, Germans have always fancied themselves as forest people. "Even the most urban Germans have a deep sense of the forest within them," explained Karen Leeder, a professor of modern German literature at the University of Oxford. "The forest is the German soul. It touches the very roots of the country." As Leeder explained, Germans' emotional connection to the woods harks back to one of the most pivotal events in European history.[5] In 9 AD, what is now Germany was inhabited by Teutonic tribes that were scattered across the densely forested hinterland. In an attempt to quell these clans and expand its territory west, the Roman army sent three of its best legions into the Teutoburg Forest in present-day Lower Saxony. Unaccustomed to fighting in this murky, inhospitable landscape, the Romans were annihilated in a defeat so devastating that it signaled the end of the empire's expansion and threatened the survival of Rome itself. By driving the Romans out of Germania, the tribes' ambush created a geographic boundary between Germanic and Latin cultures that still exists more than 2,000 years later. It also gave birth to a nascent German national spirit; as Roman historian Tacitus described, Germania was a land permeated by impenetrable forests and filled with woodland-loving tribes whose culture is bound to the trees.[6] "There's this idea of Germania straight away as 'Woodlands' and the battle of the Teutoburg Forest was seen as early Germans defending their identity," Leeder said. "This is the founding idea of Germany."

The country's mythological bond with the forest has only been strengthened over the centuries. In the 1800s, the rise of German Romanticism popularized the idea of the woods as a place of yearning, isolation, and love. From the Brothers Grimm to Goethe, a wave of writers, poets, and painters stirred the nation's collective imagination while helping to revitalize deep-seated legends of star-crossed lovers and mystical woods. Around this time, Minna and Wilhelm were wed under the Bräutigamseiche's branches, and their zeitgeist-capturing love story captivated the hearts of local readers. German Romanticism also portrayed the forest as a symbol of national unity.[7] As Napoleon's troops marched toward Germany in the early 1800s, German foresters were convinced that by planting trees along the border with France, these Romance-speaking invaders would get lost in the woods, just as the Romans did.[8] "The forest became about defending the borders and national identity," Leeder explained.

Yet, even the woods couldn't escape the shadow of National Socialism, and the Nazis exploited this idea of the timeless German forest as a metaphor for the enduring Aryan race. Speaking from his forest hunting lodge in 1935, Hitler's deputy, Hermann Göring, said, "We have become used to seeing the German nation as eternal. There is no better symbol for us than the forest, which has and always will be eternal. The eternal forest and an eternal nation—they belong together."[9] A year later, the Nazis produced the popular film *Ewiger Wald (Eternal Forest)* to portray the shared destiny of the German woods and Aryan people, and the term became one of the Nazis' most-used rallying cries alongside "*Blut und Boden*" (blood and soil).[10] The Nazis specifically latched on to Germany's national tree, "the mighty oak," as a symbol of the nation's strength. The Reich encouraged Germans to plant oak trees to honor Hitler, and at the 1936 Olympic Games in Berlin, every gold medal winner was ceremoniously given a "Hitler oak" sapling.[11] As the country grappled with its dark past in the decades after World War II and consciously rejected any symbolic connections to nationalism, it's no wonder that the legend of the Bridegroom's Oak had been all but forgotten by the time Martens began serving it.

Today, Germans have rekindled their intimate relationship with the forest, and when you look around, it's not hard to understand why. Thirty-three percent of the nation is covered in woods. Germany is home to more than 90 billion trees and has nearly three times as much protected land as the US, proportionate to the countries' sizes.[12] As Dieter Borchmeyer, a professor of modern German literature at the University of Heidelberg and the author of the book *What Is German? A Nation's Search for Itself,* writes: "For Germans, the forest poses nothing short of a landscape of longing, the epitome of protective nature—a fact frequently met with astonishment by non-Germans."[13] After living in Germany for three years myself, this hits home.

When I first arrived in Berlin in 2016, I lived down the street from one of the country's more than 1,500 government-funded *waldkitas* (forest kindergartens).[14] These open-air, wood-bound classrooms shun toys and curriculums and instead encourage children aged three to six to use rocks, leaves, and mud to connect with the forest, regardless of the weather. Many afternoons when I'd wander back to my prewar building, I'd see Jess, whose flat I was renting, and her four-year-old son in the stairwell. His face was often streaked with dirt from a day of climbing trees and following distant hoots into the woods unsupervised. Jess would frequently rhapsodize to me about the many benefits of running free in the forest and playing uninhibitedly. "What happens if a kid gets lost?" I asked her one time. "Then they'd find something new," she said.

Soon, I was getting lost with German friends on *Sonntagsspaziergänge* (Sunday strolls) through the towering conifer and alder trees of Grunewald and Spreewald forests. After trudging for 14 kilometers through the mud-slicked woods of the Sächsische Schweiz National Park in a downpour to keep up with my perpetually cheery pal Klaus, I first heard the popular German expression *"Es gibt kein schlechtes Wetter, nur schlechte Kleidung"* (There is no bad weather, only bad clothing). And as flecks of snow began to filter through the wall of spruce trees in the Harz Mountains, I learned that Germans believe that Father Christmas comes not from the North Pole but from somewhere deep in the forest.

"In no other modern country has the forest feeling remained as alive as it has in Germany," Borchmeyer argues. "The parallel rigidity of the upright trees and their density and number fill the heart of the German with a deep and mysterious delight. To this day, he loves to go deep into the forest where his forefathers lived; he feels at one with the trees."[15]

This "forest feeling" is one of the reasons Martens was drawn to the Bräutigamseiche to begin with. "You have to understand, for German people, it is always special to go in the woods," Martens said, looking at a framed picture in his den of his granddaughter climbing the oak's ladder. "Growing up in Gelting, there were many pastors in my neighborhood who were telling me that I should go to their church, and I told them, 'No thanks, I would rather go to the woods alone. There, I have my connection with nature.' It's the same at the oak." When I asked Martens why it's important to be alone at the oak, he closed his eyes for a moment and seemed to disappear somewhere deep within himself. "The tree has a certain aura. I get goose bumps just thinking about it," he said, lifting up the sleeve of his wool sweater. "I can't describe it . . . you get near it, and you have this feeling: the sound of the leaves, the singing of the birds, the running of the squirrels. It's a symphony. You can't have this special feeling if other people are around. It is absolutely necessary that you are alone and you feel your inner quietness. Only then can you feel that *waldeinsamkeit* is growing."

German is filled with delightfully descriptive expressions of melancholy that have no English equivalent, from *sehnsucht* (a yearning for something unattainable) to *heimat* (a longing for Germany and German culture). At first glance, waldeinsamkeit, a combination of the words *wald* (forest) and *einsamkeit* (loneliness), is one such expression. Yet, the literal definition of "forest loneliness" belies the true feeling of this quintessentially German concept: an enlightened sense of self that can only be achieved by being alone in the woods. "Waldeinsamkeit is the romantic idea of the lonely wanderer," Leeder said. "It's very German to find connectedness in the forest. In the aloneness, you will find a true connection to yourself, and to other living things. That's the interesting thing: you go to be alone and put your faith in the spirit of the forest in order to find something or someone." And for Germans, what better place to make these connections and find that someone than in the knothole of an oak tree?

———

Martens continued to go to the oak, day after day, month after month, and always alone. Sometimes when those whose love he'd helped sow were celebrating an anniversary or returning to Eutin on holiday, they'd invite Martens out for dinner and he'd politely accept, even if he would have rather declined. "When I'm not working, I'm the type who likes to stay home and be alone," Martens said, gazing out the window toward his impeccably manicured lawn. "I'm a private person." Then one day in 1989, a German TV station was doing a segment on the oak, and the presenter asked Martens if he himself had ever found love in its trunk. The question made Martens uneasy, but after a moment, he looked down and said, "No, I'm happily single at the moment." A few days later, while he was climbing up the ladder to deliver mail to the oak, Martens reached into his bag, pulled out a stack of letters, and happened to spot one in the pile from a woman named Renate Heinz. It was addressed to him.

The day Martens was interviewed on the TV show, Renate was 760 kilometers away in Saarbrücken, watching in her living room. A divorced mother with a spontaneous streak, Renate was drawn to Martens' mix of vulnerability and confidence. When the postman bashfully confessed that he was single, Renate turned to her son Thomas and exclaimed, "Well, I'm going to fix that!" She pulled out a gray business card, found a blue pen, and got right to the point, writing: "I would like to get to know you. You are my type. At the moment, I am also alone."

Martens was intrigued by Renate's directness. "At first, I thought this kind of letter was rather naughty, but sweet," he said, blushing as he stared at the card that he still keeps in its own page in the front of his scrapbook. Then, when Martens saw that the return address was from Saarbrücken, the postman's precision kicked in. "I thought, okay, she's living at the German-French border. It's right on the way to visit my mother. So, I called her, rather clumsily." The two were soon talking on the phone every night. "And I have the phone bills to prove it!" Martens laughed. After two months, Martens suggested they finally meet face-to-face. "I told her, I will visit you, but you have to accept my dog, Meica." Renate agreed, and for the second time in his life, Martens anxiously loaded up his Volkswagen and drove toward the French border to meet a woman he hardly knew, all thanks to a letter he happened to pull from a stack.

After a 10-hour drive, Martens and Meica arrived in Saarbrücken and waited in the parking lot where Renate had suggested they meet. From their late-night calls, Martens had a sense of what Renate looked like, but he'd never actually seen her and kept scanning the streets wondering, "Is *she* the one?" Then, an attractive woman with short blond hair wearing a knee-length flower dress approached the car. Despite being a cat person, Renate bent down to pet Meica, and then kissed Martens on the cheek. "That was it for me," he said, placing his hand over his heart. The two spent several days touring Saarbrücken and staying in Renate's small apartment. Martens found her easy to talk to, and she had a grace and warmth about her that seemed almost French. She even looked like Catherine Deneuve. Despite swearing off love, Martens could feel himself already falling for her. "More importantly," he said, raising his index finger, "Renate and Meica had a connection. Otherwise, it wouldn't have worked out." Now, all that was left was to win over Martens' mother. So Renate, Meica, and Martens piled back into the Volkswagen and drove south to Mulhouse. By the end of their three-day stay in France, Martens said Yvette and Renate had become inseparable. With Meica's tail-wagging approval and his mother's blessing, Martens built up the courage to ask Renate to move in with him on the drive back to Saarbrücken. "Two months later, on November 9, 1989, she arrived—the very day the Berlin Wall fell," Martens said. "From that point on, Renate's life was as bound by the oak as mine."

The two painted their home the same shade of yellow as the German postal service's logo and settled into a routine. They'd walk Meica through the Dodauer Forest each day, Renate would cook elaborate meals at night and bring home bottles of French Bordeaux and Burgundy from her job as a local wine purveyor, and they'd vacation in her parents' flat in the Bavarian Alps, hiking through the woods and sitting quietly among the trees.

One night after Martens took Renate bowling with his pals from the post office, they ended up at the group's favorite bar. A friend leaned over to the two of them and said, "You've been living together for almost five years. When are you finally going to get married?" Martens had promised himself that he'd never remarry after his last relationship crumbled, but he suddenly turned to Renate and popped the question—sort of. "I said, 'Yea, we should get married! I'd have gotten down on one knee and all that, but I wasn't the youngest by then." A few months later, on a sticky summer afternoon in 1994, the couple exchanged vows in the Eutin Town Hall in front of 50 people, including Yvette, who had driven up from France. They were then whisked to the Bräutigamseiche, where Martens' postal worker friends had arranged a surprise reception under the oak's branches. The local newspaper snapped a picture of the pair kissing by the tree's trunk and printed a story in the next day's paper with the headline: "Wedding of the Year."

"I felt absolute joy," Martens said, looking at a photo of Renate he keeps in his study. "It was the two loves of my life together: the oak tree and Renate." The years went on, and Martens continued to diligently serve the oak. News of the postman's own gilded love story drew more letters to its hollow, and each spring, as the oak's bare branches burst green with life, new marriages would form. Martens' hair slowly turned white, and a well-trodden footpath began to form through the 1,200-hectare forest, as more people waited for the mailman by the tree. Even after retiring in 2004 to spend more time with Renate, Martens continued to speak on the oak's behalf whenever German media came calling, fulfilling a duty he promised his superior many years ago. But Renate was a lifelong smoker, and several years ago, she was diagnosed with lung cancer. As her condition deteriorated, Martens was no longer able to take care of her and was forced to admit her to hospice care, a decision that he said broke his heart. He visited her every day, holding her hand and doing his best to comfort her. "When she was dying, there was nothing I could do," he said, looking away. Renate eventually passed in February 2019. "We were just a few months away from our silver anniversary."

These days, Martens said he can't go to the Bräutigamseiche without thinking of Renate, but the tree has a way of luring him back. The day after she died, he found himself sitting in its shadow, immersing himself in the woods as waldeinsamkeit swelled within him—a process he found remarkably therapeutic.

After several days of talking to the mailman at his home, I followed Martens' heavy footsteps through the forest toward the old oak. As a cool breeze slipped through the Dodauer's coil of knotted trunks and a cascade of yellow leaves fluttered from the canopy, I asked him how it felt to be back. "It feels like I'm coming home," he said, stopping to look around as the mist swallowed birch and elm trunks in the distance. When we approached the circular wooden fence ringing the oak, I heard a faint pattering of footsteps quickly gaining on us. Soon, a man wearing a blue hoodie with messy blond hair came tramping through the forest, kicking up leaves as he made his way toward the tree. After bounding up the ladder, he shot his forearm into the knothole, pulling out every last letter and shaking his head as he ruffled through them, one by one.

"Do you guys believe in this stuff?" he called over, before coming toward Martens and me to introduce himself. It was Jan, the 35-year-old Taurus whose letter in the bright green envelope I had read days earlier. He explained that he's a farmer from Grossenbrode, a town on the Baltic Sea, and that he drives 130 kilometers round-trip from his home to the Bridegroom's Oak twice a month to read through the letters left in the knothole. He'd even tried writing the oak recently, but no one had written him back yet, and he was ready to give up. "You can't lose hope," Martens said, patting Jan on the shoulder and recounting his own tale of how a lucky letter at the oak changed his fate. By the end of the story, Jan was shaking Martens' hand with both palms and promised to return in two weeks' time if no one had written him first.

As Jan disappeared back through the woods, Martens pointed to two signs at the edge of the clearing. Several years ago, the town of Eutin realized that Martens is really the only person alive who can speak authoritatively about the tree's history. "Mr. Martens has so much to tell about it, but he won't be around forever," Ilka Kleene, a public relations officer at Eutin Tourism, told me. "It would be really sad if all of this knowledge were to vanish." So, town officials asked him to write a condensed version of Minna and Wilhelm's forbidden love story that set German hearts aflame. "*Es began wie im Märchen . . .*" the first line starts. "It began like a fairy tale . . ." Next to it, a second sign reads MAY THIS MARRIAGE LAST A LONG TIME! In 2009, after more than 100 years of bringing people together, the Bridegroom's Oak was symbolically married to a 200-year-old chestnut tree near Düsseldorf. Though 500 kilometers apart, the trees remained together for six years until the chestnut started suffering from old age and had to be cut down, leaving the Bridegroom's Oak a widow.

"When I started coming here, the tree was stronger and healthier," Martens said, pointing up to a series of iron cables securing the oak's branches. "You can tell it's getting more ill. But I'm not so healthy, either, so I suppose we have a special connection." In 2014, arborists discovered a fungal infection inside the oak, leading them to lop off a number of its limbs to prevent the disease from spreading. Around the same time, Martens was diagnosed with leukemia. Like the tree's branches, he explained that his bones aren't so strong anymore either. "But I can still climb the ladder," he said, slowly raising himself up its rungs and reaching into the knothole. "I can't believe how many letters there are in here," he said, placing Jan's bright green envelope back in the hollow. "In my day, these would all be gone by now!"

At the edge of the forest, I asked Martens what he thought might happen if the oak's health continued to decline. "There's talk of replacing it with a regular postbox when it dies, but why? What's the tradition there?" he asked. "I can't think about what will happen to it after I'm gone. All I know is I don't think anyone will ever care about the tree the way I have." He then lowered himself into his Volkswagen and drove out of the woods, toward all the other mailboxes he'd once served.

———————

Before leaving Eutin, I returned to the Dodauer Forest one last time to wander aimlessly alone, embracing my "forest loneliness." Perhaps if I got lost, I'd find something new, as my German landlord had told me. This six-day trip was the first time I had been back to Germany since moving from Berlin to Brooklyn, and I was struck by how much heimat I had been harboring. I missed how low the German clouds seem to descend each November, shrouding the country in a dreary, delirious dream that doesn't lift until spring. I missed Germans' startling self-awareness, their sense of who they are, and who they'll never be again. But above all, I missed Germans' romantic relationship with nature. It's a national trait that seems to defy every German stereotype of stiffness and order, and it's simultaneously confusing and confounding. How can the same rule-abiding nation that sends each household a four-page manual explaining how to properly separate your recyclables also fund *Lord of the Flies*–style forest schools? How can Germans vilify those who jaywalk or talk on the quiet car of a train while evangelizing someone like forester Peter Wohlleben, the author of *The Hidden Life of Trees*, who begs his fellow Germans to veer off trails and talk to trees? And why would one of the world's most efficient postal services—an international logistics juggernaut that prides itself on delivering 95 percent of letters within one day and 99 percent within two days—maintain a letter box three meters up a tree trunk in the middle of the forest where no one lives? As Leeder told me, "The idea that they sanctioned a postman to send letters to a tree is so, so weird that it must call to something very deep." It does.

If "the forest is the German soul," as Leeder said, then the fairy tales and make-believe worlds that spring from them reveal a deeper truth about how hopeful and whimsical Germans truly are. I found the country's collective embrace of the forest to be nothing short of addictive when I lived in Germany, and ever since I left, I've consciously tried to channel this wondrous part of the German psyche into my new American life. Our apartment is only 49 square meters, but we chose it because it's within walking distance of Brooklyn's last remaining woods. Our nine-month-old son is already on the wait list to attend the city's first forest school. And on many weekends, I venture alone into a dense grove of hickory, black birch, and tulip trees in Prospect Park to continue a practice I started years earlier in Berlin's Tiergarten park: waldeinsamkeit. In a way, we're all "lonely wanderers" plodding aimlessly through the dark forest, longing for nothing more than love and light to steer our purpose. The Germans just have a word for it.

As I crunched through the woods toward the half-timbered forest keeper's house where Minna once lived, I thought about her and Wilhelm. Love, by its very nature, is such an inexplicable, uncontrollable thing, a spontaneous collision of coincidences that no algorithm can predict. It overwhelms us, terrifies us, and leads us toward behavior that is both entirely irrational and gorgeous—like slipping away from your strict father at night to leave lovestruck letters in an oak tree, sneaking into a foreign country by pretending to be someone's cousin, and driving 10 hours to a city where you've never been to meet a woman you've never met. In a way, the Bridegroom's Oak is the most sublime example of waldeinsamkeit—an enduring reminder that if you put your faith in the spirit of the forest, it can help you not only to find yourself, but to lose yourself in something greater than yourself.

The sun was starting to set, so I turned around and retraced my footsteps back toward the Bridegroom's Oak. When I came to the edge of the clearing surrounding the tree, I looked up and saw a woman standing atop the ladder, sliding something bright and green into her jacket pocket.

Acknowledgments

This book never would have happened were it not for the kindness, generosity, and patience of many people around the world—most notably, the remarkable custodians who let me into their lives. Balla, Roland, Victoriano, Paola, Raffaella, Sudhammal, Murukan, Gopakumar, Selvaraj, Gopalakrishnan, Mohan, Jhen-fa, Moriyama, Alison, Darren, Jacqualine, Odalys, Felicia, Bernardo, María Caridad, Yamamoto-san, and Karl: meeting each of you was a gift, and I can't thank you enough for sharing your time and wisdom with me.

I am also forever indebted to the many translators, historians, and experts who took time out of their lives to contribute to this project. In Mali and Guinea, I'd like to thank the Kouyaté family for welcoming me into your home as one of your own, Kevin MacDonald for his expertise on the Mali Empire, and Ibrahima Diabate and Alieu Diabate for their long memories. In Sweden, I'm thankful for Benedict Thompson's tireless translations; Tina Westergren's hospitality; Ingela Bergils's historical expertise; Fredrik Sjöstrand's friendship; and Lars Persson's, Eva Milberg's, and Ludvig Olsson's time and perspectives. In Peru, I'd like to thank Edwin Cusi for showing me a side of your home country that almost no outsiders see, Guido Jara Ugarte and Dr. Edwin Barnhart for sharing your knowledge of the Inca world, and Gregorio and Josefina for your warmth. In Sardinia, I owe a heartfelt thank you to the Abraini and Selis families, Antonio Sanna, Giovanni Fancello, Paolo Ladu, Badora Piredda, Cristiano Pili, Luca Urgu, and the entire island for its boundless hospitality and for always making me feel at home. In India, an immense thank you goes to Dax Gueizelar and Satheesh Miranda for your time, translations, and generosity. I'd also like to thank Divya Iyer for so graciously welcoming me into your home, and Dr. Sharada Srinivasan for so patiently explaining the history and science behind this wonder. In Taiwan, I will always remember the Wu family. You have opened the doors to your apartment, theater, and lives for me on two occasions, and remain my Taiwanese family. A very special thank you, as well, to Lyn for your incredible translations; Chen Pin-chuan, Ru-shou Chen, and Chris Berry for sharing your endless knowledge of Taiwanese cinema with me; and RuRu and Hao-ze for sharing a side of the master few ever see. In England, a special thanks to Alison and Steve, for patiently explaining the subtle nuances that make beekeeping so wondrous, and to Dr. Randolf Menzel for sharing his vast scientific knowledge with me. My chapter on Cuba wouldn't have been possible without Araceli Tinajero's groundbreaking book *El Lector*. Thank you as well to Gary Mormino and Louis Pérez, for your expertise. A huge, huge thank you, as well, to Nicholas Syris. Nick, you accompanied me to Cuba on a whim, introduced me to countless people throughout the country, and generously shared your incredible knowledge on all things habanos throughout our stay. This chapter is so much richer because of you. Additional thanks go to Daymi Difurniao for your exhaustive help in organizing this trip. In Japan, I would have been completely lost without Haruko Hosokawa and Mitsi Morikawa. Your translations, patience, and knowledge of Japan's past and present are remarkable. Thank you as well to Keiko Kuroshima and Dr. Andrew Gordon for adding so much depth to these pages. And in Germany, I didn't know that a chance encounter with Angelika and Peter Bethke would blossom into such an enduring friendship. You two became my family in Eutin, and I think of you frequently and fondly.

I have been incredibly fortunate to have Wendy Levinson in my corner throughout the writing and research of this book. Your patience and brilliant guidance continue to astonish me. Thank you so much for being the first reader on each of these chapters, for always steering me straight, and for taking a chance on me.

My deepest gratitude to the tireless team at St. Martin's Press, starting with Daniela Rapp, who first saw something in these pages. Michael Flamini, your careful and invaluable edits have made this book so much stronger, and I'm grateful that you chose to take this on. Ed Chapman, Kiffin Steurer, and Laurie Henderson, thank you for catching and correcting my mistakes and improving my prose. Claire Cheek, thank you for keeping everything on track with grace and kindness. Katie Bassel and

Sara Beth Haring, thank you for pushing this project out into the world. And Soleil Paz, thank you for such a stunning cover design.

I am beyond grateful for the amazing folks at the BBC. Ellie Cobb and Miriam Weiner, thank you for your thoughtful and wise edits to the BBC Travel stories that inspired four of the chapters in this book. Simon Frantz, thank you for allowing me the time and space I needed to research this book. And above all, an immense thank you to Anne Banas for believing in this book, and for believing in me. Your ongoing encouragement and support helped make this project happen, and I'll never forget that.

In addition, I am tremendously thankful to Meredith Small and David Farley for agreeing to read an early version of this manuscript, and for greatly improving it.

Finally, thank you to my family, whose unwavering love and support I carried with me throughout this journey. Mom and Dad, you are everywhere in these pages. I can't thank you enough for the time you each poured into these early drafts, for buying me my first journal as a kid, and for showing me that there is beauty and grace in simplicity. Julyssa, I don't know what I did to deserve you. Thank you for being my light, my life, my editor, and my best friend. And to Oliver, you may not read this book for many years, but if you ever do, I hope it reminds you that the world can be a wondrous place, and that one of the greatest uses of life is to spend it on something that may outlast it.

Bibliography

14ymedio. 2021. "'There is No Popular Uprising, Only an Aggression by the United States,' Says Cuba's Foreign Minister." July 14. https://translatingcuba .com/there-is-no-popular-uprising-only-an-aggression-by-the-united-states -says-cubas-foreign-minister/.

Aanmeegam. 2022. *Sabarimala Fasting Rules—Ayyappa Vratham Rules*. January 31. https://www.aanmeegam.in/en/sabarimala-fasting-rules/.

agency, DPA news (Deutsche Presse-Agentur). 2009. "Forest Love." January 23. https://www.dw.com/en/love-for-the-forests-deeply-rooted-in-german -psyche/a-3970648.

Ahmed, Dr. Nazeer. n.d. *The Atlantic Slave Trade*. History of Islam: An encyclopedia of Islamic history. https://historyofislam.com/contents/onset-of-the -colonial-age/the-atlantic-slave-trade/.

Allsop, Laura, and Lianne Turner. 2011. "Bollywood poster painters face extinction in digital age." CNN, June 23. http://www.cnn.com/2011/WORLD /asiapcf/06/23/bollywood.painted.posters/index.html.

Andrade, Tonio. 2008. *How Taiwan Became Chinese: Dutch, Spanish, and Han Colonization in the Seventeenth Century*. New York: Columbia University Press.

Armario, Christine, and Nick Miroff. 2022. "Cubans arriving in record numbers along Mexico border." *The Washington Post*, April 7. https://www .washingtonpost.com/national-security/2022/04/07/cuba-migration-border -miami/.

Association, Shodoshima Shoyu. 2021. "Shodoshima Soy Sauce Kingdom of Wooden Barrels." https://shima-shoyu.com/history_en/.

Athanassiadis, Barbara. 2018. *My Venice.* (Independently published.)

Augustine. 1998. *The City of God Against the Pagans.* Cambridge: Cambridge University Press.

Baldauf, Scott. 2010. "Timbuktu, the birthplace of blues." *The Christian Science Monitor,* March 5. https://www.csmonitor.com/World/Global-News /2010/0305/Timbuktu-the-birthplace-of-blues.

Battuta, Ibn. 1929. *The Travels of Ibn Battuta: Explorations of the Middle East, Asia, Africa, China and India from 1325 to 1354.* N.p.: Pantianos Classics.

Baudin, Louis. 1961. *A Socialist Empire: The Incas of Peru.* New York: D. Van Nostrand.

Baxter, Joan. 2000. "Africa's 'Greatest Explorer.'" December 13. http://news .bbc.co.uk/2/hi/africa/1068950.stm.

Bellows, Keith. 2013. *100 Places That Can Change Your Child's Life: From Your Backyard to the Ends of the Earth.* Washington, DC: National Geographic.

Benes, Alejandro. 1995–1996. "Samuel Clemens and His Cigars." *Cigar Aficionado* (Winter). https://www.cigaraficionado.com/article/samuel-clemens -and-his-cigars-6042.

Bennison, Amira, interview by Melvyn Bragg. 2015. "The Empire of Mali." BBC (October 29).

Berry, Chris, and Ming-yeh T. Rawnsley. 2020. "Introduction to a special issue on Taiwanese-language films (taiyupian)." *Journal of Chinese Cinemas.*

Bingham, Hiram. 1913. "The discovery of Machu Picchu." *Harper's* (April).

Bingham, Hiram. 1922. *Inca Land: Explorations in the Highlands of Peru.* Boston and New York: Houghton Mifflin Co.

Bingham, Hiram. 1948. *Lost City of the Incas: The Story of Machu Picchu and Its Builders*. New York: Duell, Sloan and Pearce.

Bloch, Hannah. 2015. "How the Inca Empire Engineered a Road Across Some of the World's Most Extreme Terrain." *Smithsonian*, June 26. https://www.smithsonianmag.com/smithsonian-institution/how-inca-empire-engineered-road-would-endure-centuries-180955709/.

Bond, Jennifer K., Claudia Hitaj, et al. 2021. "Honey Bees on the Move: From Pollination to Honey Production and Back." *Economic Research Service*.

Borchmeyer, Dieter. 2019. "A Very Special Relationship, Germans and Their Forest." *The German Times* (April). http://www.german-times.com/a-very-special-relationship-germans-and-their-forest/.

Bordewich, Fergus M. 2006. "The Ambush That Changed History." *Smithsonian* (September). https://www.smithsonianmag.com/history/the-ambush-that-changed-history-72636736/.

Boyce, Mary. 2000. *Zoroastrians: Their Religious Beliefs and Practices* (The Library of Religious Beliefs and Practices). Abingdon, Oxfordshire: Routledge.

Breuer, Rayna. 2019. "The origins of the Germans' special relation to the forest." DW, September 24. https://www.dw.com/en/the-origins-of-the-germans-special-relation-to-the-forest/a-45613711.

Britannica, The Editors of Encyclopaedia. 1998. "Inca." In *Encyclopaedia Britannica Online*, July 20. https://www.britannica.com/topic/Inca.

Britannica, The Editors of Encyclopaedia. 1998. "Mirror." In *Encyclopaedia Britannica Online*, July 20. https://www.britannica.com/technology/mirror-optics.

Britannica, The Editors of Encyclopaedia. 1998. "Pachacuti Inca Yupanqui." In *Encyclopaedia Britannica Online*, July 20. https://www.britannica.com/biography/Pachacuti-Inca-Yupanqui.

Britannica, The Editors of Encyclopaedia. 1998. "Tokugawa period." In *Encyclopaedia Britannica Online*, July 20. https://www.britannica.com/event /Tokugawa-period.

Britannica, The Editors of Encyclopaedia. 1999. "Domestic Honeybee." In *Encyclopaedia Britannica Online*, May 4. https://www.britannica.com/animal /bee.

Britannica, The Editors of Encyclopaedia. 2000. "Chiang Kai-shek." In *Encyclopaedia Britannica Online*, January 12. https://www.britannica.com /biography/Chiang-Kai-shek.

Brodeur, Jean-Paul, and William Francis Walsh. 1999. "The decline of constabulary police." In *Encyclopaedia Britannica*, July 26. https://www.britannica .com/topic/police/The-decline-of-constabulary-police.

Brodeur, Jean-Paul, and William Francis Walsh. 1999. "The French Police Under the Monarchy." In *Encyclopaedia Britannica Online*, July 26. https:// www.britannica.com/topic/police/The-decline-of-constabulary-police.

Brodeur, Jean-Paul, William Francis Walsh, George L. Kelling, Michael Parker Banton, and Thomas Whetstone. 1999. "Early police in the United States." In *Encyclopaedia Britannica*, July 26. https://www.britannica.com /topic/police/Early-police-in-the-United-States.

Bromwich, Rachel. 2014. *Trioedd Ynys Prydein: The Triads of the Island of Britain*. Cardiff: University of Wales Press.

Buettner, Dan. 2004. "Sardinia, Italy: Home to the world's longest-living men." https://www.bluezones.com/explorations/sardinia-italy/.

Carrington Bolton, H. 1893. "A Modern Oracle and Its Prototypes. A Study in Catoptromancy." *The Journal of American Folklore* (American Folklore Society).

Cartwright, Mark. 2014. "Inca Civilization." In *World History Encyclopedia*, September 15. https://www.worldhistory.org/Inca_Civilization/.

Cartwright, Mark. 2014. "The Inca Road System." In *World History Encyclopedia*, September 8. https://www.worldhistory.org/article/757/the-inca-road-system/.

Cartwright, Mark. 2015. "Inca Textiles." In *World History Encyclopedia*, February. https://www.worldhistory.org/article/791/inca-textiles/.

Cartwright, Mark. 2018. "Pachacuti Inca Yupanqui." In *World History Encyclopedia*, 18 July. https://www.worldhistory.org/Pachacuti_Inca_Yupanqui/.

Castro, Jason. 2012. "You Have a Hive Mind." *Scientific American*, March 1. https://www.scientificamerican.com/article/you-have-a-hive-mind/.

Census, Japanese. 2018. "Statistics of Foreign Residents (Former Statistics of Registered Foreigners)." E-Stat, December. https://www.e-stat.go.jp/stat-search/files?page=1&layout=datalist&toukei=00250012&tstat=000001018034&cycle=1&year=20180&month=24101212&tclass1=000001060399&tclass2val=0.

Central Water Commission, Sewa Bhawan, and R. K. Puram. 2020. *Flood Forecasting and Warning Network Performance Appraisal Report 2018*. New Delhi: Government of India Central Water Commission Flood Forecast Monitoring Directorate.

Charles-Edwards, Thomas, and Fergus Kelly. 1983. "Bechbretha: An old Irish law-tract on bee-keeping." Dublin Institute for Advanced Studies.

Cheng, Dr. Isabelle 2018. "Saving the Nation by Sacrificing Your Life: Authoritarianism and Chiang Kai-shek's War for the Retaking of China." *Journal of Current Chinese Affairs*.

Cheung, Han. 2016. "Taiwan in Time: The great retreat." *Taipei Times,* December 4. https://www.taipeitimes.com/News/feat/archives/2016/12/04 /2003660529.

China, Ministry of Foreign Affairs of the People's Republic of. 2022. "Foreign Ministry Spokesperson Wang Wenbin's Regular Press Conference on August 8, 2022." August 8. https://www.fmprc.gov.cn/mfa_eng/xwfw_665399 /s2510_665401/202208/t20220808_10737507.html.

Chinta, Indu. 2020. "Mirroring the Past in Present." September 24. https: //www.newindianexpress.com/cities/kochi/2020/sep/24/mirroringthe-past -in-present-2200953.html.

Chiu, Wen-Ta, Jeremiah Scholl, Yu-Chuan Jack Li, and Jonathan Wu. 2021. "So Few COVID-19 Cases in Taiwan: Has Population Immune Health Played a Role?" *Frontiers in Public Health.*

CIA. n.d. *The World Factbook.* https://www.cia.gov/the-world-factbook /countries/peru/#geography.

Cieza de León, Pedro. 1999. *The Discovery and Conquest of Peru.* Durham: Duke University Press.

Cole, Pamela McArthur. 1893. "New England Weddings." *The Journal of American Folklore* (April–June).

Coleman de Graft-Johnson, John. 2022. "Musa I of Mali." In *Encyclopaedia Britannica.* https://www.britannica.com/biography/Musa-I-of-Mali.

—. 2022. "Musa I of Mali." https://www.britannica.com/biography/Musa-I -of-Mali.

Collector, The Poster. 2016. "History of Movie Posters." November 9. https: //postercollector.co.uk/articles/history-of-movie-posters/.

Columbus, Christopher, and Clements R. Markham. 2010. *The Journal of Christopher Columbus (during his First Voyage, 1492–93): And Documents relating to the Voyages of John Cabot and Gaspar Corte Real.* London: Hakluyt Society.

Commission, Central Water. 2018. *Report On Kerala Floods & Solutions.* Indian Government.

Companies Market Cap. 2023. "Market capitalization of Kikkoman." February. https://companiesmarketcap.com/kikkoman/marketcap/.

Conservancy, The Language. 2020. "Languages on the Edge of Extinction." January 13. https://languageconservancy.org/language-loss/.

Cook, Arthur Bernard. 1895. "The Bee in Greek Mythology." *The Journal of Hellenic Studies.*

Colnect.com. n.d. "Robaina with Cigar and Tobacco Field." https://colnect.com/en/stamps/stamp/574427-Robaina_with_Cigar_and_Tobacco_Field-93rd_Birth_Anniversary_of_Alejandro_Robaina-Cuba.

Cooper, Adrian. 2019. "How Robots Change the World." Oxford Economics. https://www.oxfordeconomics.com/resource/how-robots-change-the-world/.

Coote Lake, E. F. 1961. "Folk Life and Traditions." *Folklore.*

Correspondent, Special, *The Hindu.* 2019. "Poor dam management blamed for Kerala floods." April 3. https://www.thehindu.com/news/national/kerala/amicus-curiae-for-panel-to-identify-flood-causes/article26726699.ece.

Corson, Richard. 2005. *Fashions in Makeup: From Ancient to Modern Times.* London: Peter Owen Publishers.

Council, National Lightning Safety. 2022. "What are the Odds of Becoming a Lightning Victim." http://lightningsafetycouncil.org/Odds.pdf.

Council, National Safety. 2020. "Odds of Dying." https://injuryfacts.nsc.org /all-injuries/preventable-death-overview/odds-of-dying/.

Crane, Eva. 1999. *The World History of Beekeeping and Honey Hunting*. New York: Routledge.

Critchley, Thomas Alan. 1967. *A History of Police in England and Wales, 900–1966*. N.p.: Patterson Smith.

Crittenden, Alyssa N. 2011. "The Importance of Honey Consumption in Human Evolution." *Food and Foodways*.

Culture, Taiwan Ministry of. 2022. "National treasure movie poster artist Chen Tzu-fu passes away at 97." October 26. https://www.moc.gov.tw/en /information_196_149103.html.

D'Altroy, Terence N. 1985. "Staple Finance, Wealth Finance, and Storage in the Inka Political Economy." *Current Anthropology* (April).

Dangerous Minds. 2017. "Amazing Hand-Painted Movie Posters by Legendary Thai Artist Tongdee Panumas." May 19. https://dangerousminds .net/comments/hypnotically_colorful_hand-painted_movie_posters_by _legendary_thai_artist_t.

de la Vega, Garcilaso. 1994. *Royal Commentaries of the Incas and General History of Peru*. Austin: University of Texas Press.

De Montaud, Inés Roldán. 2002. "Spanish Fiscal Policies and Cuban Tobacco During the Nineteenth Century." *Cuban Studies*.

de Souza Amorim, D., B. V. Brown, and D. Boscolo et al. 2022. "Vertical stratification of insect abundance and species richness in an Amazonian tropical forest." *Scientific Reports*.

Deledda, Grazia. 2020. *Elias Portolu*. Translated by Kevan Houser. ISBN Services.

Denselow, Robin. 2006. "Obituary: Ali Farka Toure." *The Guardian*, March 8. https://www.theguardian.com/news/2006/mar/08/guardianobituaries .artsobituaries.

Department, Town of Plymouth Police. 2006. "A Brief History of the Plymouth, Massachusetts, Police Department." November 30. https://web.archive .org/web/20070814000306/http://www.plymouthpolice.com/ourhist.htm.

Desk, India Today Web. 2019. "Death toll in flood-hit Kerala rises to 121, 40 injured." *India Today,* August 19. https://www.indiatoday.in/india/story/death -toll-in-flood-hit-kerala-rises-to-121-40-injured-1582258-2019-08-19.

Diep, C. 2020. "Number of businesses manufacturing soy sauce in Japan from 2010 to 2019." Statista (September). https://www.statista.com/statistics /1275945/japan-soy-sauce-manufacturer-number/.

Dillon, Michael E., and Robert Dudley. 2014. "Surpassing Mt. Everest: Extreme flight performance of alpine bumble-bees." *Biology Letters*.

Division, National Emergency Response Centre: Ministry of Home Affairs Disaster Management. 2020. "Situation report as on 18th August 2020 at 1900 Hrs." National Emergency Response Centre.

Drake, Samuel Adams. 1901. *A book of New England legends and folk-lore in prose and poetry*. Boston: Little, Brown and Company.

Dunn, Ross E. 2012. *The Adventures of Ibn Battuta: A Muslim Traveler of the Fourteenth Century*. Berkeley: University of California Press.

Economics, Trading. 2023. "Germany-Terrestrial Protected Areas (% of Total Land Area)." February. https://tradingeconomics.com/germany/terrestrial -protected-areas-percent-of-total-land-area-wb-data.html.

Economist, The. 2017. "The people who read to Cuban cigar-factory workers." October 14. https://www.economist.com/the-americas/2017/10/12/the -people-who-read-to-cuban-cigar-factory-workers.

Editors, History.com. 2022. "Inca." July 26. https://www.history.com/topics /south-america/inca.

El-Soud, Neveen Helmy Abou. 2012. "Honey Between Traditional Uses and Recent Medicine." *Macedonian Journal of Medical Sciences.*

Elder, Pliny the. n.d. *The Natural History of Pliny.* Translated by John Bostock, and Henry T. Riley. London: Taylor and Francis.

English, Colleen. 2018. "Telling the Bees." September 5. https://daily.jstor .org/telling-the-bees/.

Ermlich, Günter. 2006. "Postilion d'Amour." *Zeit,* August 24.

Ernst, A. 1889. "On the Etymology of the Word Tobacco." *American Anthropologist.*

Eteraf-Oskouei, Tahereh, and Moslem Najafi. 2013. "Traditional and Modern Uses of Natural Honey in Human Diseases: A Review." *Iranian Journal of Basic Medical Sciences.*

Factbook, The Library of Congress Country Studies and the CIA World. 1992. "Peru: The Andean Highlands." https://photius.com/countries/peru /society/peru_society_the_andean_highlands.html.

Fancello, Giovanni. 2012. *Pasta: Storia ed Avventure di un Cibo tra Sardegna e Mediterraneo.* N.p. EDES.

Femmes, Fatales & Fantasies, Inc. n.d. "History of Movie Posters." https://fffmovieposters.com/history-of-movie-posters/.

Filkins, Dexter. 2022. "A Dangerous Game Over Taiwan." *The New Yorker*, November 14.

Fisher, Max. 2013. "A revealing map of the world's most and least ethnically diverse countries." *The Washington Post*, May 26. https://www.washingtonpost.com/news/worldviews/wp/2013/05/16/a-revealing-map-of-the-worlds-most-and-least-ethnically-diverse-countries/.

Fletcher, Pascal. 2021. "Cuba protests: Frustration at government runs deep." BBC, July 14. https://www.bbc.com/news/world-latin-america-57823130.

Florek, Dr. Stan. 2018. "Chinese Bronze Mirrors." November 14. https://australian.museum/learn/cultures/international-collection/chinese/chinese-bronze-mirrors/.

Foer, Joshua. 2011. "The Last Incan Grass Bridge." Slate.com, February 22. http://www.slate.com/articles/life/world_of_wonders/2011/02/the_last_incan_grass_bridge.html.

Folger, Tim, and Roger Ressmeyer. 1991. "The Big Eye." *Discover* (November).

Forman, Werner, and Stephen Quirke. 1996. *Hieroglyphs and the Afterlife in Ancient Egypt*. Norman: University of Oklahoma Press.

Foundation, Planet Bee. 2017. "The Sacred Bee: Ancient Egypt." *Planet Bee* (blog), November 6. https://www.planetbee.org/planet-bee-blog//the-sacred-bee-bees-in-ancient-egypt.

France-Presse, Agence. 2018. "Facing US$3 billion in Kerala flood damage, India rejects UAE's US$100 million offer." August 23. https://www.scmp.com/news/asia/south-asia/article/2160925/facing-us3-billion-kerala-flood-damage-india-rejects-uaes-us100.

Franco, Ana Paula, Sebastian Galiani, and Pablo Lavado. 2021. "Long-Term Effects of the Inca Road." *National Bureau of Economic Research.*

Fudala, Ayla. 2017. "The Sacred Bee: Ancient India." *Planet Bee* (blog), December 5. https://www.planetbee.org/planet-bee-blog//the-sacred-bee-bees-in-ancient-india-and-china-7tmcx.

Fudala, Ayla. 2018. "The Sacred Bee: The British Isles." *Planet Bee* (blog), March 9. https://www.planetbee.org/planet-bee-blog//bees-in-the-british-isles.

Good, Bee. n.d. "The Tradition of 'Telling the Bees.'" *Bee Good* (blog) https://beegood.co.uk/blog/the-tradition-of-telling-the-bees/.

Gordon, Andrew. 2002. *A Modern History of Japan: From Tokugawa Times to the Present.* Oxford: Oxford University Press.

Goto-Jones, Christopher. 2009. *Modern Japan: A Very Short Introduction.* Oxford: Oxford University Press.

Graber, Cynthia. 2011. "Farming Like the Incas." *Smithsonian,* September 6. https://www.smithsonianmag.com/history/farming-like-the-incas-70263217/.

Gregory, Alice. 2017. "Running Free in Germany's Outdoor Preschools." *The New York Times,* May 18. https://www.nytimes.com/2017/05/18/t-magazine/germany-forest-kindergarten-outdoor-preschool-waldkitas.html.

Gross, Michelle. 2018. "Lorighittas: An all-but-lost Sardinian dish." BBC Travel, June 26. https://www.bbc.com/travel/article/20180625-lorighittas-an-all-but-lost-sardinian-dish.

Guides, Library of Congress Research. n.d. "Birth of Ybor City, the Cigar Capital of the World." https://guides.loc.gov/this-month-in-business-history/ybor-city.

Guion, David. 2014. "Medieval Night Watchmen and the Modern Wind Band." *Musicology for Everyone* (blog), June 16. https://music.allpurposeguru .com/2014/06/medieval-night-watchmen-and-the-modern-wind-band/.

Haley, Alex. 1976. *Roots*. Garden City, NY: Doubleday.

Hallfahrt, Philipp. 2018. "Forest cultural heritage in Germany." September 24. https://www.deutschland.de/en/topic/environment/how-large-are -germanys-forests-facts-and-figures.

Hammer, Elizabeth. n.d. "Buddhism in Japan." https://asiasociety.org /education/buddhism-japan.

Healy, Paul F., and Marc G. Blainey. 2011. "Ancient Maya Mosaic Mirrors: Function, Symbolism, and Meaning." *Ancient Mesoamerica*.

Heaney, Christopher. 2011. *Cradle of Gold: The Story of Hiram Bingham, a Real-Life Indiana Jones, and the Search for Machu Picchu*. New York: St. Martin's Griffin.

Heidborn, Tina. 2010. "Dancing with Bees." *Max Planck Research* (February).

Hendricks, Scotty. 2018. "Was the Incan Empire a socialist paradise?" Big Think, February 21. https://bigthink.com/politics-current-affairs/was-the -inca-empire-a-socialist-paradise-the-curious-case-of-the-inca-economy -and-how-it-worked/.

Henry, Zane. 2021. "A beginner's guide to mead, the drink shaking off its 'ye olde' image." *National Geographic*, November 5. https://www.national geographic.co.uk/travel/2021/11/a-beginners-guide-to-mead-the-drink -shaking-off-its-ye-olde-image#.

Hill, Margari. 2009. "The Spread of Islam in West Africa: Containment, Mixing, and Reform from the Eighth to the Twentieth Century." SPICE (January).

https://spice.fsi.stanford.edu/docs/the_spread_of_islam_in_west_africa_containment_mixing_and_reform_from_the_eighth_to_the_twentieth_century.

Horn, Tammy. 2005. *Bees in America: How the Honey Bee Shaped a Nation*. Lexington: University Press of Kentucky.

Hrbek, Ivan. 2023. *Ibn Battuta*. In *Encyclopaedia Britannica*, February 2. https://www.britannica.com/biography/Ibn-Battuta.

Hsiau, A-Chin. 2005. *Contemporary Taiwanese Cultural Nationalism*. London: Routledge Press.

Hsin-yu, Wang, and James Lo. 2022. "National treasure movie poster painter dies at 96." Focus Taiwan, October 25. https://focustaiwan.tw/culture/202210250025.

India, Press Trust of. 2019. "Lapses In Dam Management Worsened Kerala Floods: Amicus Curiae Report." April 3. https://www.huffpost.com/archive/in/entry/lapses-in-dam-management-worsened-kerala-floods-amicus-curiae-report_in_5ca4adeee4b079824025445f.

Indian, Smithsonian National Museum of the American. 2015. "Ancestors of the Inka." https://americanindian.si.edu/inkaroad/ancestors/beginningsoftheroad/introduction.html.

Indian, Smithsonian National Museum of the American. 2015. "The Four Suyus." https://americanindian.si.edu/inkaroad/engineering/activity/four-suyus.html.

Indian, Smithsonian National Museum of the American. 2015. "The Chaski: Official Messengers of the Inka Empire." https://americanindian.si.edu/nk360/inka/pdf/inka-teachers-guide.pdf.

Indian, Smithsonian National Museum of the American. n.d. "The Great Inka Road: Engineering an Empire." https://americanindian.si.edu/inkaroad/.

Indian, Smithsonian National Museum of the American. 2015. "Inka Universe." June. https://americanindian.si.edu/inkaroad/inkauniverse/inkaroadexpansion /building-road.html.

Institute, South African National Biodiversity. n.d. "Bees Are at the Heart of Biodiversity." https://www.sanbi.org/news/bees-are-at-the-heart-of -biodiversity/.

Instituto Nacional de Estadística e Informática, Peru. 2017. *Canas*. https: //www.citypopulation.de/en/peru/admin/cusco/0805__canas/.

J, Noake. 1884. "More Worcestershire Superstitions." *The Gentleman's Magazine*, January to June.

Jackson, Kellie Carter. 2019. "The true story behind 'The Lion King.'" *The Washington Post*, July 17. https://www.washingtonpost.com/outlook/2019/07 /17/true-story-behind-lion-king/.

Jamshidi, Jamshid. 2021. "Double Police Efforts Ahead of the Release of the Gryningspyromanen." *Aftonbladet*, November 20. https://www.aftonbladet .se/nyheter/krim/a/EaB6X2/dubbla-polisinsatser-infor-frislappandet-av -gryningspyromanen.

Japan, Soy Sauce. 2020. "History of soy sauce." *Soy Sauce Japan* (blog), February 26. https://soysauce-japan.com/blogs/soy-sauce-museum/history-of-soy-sauce.

Japan, Statistics Bureau. 2020. *Japan: Kagawa*. https://www.citypopulation .de/en/japan/kagawa/.

Johnson, Ben. n.d. "Give Us Our Eleven Days." https://www.historic-uk .com/HistoryUK/HistoryofBritain/Give-us-our-eleven-days/.

Johnston, Eric. 2015. "Is Japan becoming extinct?" *Japan Times*, May 16. https://www.japantimes.co.jp/news/2015/05/16/national/social-issues/japan -becoming-extinct/#.WlHK_iOB3aZ.

Kai, Dr. Nubia. 2015. *The Oral Historiography of the Mali Empire*. Performed by Dr. Nubia Kai. Library of Congress, Washington, DC, May 6.

Kase, Aaron. 2016. "How to Raise Bees in the Driest Place on Earth." Vice.com, February 16. https://www.vice.com/en/article/wnbydw/how-to-raise-bees-in-the-driest-place-on-earth.

Kelleher, Katy. 2023. *The Ugly History of Beautiful Things: Essays on Desire and Consumption*. New York: Simon & Schuster.

Kikkoman. n.d. "Second Semi-Fermented Soy Sauce Manufacturing Method and Patent Available for Free." https://www.kikkoman.com/en/quality/ip/topics2.html.

Kikkoman. 2023. "Soy Sauce Business." https://www.kikkoman.com/en/corporate/about/group/soysauce.html.

Kite, W. 1889. "Telling the Bees." *The Magazine of American History with Notes and Queries* (January–June).

Knight, Rosie. 2020. "The Fascinating World of Hand-Painted Ghanaian Movie Posters." Nerdist.com, April 28. https://nerdist.com/article/hand-painted-ghanaian-movie-posters/.

Knowles, Andrew. 2016. "Georgian watchmen—security on the night-time streets." Regency History, August 4. https://www.regencyhistory.net/2016/08/georgian-watchmen-security-on-night.html.

Kritsky, Gene. 2015. *The Tears of Re: Beekeeping in Ancient Egypt*. Oxford: Oxford University Press.

Kurihara, Kenzo. 2015. "Umami the Fifth Basic Taste: History of Studies on Receptor Mechanisms and Role as a Food Flavor." *Biomed Res Int*.

Küster, Hansjörg. 2004. "Forests Against France. An important impetus for German forest plantations in the 19th century." *Revue de géographie historique.*

Laver, Michael. 2020. *The Dutch East India Company in Early Modern Japan: Gift Giving and Diplomacy.* London: Bloomsbury Academic.

Lawrence, D. H. 1921. *Sea and Sardinia.* New York: Thomas Seltzer.

Lee, Robert G., and Sabine Wilke. 2005. "Forest as Volk: Ewiger Wald and the Religion of Nature in the Third Reich." *Journal of Social and Ecological Boundaries.*

Levine, David. n.d. "The Population of Europe: Early Modern Demographic Patterns." In Encyclopedia.com. https://www.encyclopedia.com /international/encyclopedias-almanacs-transcripts-and-maps/population -europe-early-modern-demographic-patterns#:~:text=can%20be%20appre ciated.-,POPULATION%20GROWTH,almost%20300%20million%20 in%201900.

Levtzion, N. 1963. "The Thirteenth- and Fourteenth-Century Kings of Mali." *The Journal of African History.*

Linckersdorff, Sophie. 2021. "Der Türmer von Nördlingen." *Süddeutsche Zeitung,* May 21.

Lindelöw, Per. 2011. "So the police cracked the dawn pyromaniac." *Expressen,* June 22. https://www.expressen.se/kvallsposten/sa-knackte-polisen -gryningspyromanen/.

Local, The. 2011. "'Dusk and dawn pyromaniac' faces court." *The Local,* March 14. https://www.thelocal.se/20110314/32568/.

Local, The. 2019. "Group of friends buy entire abandoned Spanish village to fulfil retirement dream." *The Local,* August 14. https://www.thelocal.es /20190814/group-of-friends-buy-entire-abandoned-spanish-village-to-fulfil -retirement-dream/.

London, Museum of. n.d. "The Great Fire of London 1666." https://www .museumoflondon.org.uk/discover/great-fire-london-1666.

Lunazzi, José J. 2007. "Olmec mirrors: An example of archaeological American mirrors." Universidade Estadual de Campinas-Instituto de Física.

MacDonald, K., S. Camara, and S. Canós et al. 2011. "Sorotomo: A Forgotten Malian Capital?" *Archaeology International.*

MacEacheran, Mike. 2021. "Waldeinsamkeit: Germany's cherished forest tradition." BBC, March 15. https://www.bbc.com/travel/article/20210314 -waldeinsamkeit-germanys-cherished-forest-tradition.

Magie, David 1921. *The Scriptores historiae augustae with an English translation.* Cambridge, MA: Harvard University Press.

Mallory, Lester D. 1960. "499. Memorandum from the Deputy Assistant Secretary of State for Inter-American Affairs (Mallory) to the Assistant Secretary of State for Inter-American Affairs (Rubottom)." US Dept. of State: Office of the Historian, April 6. https://history.state.gov/historicaldocuments /frus1958-60v06/d499.

Manthorpe, Jonathan. 2008. *Forbidden Nation: A History of Taiwan.* New York: St. Martin's Griffin.

Mastino, Attilio. 2021. *The Making of Medieval Sardinia.* Leiden: Brill.

Mattos, Ramiro. 2015. "El Qhapaq Ñan del Tawantinsuyu: Reflexiones sobre su significado político y social en el presente andino." *Revista de Antropología del Museo de Entre Ríos,* December 20.

McGreevy, Nora. 2021. "Machu Picchu Is Older Than Previously Thought, Radiocarbon Dating Suggests." *Smithsonian,* August 5. https://www .smithsonianmag.com/smart-news/radiocarbon-dating-reveals-machu -picchu-older-previously-thought-180978360/.

Meggers, Georg. 2017. "An Den Zufall Adressiert." *Marie,* November 22.

Meghji, Shafik. 2021. "The innovative technology that powered the Inca." BBC, December 13. https://www.bbc.com/travel/article/20211212-the -innovative-technology-that-powered-the-inca.

Meinert, Julian. 2021. "The Insane History of Polish Movie Posters." Sabukaru, March 28. https://sabukaru.online/articles/the-insane-history-of -polish-movie-posters.

Melchior-Bonnet, Sabine. 2002. *The Mirror: A History.* New York: Routledge.

Melechi, Antonio. 2020. "Sardinia: The legacy of the notorious shepherd-bandits of the mountains." *BBC World Histories Magazine* (May).

Metcalfe, Alex, Hervin Fernández-Aceves, and Marco Muresu, eds. 2021. *The Making of Medieval Sardinia.* Leiden: Brill.

Michaels, Samantha. 2013. "In Postcards, Movie Posters and Paintings, an Alternative Look at Burma's Past." The Irrawaddy, May 11. https://www .irrawaddy.com/news/burma/in-postcards-movie-posters-and-paintings-an -alternative-look-at-burmas-past.html.

Mille, Richard. 2022. "Forbes World's Billionaires List: The Richest in 2022." https://www.forbes.com/billionaires/.

Mohamud, Naima. 2019. "Is Mansa Musa the richest man who ever lived?" BBC, March 10. https://www.bbc.com/news/world-africa-47379458.

Morgan, Thaddeus. 2018. "This 14th-Century African Emperor Remains the Richest Person in History." History.com, August 31. https://www.history .com/news/who-was-the-richest-man-in-history-mansa-musa.

Mortimer, Ian. 2016. *Millennium: From Religion to Revolution: How Civilization Has Changed over a Thousand Years.* New York: Simon & Schuster.

Müller, Sarah. 2022. *Promis Rätseln In TV-Show: Welches Geheimnis Steckt Hinter Dieser Sächsischen Familie?* November 7. https://www.tag24 .de/nachrichten/regionales/erzgebirge-nachrichten/promis-raetseln-in -tv-show-welches-geheimnis-verbirgt-dieses-saechsische-ehepaar -2538459.

Murdock, George Peter. 1934. "The Organization of Inca Society." *The Scientific Monthly* (March).

Murra, John V. 1998. *Andean Peoples.* In *Encylcopaedia Britannica*, September 18. https://www.britannica.com/topic/Andean-peoples.

Museum, National Human Rights. n.d. "White Terror Period." https://www .nhrm.gov.tw/w/nhrmEN/White_Terror_Period.

N/A. 1956. "Bees Join Mourners at Funeral Today." *The North Adams Transcript*, April 27.

Needleman, Deborah. 2017. "Who Will Save These Dying Italian Towns?" *The New York Times,* September 7. https://www.nytimes.com/2017/09/07/t -magazine/abandoned-italian-towns.html.

News, ABS-CBN. 2018. "The lost art of hand-painted movie posters." September 5. https://news.abs-cbn.com/life/09/05/18/the-lost-art-of-hand -painted-movie-posters.

News, SVT. 2018. "The dawn pyromaniac is sentenced to prison—the Court of Appeal lowers the sentence." October 8. https://www.svt.se/nyheter/lokalt /vastmanland/gryningspyromanen-doms-till-fangelse-hovratten-sanker -straffet.

Niane, DT. 1984. *The Decline of the Mali Empire.* UNESCO.

Nijhawan, Surabhi. 2015. "Himalayas Are Home to the World's Largest Bees Which Produce a Potent Variety of Honey." *India Times,* November

12. https://www.indiatimes.com/news/weird/himalayas-are-home-to-the
-world-s-largest-bees-which-produce-a-potent-variety-of-honey-247203
.html.

Nippel, Wilfried. 1995. *Public Order in Ancient Rome*. Cambridge: Cambridge University Press.

Nippon.com. n.d. *Japan Continues to Gray: Baby Boomers Reach 75*. https://www.nippon.com/en/japan-data/h01446/.

Noble Wilford, John. 2007. "How the Inca Leapt Canyons." *The New York Times*, May 8. https://www.nytimes.com/2007/05/08/science/08bridg.html/.

Norman, Mark. 2020. *Telling the Bees and Other Customs: The Folklore of Rural Crafts*. Cheltenham: The History Press.

Ochsendorf, Dr. John 2005. "Engineering in the Andes Mountains: History and Design of Inca Suspension Bridges." *Library of Congress, and Sponsoring Body Library of Congress*. Washington, DC, December 8.

Ogden, Daniel. 2019. *Greek and Roman Necromancy*. Princeton, NJ: Princeton University Press.

Ölander, Micke. 2015. "Gryningspyromanens hot: 'Ska brinna igen.'" *Expressen*, March 23. https://www.expressen.se/kvallsposten/gryningspyro
manens-hot-ska-brinna-igen/.

Ölander, Micke. 2021. "Ulf Borgström Is Released—the Threat: 'Do What I Want.'" *Expressen*, April 10. https://www.expressen.se/kvallsposten/krim
/ulf-borgstrom-slapps-fri-hotet-gor-vad-jag-vill/.

Ölander, Micke. 2015. "The Dawn Pyro Novel: Revenge, it's sweet." *Expressen*, March 24. https://www.expressen.se/kvallsposten/gryningspyromanen
-hamnden-den-ar-ljuv/.

Ölander, Micke. 2015. "The threat of the dawn pyromaniac: 'Will burn again.'" *Expressen,* March 23. https://www.expressen.se/kvallsposten/gryningspyroma nens-hot-ska-brinna-igen/.

Oldstone, Michael B. A. 1998. *Viruses, Plagues, and History.* Oxford: Oxford University Press.

Orr, Michael C., Terry Griswold, James P. Pitts, and Frank D. Parker. n.d. "A new bee species that excavates sandstone nests." *Current Biology.* https:// ucanr.edu/sites/PollenNation/Meet_The_Pollinators/Bees_496.

Overbye, Dennis, Kenneth Chang, and Joshua Sokol. 2022. "Webb Telescope Reveals a New Vision of an Ancient Universe." *The New York Times,* July 12. https://www.nytimes.com/2022/07/12/science/james-webb-telescope -images-nasa.html.

Parpola, Asko. 2019. "The Mirror in Vedic India: Its Ancient Use and Its Present Relevance in Dating Texts." Helsinki: Finnish Oriental Society.

Patowary, Kaushik. 2019. "The Adorable Custom of 'Telling The Bees.'" April 23. https://www.amusingplanet.com/2019/04/the-adorable-custom-of -telling-bees.html.

PBS. 1998. *Tug of War: The Story of Taiwan.*

Pendergrast, Mark. 2004. *Mirror, Mirror: A History of the Human Love Affair with Reflection.* New York: Basic Books.

Persson, Daniel. 2018. "Ulf Borgström is charged with new crimes." May 17. https://sverigesradio.se/artikel/6948345.

Peruviano, Gobierno. 2007. "Frequencias: Preguntas de Población." *Censos Nacionales 2007.*

Planet, Protected. n.d. *United States of America*. https://www.protectedplanet.net/country/USA.

Potts, Mary Anne. 2010. "Finding Machu Picchu: A Look at Explorer Hiram Bingham, A Real-Life Indiana Jones." *National Geographic*, May 26. https://www.nationalgeographic.com/adventure/article/machu-picchu-hiram-bingham.

Pozzetta, George E., and Gary R. Mormino. 1998. "The Reader and the Worker: *Los Lectores* and the Culture of Cigarmaking in Cuba and Florida." *International Labor and Working-Class History*.

Prisco, Jacopo. 2020. "The unexpected art of Ghana's hand-painted movie posters." CNN, November 4. https://www.cnn.com/style/article/ghana-film-posters/index.html.

Ransome, Hilda M. 2004. *The Sacred Bee in Ancient Times and Folklore*. Mineola, NY: Dover Publications.

Rawcliffe, Carole, and Claire Weeda. 2019. *Policing the Urban Environment in Premodern Europe*. Amsterdam: Amsterdam University Press.

Reed, Lawrence W. 2022. "What Caused Japan's Post-War Economic Miracle?" August 26. https://fee.org/articles/what-caused-japan-s-post-war-economic-miracle/.

Rees, G. E. 1917. "Telling the Bees." In *A Treasury of War Poetry: British and American Poems of the World War, 1914–1919*. Edited by George Herbert Clarke. London, New York, Toronto: Hodder and Stoughton.

Resources, University of California: Division of Agriculture and Natural. n.d. "Bees." https://ucanr.edu/sites/PollenNation/Meet_The_Pollinators/Bees_496/.

Rivero Muñiz, José. 1951. *La lectura en las tabaquerías*. *Revista de la Biblioteca Nacional* (October–December).

Rostworowski de Diez Canseco, Maria. 1999. *History of the Inca Realm.* Cambridge: Cambridge University Press.

Roud, Steve. 2003. *The Penguin Guide to the Superstitions of Britain and Ireland.* Penguin UK.

Rozman, Gilbert. 1974. "Edo's Importance in the Changing Tokugawa Society." *Journal of Japanese Studies.*

Rubinstein, Murray A. 2017. *Taiwan: A New History.* London: Routledge.

Sabarimala. n.d. *Rituals.* https://sabarimala.kerala.gov.in/rituals.

Sachs, Andrea. 2001. *A Book of Life. TIME,* October 22. https://content.time .com/time/subscriber/article/0,33009,1001056-2,00.html.

Saed, Omnia. 2021. "Found: A 7,500-Year-Old Cave Painting of Humans Gathering Honey." Atlas Obscura, December 16. https://www.atlasobscura .com/articles/honey-cave-painting.

Samson, David R. 2021. "The Human Sleep Paradox: The Unexpected Sleeping Habits of *Homo sapiens.*" *Annual Review of Anthropology.*

Sánchez de la Hoz, Pedro. 1917. *An Account of the Conquest of Peru.* New York: Cortes Society.

Sanchez-Parodi, Julie. 2009. "The Eleusinian Mysteries and the Bee." *Rosicrucian Digest.*

Sandel, Todd L. 2003. "Linguistic Capital in Taiwan: The KMT's Mandarin Language Policy and Its Perceived Impact on Language Practices of Bilingual Mandarin and Tai-gi Speakers." *Language in Society.*

Sarmiento de Gamboa, Pedro. 2014. *The History of the Incas.* CreateSpace Independent Publishing Platform.

Sauce, The History of Soy. n.d. "The Roots of Soy Sauce Are in China." https://www.soysauce.or.jp/en/the-history-of-soy-sauce.

Schiller, Tom. 2022. "Japan's humble birthplace of soy sauce." BBC, March 24. https://www.bbc.com/travel/article/20220323-japans-humble-birthplace -of-soy-sauce.

Schultz, Colin. 2012. "Honey Was the Wonder Food That Fueled Human Evolution (And Now It's Disappearing)." *Smithsonian,* September 20. https://www.smithsonianmag.com/smart-news/honey-was-the -wonder-food-that-fueled-human-evolution-and-now-its-disappearing -44399150/.

Sciences, Nasa: Earth Science Applied. n.d. "Kerala India Flood 2018." https://appliedsciences.nasa.gov/what-we-do/disasters/disasters-activations /kerala-india-flood-2018.

Sciolino, Elaine. 2005. *Persian Mirrors: The Elusive Face of Iran.* New York: Free Press.

Seeley, Thomas D. 2010. *Honeybee Democracy.* Princeton, NJ: Princeton University Press.

Service, National Park. n.d. "Ybor City Historic District Tampa, Florida." https://www.nps.gov/nr/travel/american_latino_heritage/ybor_city_historic _district.html.

Service, National Park. n.d. "Ybor City: Cigar Capital of the World." https://www.nps.gov/teachers/classrooms/upload/TWHP-Lessons _51ybor.pdf.

Sesin, Carmen, and Julia Ainsley. 2022. "Cuban migrants outpace Central Americans arriving at U.S. border." NBC News, April 8. https://www .nbcnews.com/news/latino/cuban-migrants-outpace-central-americans -arriving-us-border-rcna23644.

Shakespeare, William. 2005. *Much Ado about Nothing*. London: Penguin.

Shally-Jensen, Michael. 2017. *The Ancient World : Extraordinary People in Extraordinary Societies*. Ipswich: Salem Press.

Shurtleff, William, and Akiko Aoyagi. 2004. "History of Soy Sauce, Shoyu, and Tamari." Soy Info Center. https://www.soyinfocenter.com/HSS/soy _sauce1.php.

Siddharth, Gaurav. 2017. "My Quick Visit to Sabarimala—World's second largest pilgrimage in Kerala." March 30. https://www.theindia.co.in /travelogues/about-sabarimala-worlds-second-largest-pilgrimage-in-kerala.

Simon, Aneetta. 2018. "Craft Documentation: Metal Mirrors." July 12. https://issuu.com/aneettasimon/docs/book.

Singapore, Sree Narayana Mission. n.d. "About Sree Narayana Guru." https: //sreenarayanamission.org/about-us/about-sree-narayana-guru/.

Slaven, James. 2022. "The Honey Bee." August 11. https://owlcation.com /humanities/Celtic-Lore-of-the-Honey-Bee.

Slow Food Foundation for Biodiversity. n.d. Ark of Taste. https://www .fondazioneslowfood.com/en/what-we-do/the-ark-of-taste/.

Smith, Bardwell L. 1976. *Religion and Social Conflict in South Asia*. Leiden: Brill.

Smith, William. 1875. *A Dictionary of Greek and Roman Antiquities*. London: John Murray.

Smithsonian. 2011. "Quipu." November 8. https://www.si.edu/newsdesk /snapshot/quipu.

Spufford, Peter. 2002. *Power and Profit: The Merchant in Medieval Europe*. London: Thames & Hudson.

Squires, Graham. 2022. "Edo Period." October 11. https://www.worldhistory
.org/Edo_Period/.

Staff, *BK*. 2017. "The man keeping Thailand's hand-drawn movie poster art
alive." October 17. https://bk.asia-city.com/city-living/news/thai-movie-poster
-art.

Stein, Eliot. 2009. *Sardinia*. Bath: Footprint.

Stein, Eliot. 2018. "The 96-year-old painter who saved a village." BBC, November 29. https://www.bbc.com/travel/article/20181128-the-96-year-old
-painter-who-saved-a-village.

Stein, Gary. 2019. *Touring the Shadow Factory*. Columbus: Brick Road Poetry
Press.

Steves, Rick. 2020. "For the Love of Europe". Rick Steves' Europe. https:
//www.ricksteves.com/watch-read-listen/read/articles/rothenburg-night
-watchman.

Stewart, Jocelyn Y. 2006. "Ali Farka Toure, 67; Malian Guitarist Was Hailed
in U.S. as the 'Desert Bluesman." *The Los Angeles Times*, March 8. https://
www.latimes.com/archives/la-xpm-2006-mar-08-me-toure8-story.html.

Stewart, Jules. 1985. "Madrid Reviving 400-Year Tradition of Night
Watcher." *The Los Angeles Times*, December 29.

Stone Fish, Isaac. 2016. "Stop Calling Taiwan a 'Renegade Province," *Foreign Policy*, January 15. https://foreignpolicy.com/2016/01/15/stop-calling
-taiwan-a-renegade-province/.

Strochlic, Nina. 2017. "These Stunning Pictures Revealed Machu Picchu to
the World." *National Geographic*, July 24. https://www.nationalgeographic
.com/photography/article/machu-picchu-panoramas-henry-bingham
-discovery.

Suckling, James. 2010. "Legendary Cuban Farmer Alejandro Robaina Dies." *Cigar Afficionado,* April 19. https://www.cigaraficionado.com/article/legendary-cuban-farmer-alejandro-robaina-dies-3871

Sui, Cindy. 2016. "Taiwan Kuomintang: Revisiting the White Terror years." BBC, March 13. https://www.bbc.com/news/world-asia-35723603.

The Sun. 2017. "The surprising history behind honeymoons." April 24. https://nypost.com/2017/04/24/the-surprising-history-behind-honeymoons/.

Survey, U.S. Geological. n.d. "Do native bees occur on every continent on the planet?" https://www.usgs.gov/faqs/do-native-bees-occur-every-continent-planet.

Szczepanski, Kallie. 2017. "The Invention of the Mirror." ThoughtCo, March 8. https://www.thoughtco.com/the-invention-of-the-mirror-195163#.

Tai-lin, Huang. 2005. "White Terror exhibit unveils part of the truth." *Taipei Times,* May 20. https://www.taipeitimes.com/News/taiwan/archives/2005/05/20/2003255840.

Taiwan, Government of. 2022. "History." https://www.taiwan.gov.tw/content_3.php.

Taiwan, Ministry of Foreign Affairs Republic of China. 2020. "Diplomatic Allies." https://en.mofa.gov.tw/AlliesIndex.aspx?n=1294&sms=1007.

Tampapix.com. n.d. "The Cigar That Sparked a Revolution." https://tampapix.com/revolution.htm.

Taylor, Rabun. 2008. *The Moral Mirror of Roman Art.* New York: Cambridge University Press.

Telescope, James Webb Space. n.d. "Webb's Mirrors." NASA. https://webb.nasa.gov/content/observatory/ote/mirrors/index.html.

Times, Special to *The New York Times*. 1957. "Madrid Serenos Keep Night Peace: City's Street Watchmen Are a Beloved Heritage of the Middle Ages." May 12.

Thompson, Carol. 1998. *The Empire of Mali*. N.p. Franklin Watts.

Tikkanen, Amy. n.d. *New Seven Wonders of the World*. In *Encyclopaedia Britannica*. https://www.britannica.com/list/new-seven-wonders-of-the-world.

Tinajero, Araceli. 2010. *El Lector: A History of the Cigar Factory Reader*. Austin: University of Texas Press.

Torstensson, Ebba. 2021. "The 'Dawn Pyroman' has escaped—cut off the shackles." *Expressen*, October 21. https://www.expressen.se/kvallsposten/gryningspyromanen-har-rymt/.

Tourism, Kerala. n.d. "Sree Narayana Guru." https://www.keralatourism.org/varkala/sree-narayana-guru.php.

Tourisme, Lausanne. 2019. "The voice of the Cathedral." November 28. https://www.lausanne-tourisme.ch/en/the-lausanner/articles/the-voice-of-the-cathedral/.

Travel, Kraków. n.d. "The legend of the bugle call from St Mary's." http://krakow.travel/en/artykul/116/the-legend-of-the-bugle-call-from-st-marys.

UNESCO. 2009. "Manden Charter, proclaimed in Kurukan Fuga." https://ich.unesco.org/doc/src/28118-EN.doc.

Urgu, Luca. 2022. "In cammino per Santu Frantziscu." *La Nuova Sardegna*, May 3.

Vega-Hidalgo, Á., Y. Añino and E. Krichilsky et al. 2020. "Decline of native bees (Apidae: Euglossa) in a tropical forest of Panama." *Apidologie*.

Venkataraman, Ayesha, Suhasini Raj, and Maria Abi-Habib. 2018. "After Worst Kerala Floods in a Century, India Rejects Foreign Aid." *The New York Times*, August 23. https://www.nytimes.com/2018/08/23/world/asia/india -kerala-floods-aid-united-arab-emirates.html.

Version, Authorized King James. 1998. *The Bible*. Oxford UP.

Vinay, Harsha. 2019. "Mirrors of Malabar." *The Hindu*, September 21.

W. von Hagen, Victor. 1952. "America's Oldest Roads." *Scientific American*, (July).

Waitman, Alixandra. n.d. "José Martí y El Pueblo Fiel." https://tampahistorical .org/items/show/43.

Warner Morley, Margaret. 1899. *The Honey-Makers*. Chicago: A. C. McClurg & Company.

Warwick, Sarah. 2022. "Feng shui mirror rules—for wealth, prosperity and well-being." September 26. https://www.homesandgardens.com/interior -design/feng-shui-mirror-rules.

Westin, Adam. 2018. "Dawn pyromaniac detained on suspicion of attempted arson." *Aftonbladet*, January 19. https://www.aftonbladet.se/nyheter/a/jPzbgq /gryningspyromanen-haktad-misstankt-for-forsok-till-mordbrand.

Whittier, John Greenleaf. 1894. *The Complete Poetical Works of John Greenleaf Whittier*. Boston and New York: Houghton Mifflin.

Wiklund, David, interview by Radio Sweden. 2012. "From bullied teenager to Sweden's worst arsonist." February 13.

Wingfield-Hayes, Rupert. 2022. "Defiant Taiwan's identity is moving away from China." BBC, October 10. https://www.bbc.com/news/world-asia -63196482.

World, R&I. 2021. "Researchers Unearth the Most Well-Preserved Cave Painting of Gathering Honey." July 7. https://ruvid.org/ri-world/researchers -unearth-the-most-well-preserved-cave-painting-of-gathering-honey/.

Yu, Verna. 2009. "Untold Stories of China and Taiwan." *The New York Times*, October 5. https://www.nytimes.com/2009/10/06/world/asia/06iht-taiwan .html.

Zarodimos, Vasileios. 2019. "Cuban Cigars meet Great Literature: Cigar Smoking Authors." February 12. https://us.egmcigars.com/blogs/the-cuban -cigars-blog-by-egm-cigars/cuban-cigars-meet-great-literature-popular -cigar-smoking-authors.

Zene, Cosimo. 2007. "S'imbiatu: Gift and community in central Sardinia." *Culture and Religion: An Interdisciplinary Journal* vol. 8 (3).

Author's Note

Four chapters in this book ("The World's Rarest Pasta," "Asia's Last Film Poster Painter," "The Man Trying to Save Japanese Food," and "The Most Romantic Job in Europe") were adapted from previous stories I wrote for the BBC. To expand and deepen them, I returned to spend additional time with each custodian. In certain instances, I have incorporated details I learned about them and the traditions they maintain from my first reporting trip in order to more fully capture their stories and provide a more complete account of my time spent with them.

Endnotes

Introduction

1. (Conservancy 2020)
2. (Cooper 2019)
3. (Local 2019)
4. (Combs 2020)
5. (Johnston 2015)

Chapter 1: The Living Libraries of West Africa

1. In the book, Haley embarks on a trip up the Gambia River to the village of Juffure after learning that a griot would assist him on his search to retrace his family lineage. There, he says he met a griot who was able to trace Haley's lineage back to his ancestor Kunta Kinte, whose family had lived in the Mali Empire.

2. I determined this by going through each of the 678 inscriptions, one by one, and following up with UNESCO Project Officer Juliette Hopkins, to verify it.

3. (Jackson 2019)

4. There is no single version of the *Epic of Sundiata*, and its details vary based on geography, djeli, and audience. The most "standard" version of the oral epic is generally attributed to D. T. Niane, and my condensed recalling of its main premise here is taken from his 1965 English translation, as well as additional details recounted to me in person by one of Mali's greatest living djelis, Alieu Diabate.

5. Interview with Alieu Diabate.

6. (UNESCO 2009)

7. (Bennison 2015)

8. (Baxter, Africa's "greatest explorer" 2000)

9. (Battuta 1929)

10. (Mohamud 2019)

11. (Mille 2022)

12. (Hill 2009)

13.   (Coleman de Graft-Johnson 2022)

14.   (Coleman de Graft-Johnson, Musa I of Mali 2022)

15.   (Levtzion 1963)

16.   (Morgan 2018)

17.   (Hrbek 2023)

18.   (Dunn 2012)

19.   (Battuta 1929, *The Travels of Ibn Battuta: Explorations of the Middle East, Asia, Africa, China and India from 1325 to 1354*)

20.   (Battuta 1929, *The Travels of Ibn Battuta: Explorations of the Middle East, Asia, Africa, China and India from 1325 to 1354*)

21.   (Ahmed n.d.) Portugal is believed to have conducted slave raids in Africa as early as 1444, but this is often cited as the first example of slavery through direct negotiations with a West African leader, which would be the model of the trans-Atlantic slave trade moving forward.

22.   (Thompson 1998, *The Empire of Mali*)

23.   (Niane 1984)

24.   (Kai 2015)

25.   (K. MacDonald 2011)

26.   (Baldauf 2010), (Denselow 2006)

27.   (Denselow, Obituary: Ali Farka Toure 2006)

Chapter 2: Scandinavia's Last Night Watchman

1.   (Samson 2021)

2.   (Version 1998)

3.   (Nippel 1995)

4.   Interview with Rawcliffe.

5.   Most of the information about the weapons night watchmen wielded comes from an interview with Thier, the head of the European Guild of Night Watchmen and Tower Guards. I then cross-referenced what he said with images of the current reenactors in these cities or countries who, while no longer performing a true job, have stayed true to how these individuals dressed and the weaponry they carried.

6.   (Guion 2014)

7.   (Times 1957), (Stewart 1985)

8.   (Critchley 1967)

9.   (Knowles 2016) and an interview with Rawcliffe.

10. (Brodeur et al. 1999), (Department 2006)

11. (Levine n.d.)

12. (Steves 2020)

13. (Knowles 2016), (Rawcliffe and Weeda 2019), (Shakespeare 2005)

14. (London n.d.)

15. (Brodeur and Walsh, "The decline of constabulary police" 1999), (Brodeur and Walsh, "The French police under the monarchy" 1999)

16. (Tourisme 2019)

17. (Travel n.d.)

18. (Linckersdorff 2021)

19. (Müller 2022)

20. Interview with Saljé.

21. (Ölander, "Gryningspyromanens hot: 'Ska brinna igen'" 2015)

22. (Wiklund 2012), (Local 2011), (News 2018), (Persson 2018), (Westin 2018), (Torstensson 2021), (Ölander 2021), (Ölander, "The Dawn Pyro Novel: Revenge, it's sweet" 2015), (Ölander, "The threat of the dawn pyromaniac: 'Will burn again'" 2015), (Lindelöw 2011)

23. (Jamshidi 2021)

Chapter 3: The Last Inca Bridge Master

1. (Editors 2022), (Britannica 1998), (Shally-Jensen 2017), (Indian n.d.), as well as interviews with Barnhart, Barreiro, Jara Ugarte; and also Betshy Apaza Huamani, an Andean archaeologist from Peru's University of Trujillo.

2. (Indian, "Inka Universe" 2015), (Cartwright, "The Inca Road System" 2014), (W. von Hagen 1952)

3. (Ochsendorf 2005), (Rostworowski de Diez Canseco 1999), (Bloch 2015)

4. (Noble Wilford 2007), (Ochsendorf 2005)

5. (Bingham 1948), (Bingham, *Inca Land: Explorations in the Highlands of Peru* 1922), (Heaney 2011)

6. (Bingham, *Inca Land: Explorations in the Highlands of Peru* 1922)

7. (Bingham, *Inca Land: Explorations in the Highlands of Peru* 1922)

8. (Bellows 2013)

9. (Tikkanen n.d.)

10. (Strochlic 2017)

11. (Bingham, *The Discovery of Machu Picchu* 1913)

12. (Bingham, *Inca Land: Explorations in the Highlands of Peru* 1922)
13. (Ochsendorf 2005)
14. (Ochsendorf 2005)
15. (Sánchez de la Hoz 1917)
16. (Cieza de León 1999)
17. This statistic comes from a report Ochsendorf wrote for the National Museum of the American Indian, in which he states: "Each main cable, as thick as a man's thigh, can hold 5,175 pounds, or 2,347 kilograms." Since there are four base cables, I've multiplied the kilograms by four and divided that number by 110, which equals 85.34 kilograms, or roughly the size of an average adult man.
18. (de la Vega 1994)
19. (Cartwright 2015), (Foer 2011)
20. (Smithsonian 2011)
21. (Indian, "Ancestors of the Inka" 2015), (Indian, "The Four Suyus" 2015), (Cartwright, "Inca Civilization" 2014)
22. (Cartwright, "Pachacuti Inca Yupanqui" 2018), (Cartwright, "Inca Civilization" 2014), (Britannica, "Pachacuti Inca Yupanqui" 1998), (McGreevy 2021), as well as interviews with Barnhart and Barreiro.
23. Interview with Barnhart.
24. (Franco, Galiani, and Lavado 2021), (Cartwright, "The Inca Road System" 2014)
25. (Indian, "The Chaski: Official Messengers of the Inka Empire" 2015)
26. The Inca did have llamas, which some might characterize as draft animals, though I'm referring to animals trained specifically to pull heavy loads, such as oxen or horses.
27. (Baudin 1961), (Murdock 1934)
28. (Baudin 1961), (Murdock 1934), (Hendricks 2018), and an interview with Barnhart.
29. (D'Altroy 1985)
30. (Oldstone 1998), (Bloch 2015)
31. (Peruviano 2007)
32. (Instituto Nacional de Estadística e Informática 2017)
33. (Ochsendorf 2005)

Chapter 4: The World's Rarest Pasta

1. (Biodiversity n.d.)
2. (Lawrence 1921)

3. (Stein 2009) I lived in Sardinia for several years and have written a lot about the island. Much of the island's historical, cultural, and ethnographic information here comes from the guidebook I wrote while living there.

4. (Metcalfe 2021)

5. (Stein, *Sardinia* 2009)

6. (Stein, *Sardinia* 2009)

7. (Buettner 2004)

8. (Mastino 2021)

9. (Stein, *Sardinia* 2009)

10. (Melechi 2020)

11. (Zene 2007)

12. (Deledda 2020)

13. This comes from the Museo Deleddiano, Deledda's former home and birthplace in the center of Nuoro.

14. (Stein, *Sardinia* 2009)

15. (Stein, *Sardinia* 2009), (Gross 2018)

16. (Fancello 2012)

17. (Urgu 2022)

Chapter 5: The Mirror That Reveals Your Truest Self

1. (Britannica 1998), (Folger and Ressmeyer 1991)

2. We may never know when the Aranmula kannadi began to be manufactured. But based on the fact that Srinivasan told me she has personally analyzed an Aranmula kannadi from the 1600s–1700s, I believe it's fair to say that the tradition goes back at least 300 years.

3. (Simon 2018)

4. (Simon 2018), (Vinay 2019)

5. (Kelleher 2023)

6. (Kelleher 2023), (Szczepanski 2017), (Melchior-Bonnet 2002), (Pendergrast 2004)

7. (Melchior-Bonnet 2002), (Pendergrast 2004), (Kelleher 2023)

8. (Pendergrast 2004)

9. (Kelleher 2023), (Pendergrast 2004), (Lunazzi 2007)

10. (Healy and Blainey 2011), (Kelleher 2023), (Pendergrast 2004)

11. (Kelleher 2023), (Florek 2018)

12.   (Melchior-Bonnet 2002)

13.   (Kelleher 2023)

14.   (Augustine 1998)

15.   (Carrington Bolton 1893), (Smith 1875), (Taylor 2008)

16.   (Kelleher 2023)

17.   Magie, *The Scriptores historiae augustae with an English translation* 1921)

18.   (Ogden 2019)

19.   (Melchior-Bonnet 2002), (Kelleher 2023)

20.   (Melchior-Bonnet 2002), (Kelleher 2023), (Athanassiadis 2018)

21.   (Melchior-Bonnet 2002)

22.   (Mortimer 2016)

23.   (Mortimer 2016)

24.   (Parpola 2019), (Corson 2005), as well as interviews with Srinivasan.

25.   (Sabarimala n.d.), (Siddharth 2017) Estimates vary wildly for how many people attend Sabarimala annually. Some publications state 10 million and others claim 100 million. According to the guides who accompanied me on this trip and an official for Kerala Tourism, it is likely closer to 10 to 15 million, with as many as 20 million attending each year.

26.   (Sabarimala n.d.), (Sabarimala Fasting Rules—Ayyappa Vratham Rules 2022), as well as an interview with the president of the Aranmula Development Society, Radha Krishnan P. R.

27.   (Vinay 2019), (Chinta 2020)

28.   (B. L. Smith 1976), (Singapore n.d.), (Tourism n.d.), and an interview with the president of the Aranmula Development Society, Radha Krishnan P. R.

29.   (Sciences n.d.), (Venkataraman, Raj, and Abi-Habib 2018), (France-Presse 2018)

30.   (Desk 2019), (Division 2020), (Correspondent 2019), (India 2019)

31.   (Commission 2018), (Central Water Commission Sewa Bhawan 2020)

Chapter 6: Asia's Last Film Poster Painter

1.   (Taiwan 2020)

2.   (Filkins 2022)

3.   (China 2022)

4.   (Stone Fish 2016)

5.   (Hsiau 2005), (Wingfield-Hayes 2022)

6.   (Collector 2016), (Femmes n.d.)

7.   (Allsop and Turner 2011)

8.   (Prisco 2020), (Knight 2020)

9.   (Meinert 2021)

10. ("Amazing Hand-Painted Movie Posters by Legendary Thai Artist Tongdee Panumas" 2017), (Staff 2017), (Michaels 2013), (News 2018)

11. (Andrade 2008), (G. O. Taiwan 2022), (PBS 1998), (Rubinstein 2017)

12. (PBS 1998), (Rubinstein 2017), (G. o. Taiwan 2022)

13. (PBS 1998), (G. O. Taiwan 2022), (Rubinstein 2017), (Yu 2009), (Cheung 2016) It's hard to quantify exactly how many Taiwanese migrated from mainland China to Taiwan during this period. The official Taiwanese government website cites 1.2 million. The cited *New York Times* article here states "some two million." And the cited *Taipei Times* article here states, ". . . a total of 1 million, but other estimates have gone as high as 2.5 million."

14. (Britannica 2000), (Cheng 2018), (Museum n.d.), (Rubinstein 2017), (Tai-lin 2005), (Sui 2016) Most sources state that approximately 3,000 to 4,000 people were executed during the White Terror era. The vast majority of killings under Chiang came during the so-called 228 Incident (or 228 Massacre) in 1947, in which it's thought as many as 18,000 were killed. Here, I am relying on the estimates listed in the cited BBC article.

15. (Rubinstein 2017), (Manthorpe 2008)

16. (Sandel 2003)

17. (Berry and Rawnsley 2020)

18. (Culture 2022), (Hsin-yu and Lo 2022), and interviews with Dr. Chen Ya-wen Funnily enough, Tze-fu's age is misstated in the cited article from the Ministry of Culture. He died just short of his 97th birthday.

19. Interviews with Dr. Chen Ya-wen. She also sent me a photocopy of the newspaper article Tze-fu wrote in Japanese, which I sent to a professional translator. The headline is "No regret as Japanese / My lost youth by Mr. Chen."

20. (Berry and Rawnsley 2020)

21. (Wingfield-Hayes 2022)

22. Interview with Chen Pin-chuan, the former director of the Taiwan Film and Audiovisual Institute (previously called the Taiwan Film Institute).

23. (Chiu et al. 2021)

Chapter 7: Where Bees Are a Part of the Family

1. (English 2018), (Norman 2020), (Roud 2003), (Drake 1901)

2. (Cook 1895), (Norman 2020), (Ransome 2004)

3. (Cook 1895), (Kritsky 2015)

4. (English 2018)

5. (El-Soud 2012), (Eteraf-Oskouei and Najafi 2013)

6. (Henry 2021)

7. (World 2021)

8. (Schultz, "Honey Was the Wonder Food That Fueled Human Evolution [And Now It's Disappearing]" 2012), (Crittenden 2011)

9. (Kritsky 2015)

10. (Ransome 2004), (Kritsky 2015), (Forman and Quirke 1996)

11. (Norman 2020)

12. (Ransome 2004), (Fudala 2017)

13. (Fudala 2017)

14. (Norman 2020)

15. (Cook 1895), (Ransome 2004), (Sanchez-Parodi 2009)

16. (Ransome 2004), (Fudala 2017), (Boyce 2000)

17. (Sun 2017)

18. (Crane 1999)

19. Interview with Sapoznik.

20. (Slaven 2022)

21. (Bromwich 2014)

22. (Slaven 2022), (Fudala, "The Sacred Bee: The British Isles" 2018), (Ransome 2004)

23. (Charles-Edwards and Kelly 1983)

24. (Slaven 2022)

25. (Norman 2020), (Good n.d.), (Slaven 2022), (Johnson n.d.)

26. (Good, "The Tradition of 'Telling the Bees'" n.d.)

27. (Patowary 2019)

28. (Horn 2005)

29. (Warner Morley 1899)

30. (Roud 2003)

31. (Roud 2003)
32. (Roud 2003)
33. (Horn 2005)
34. (J 1884)
35. (J 1884)
36. (Warner Morley 1899)
37. (Cole 1893)
38. (Warner Morley 1899)
39. (Rees 1917)
40. (Whittier 1894)
41. (English 2018)
42. (N/A 1956)
43. (Coote Lake 1961)
44. (Council 2022), (N. S. Council 2020)
45. (Survey n.d.), (Nijhawan 2015), (Kase 2016), (Vega-Hidalgo 2020)
46. (Dillon and Dudley 2014)
47. (de Souza Amorim 2022)
48. (Orr et al. n.d.)
49. (Resources n.d.), (Britannica 1999)
50. (Seeley 2010)
51. Interview with Wakeman.
52. Interview with Wakeman.
53. (Seeley 2010)
54. (Seeley 2010)
55. Interview with Wakeman.
56. (Heidborn 2010)
57. Interview with Wakeman.
58. (Seeley 2010)
59. (Castro 2012)
60. Interview with Wakeman.
61. (Institute n.d.)
62. (Bond, Hitaj et al. 2021)
63. (Stein 2019)

Chapter 8: The Only Democratic Job in Cuba

1.   (Tinajero 2010)

2.   (Economist 2017)

3.   (Zarodimos 2019)

4.   (Sachs 2001)

5.   (Benes 1995–1996)

6.   (Columbus and Markham 2010)

7.   (Columbus and Markham 2010)

8.   (Ernst 1889)

9.   (De Montaud 2002)

10.   (De Montaud 2002)

11.   (De Montaud 2002)

12.   (Tinajero 2010)

13.   (Tinajero 2010)

14.   (Tinajero 2010)

15.   (Tinajero 2010)

16.   (Tinajero 2010)

17.   (Tinajero 2010)

18.   (Rivero Muñiz 1951) *La Lectura en las Tabaquerias* is a 22-page pamphlet written by José Rivero Muñiz in 1942 but not published until 1951. Its full text was uploaded on the site CubaMuseo.net, but has since been removed. In my translated version, I'd noted that the site described its publication "as part of an offprint from the National Library," and that Muñiz's 1964 book *Tobacco, Its History in Cuba* is described as "the bible of the tobacco researcher."

19.   (Rivero Muñiz 1951)

20.   (Rivero Muñiz 1951)

21.   (Pozzetta 1998)

22.   (Pozzetta 1998)

23.   (Tinajero 2010)

24.   (Pozzetta 1998)

25.   (Tinajero 2010)

26.   (Pozzetta 1998)

27.   (Tinajero 2010)

28.   (Pozzetta 1998), (Tinajero 2010), (Guides n.d.), (Service n.d.)

29. (Tinajero 2010), (Pozzetta 1998)

30. Interview with Mormino

31. (Tinajero 2010)

32. (Tinajero 2010)

33. (Waitman, "José Martí" n.d.)

34. (Service, "Ybor City: Cigar Capital of the World" n.d.), (Pozzetta 1998)

35. ("The Cigar That Sparked a Revolution" n.d.), (Waitman, "José Martí y El Pueblo Fiel" n.d.)

36. ("The Cigar That Sparked a Revolution" n.d.), (Waitman, "José Martí y El Pueblo Fiel" n.d.)

37. (Robaina with Cigar and Tobacco Field n.d.)

38. (Suckling 2010)

39. From interviews with Syris and the Robaina family.

40. (14ymedio 2021)

41. (Fletcher 2021)

42. (Armario and Miroff 2022)

43. (Sesin and Ainsley 2022)

44. (Mallory 1960)

Chapter 9: The Man Trying to Save Japanese Food

1. (Kurihara 2015)

2. Interview with Yamamoto.

3. (Shurtleff and Aoyagi 2004)

4. (Shurtleff and Aoyagi 2004)

5. (Hammer n.d.)

6. (Schiller 2022)

7. (Schiller 2022)

8. (Sauce n.d.), (Shurtleff and Aoyagi 2004)

9. (Association 2021)

10. (Britannica 1998), (Squires 2022), (Gordon 2002)

11. (Japan 2020), (Shurtleff and Aoyagi 2004), (Sauce n.d.)

12. (Shurtleff and Aoyagi 2004)

13. (Shurtleff and Aoyagi 2004)

14. (Association 2021)

15. Interviews with Yamamoto, Kitishimoto Hitoshi, and Fujii Yasuto.

16. (Association 2021), as well as interviews with Yamamoto, Kitishimoto Hitoshi, and Fujii Yasuto.

17. (Shurtleff and Aoyagi 2004)

18. (Shurtleff and Aoyagi 2004)

19. (Goto-Jones 2009), (Laver 2020)

20. Interview with Sugibayashi.

21. (Gordon 2002), as well as an interview with Gordon.

22. (Reed 2022)

23. (Reed 2022)

24. (Kikkoman n.d.)

25. (Kikkoman n.d.)

26. (Kikkoman n.d.)

27. (Kikkoman, "Soy Sauce Business" 2023)

28. (Diep 2020)

29. (S. B. Japan, Japan: Kagawa 2020), (Nippon.com n.d.) The 43 percent figure for the island comes from a report that one of my guides, Haruko Hosokawa, shared with me.

Chapter 10: The Most Romantic Job in Europe

1. (Meggers 2017)

2. (Meggers 2017)

3. (Meggers 2017)

4. (Ermlich 2006)

5. (Bordewich 2006)

6. (MacEacheran 2021), (Bordewich 2006)

7. (Breuer 2019)

8. (Küster 2004)

9. (Agency 2009)

10. (Lee and Wilke 2005)

11. (MacEacheran 2021)

12. (Hallfahrt 2018), (Economics 2023), (Planet n.d.)

13. (Borchmeyer 2019)

14. (Gregory 2017)

15. (Borchmeyer 2019)

Index

NOTE: *Taiwanese names (Chapter 6) are indexed as they appear in the text;
surname first and without inversion.*

Julyssa Lopez

Eliot Stein is a journalist and editor at the BBC. *Custodians of Wonder* is inspired by a column he created for BBC Travel called Custom Made, in which he profiles remarkable people upholding ancient traditions around the world. His work has appeared in *The New York Times, Wired, The Guardian, The Washington Post, National Geographic, The Independent,* and elsewhere. He currently lives in Brooklyn with his wife and young son.